Trooper in the Far North-West

Other Spectra titles

Trooper in the Far North-West

Recollections of Life in the North-West Mounted Police, Canada, 1884-1888

John G. Donkin

Foreword to the Spectra edition by Murray Malcolm

Western Producer Prairie Books
Saskatoon, Saskatchewan

Originally published by Sampson Low, Marston, Searle & Rivington,
  London, England, in 1889
Facsimile edition published by Coles Publishing Company, Toronto,
  in 1973

Cover photograph courtesy RCMP Museum, Regina, Saskatchewan
Cover design by John Luckhurst/GDL
Printed and bound in Canada

Western Producer Prairie Books is a unique publishing venture
located in the middle of western Canada and owned by a group of
prairie farmers who are members of Saskatchewan Wheat Pool.
From the first book in 1954, a reprint of a serial originally carried
in the weekly newspaper *The Western Producer,* to the book before
you now, the tradition of providing enjoyable and informative reading
for all Canadians is continued.

Canadian Cataloguing in Publication Data
Donkin, John G. (John George), 1853-1890
    Trooper in the far North-West

    Originally published as: Trooper and Redskin in
    the far North-West. London : S. Low, Marston,
    Searle & Rivington, 1889.
    ISBN 0-88833-246-7

1. Donkin, John G. (John George), 1853-1890.   2. North
West Mounted Police (Canada) – Biography.   3. Northwest,
Canadian – Description and travel – 1871-1905.*   4. Riel
Rebellion, 1885 – Personal narratives, Canadian.
Police – Prairie Provinces – Biography.   I. Title.
FC3216.3.D64A3 1987   363.2'092'4   C87-098083-1
HV7911.D64A3 1987

CONTENTS

FOREWORD TO THE SPECTRA EDITION xi

INTRODUCTION I

CHAPTER I.

Winnipeg—An unlucky squaw—A contrast—Fort Osborne Barracks—Accepted—A reminiscence—The ups and downs of life—Off to Regina—The journey West . . 8

CHAPTER II.

Extent of the North-West Territory—Regina—The Barracks —An expedition—Quarters and comrades . . . 18

CHAPTER III.

Organization of N.W.M.P.—General fatigue—Indian Summer —Cold—Provost guard—Prisoners—Escape of Sioux— The Broncho—All sorts and conditions of men—Horse-thieves—Pay—Fever—The irate doctor 29

CHAPTER IV

Winter—Volunteers for Saskatchewan—Jumpers and moc-casins—To Qu'Appelle—Intense cold—A model hotel— Tent pegs or beefsteaks ?—A terrible march . . . 43

CHAPTER V.

The bear—Touchwood Hills—A native gentleman—The great salt plains—Sixty-two below zero—Played out—A

rest—Humboldt—Timber wolves—Hoodoo—Christmas
Day 60

CHAPTER VI.

Leave Hoodoo—Manitchinass Hill—A splendid view—Our
Christmas dinner—Batoche—The South Saskatchewan
—Duck Lake—Fort Carlton 68

CHAPTER VII.

Carlton to Prince Albert—Frozen wheat—A digression—A
splendid grazing country—" Johnnie Saskatchewan's "
palace—Brick barracks—Freedom of social life—A look
round 81

CHAPTER VIII.

1885—Inspection—Our surroundings—Clear Sky Land—
Rabbits and lynx—Easy routine—A whisky desperado—
Precious snow—North-West liquor law—Curling—Skating
—Dog trains—An Indian swell—Mother Smoke—Night
picquet—A night scene—Night thoughts 88

CHAPTER IX.

An unwelcome prisoner—Riel busy—Seditious meetings—
Threats—The Metis—Louis David Riel—A prophet—A
council of State—The provisional government—A new
religion — Red Tape — Urgent despatches — Carlton
strengthened—A convenient eclipse—Arrival of arms—
The volunteers—Scouts—A man who wanted gore—A
meddling official—The rebellion inaugurated—Officials
imprisoned—A Batoche farce—Arrival of Colonel Irvine
—Frostbite—Snow blindness 99

CHAPTER X.

Colonel Irvine departs—The fight at Duck Lake . . . 114

CHAPTER XI.

Prince Albert after the fight—Settlers summoned together—
Church fortified—Scenes within the stockade—Exalted

warriors—Inside the church—A sortie for grub—A flutter
in the dove-cot—The burning of Fort Carlton—A retreat
—An excited Scotchman and an astonished parade—A
false alarm—Inaction—Colonel Irvine 123

CHAPTER XII.

Dreary days—Defence organized—Strange weapons of war—
Patriots—An arrival—Bad news—Battleford burnt—A
fighting rig—Dead disfigured—Fighting corrals—
Rumours—A sortie and a countermarch—Ice breaks up
—Frog Lake massacre—Retreat from Fort Pitt—Leave
barracks—Fish Creek—A Jingo Bishop—The Zoo—
Battle of Batoche 134

CHAPTER XIII.

Battle of Cut-Knife Creek—Painted horses—Capture of transport—General Middleton enters Prince Albert—
" Gophers "—An invidious comparison—Martial music—
Saskatchewan steamers—Departure of troops—A strange
coincidence—Pursuit of Big Bear—Hot weather—Mosquitoes—Fish—Big Bear captured—Return of Green
Lake column 145

CHAPTER XIV.

Troops homeward bound—Big Bear goes to Regina—Mutual
Admiration Society—A good word for the police—*Esprit
de corps*—Sioux teepes—Squaws bathing—Riel sentenced
—Indian summer—The verge of the wilderness—Good-
bye to Prince Albert—Batoche bush-fires—A pleasant
camp—A chorus of coyotes 159

CHAPTER XV.

Humboldt—A strange caravan—The salt plains again—The
springs—An unpleasant situation—Indian camp—Chil-
dren—An Indian masher—Fire bags—A game preserve
—An early reveillé—Skunk Bluffs—Qu'Appelle—Lord
Lansdowne—Cigars—An Indian legend — Harvest—
Prairie fires—Pieapot's reserve—The great prairie—
Regina—A change—Leave of absence 172

CHAPTER XVI.

Louis Riel in prison—The guard-room—Guard increased—Riel doomed—Duty heavy—New organization—Mud and rain—A way to take up land—A *contretemps*—Riel's politeness—His devotions—*Apologia pro vita sua*—A prophet—Père André—Riel sane—St. Peter appears to Riel—An early breakfast—Exercise—The scaffold—Patrol—The execution 182

CHAPTER XVII.

A miserable guard—Grand rounds—Riel's grave—Winter—1886—A ball—Blizzards—Their power—Electric storms—Fatalities—Newspaper amenities and fibs—Fort Macleod—Calgary—Alberta—A garden—God's country—Chinook winds—Spring—Usual rumours—Leave Regina—Moosejaw—A festive camp—Easter Sunday—Out on the desert—Old Wives Lake—Musings—Solitude—Wood Mountain 195

CHAPTER XVIII.

Life at Wood Mountain—Unseasonable snow—Delights of roughing it—A capture—Gros Ventre Indians—Dirt—The old fort—Dust—Short rations—Fine weather—Patrols—Heat—A stampede—Antelope and sage hens—A sandhill crane—A primitive meal for a hungry man—Indian spies—Sign language—On sentry—Dawn—Gambling—Field-days—Indian graves—A ranche—Cowboys—A suggestion on dress—"Toughs"—Indian depredation and a skirmish 209

CHAPTER XIX.

Bird life—Fireflies—Prairie fires—A surprised broncho—Sioux Indians—Indian treaties—Reserves—Agents—A Sioux beauty—Sweet grass—A lonely view—Thunderstorms—Hay-Spear grass—Winchester carbines—A mail robbery—Arrest—Sentence—A cyclone 225

CHAPTER XX.

March from Wood Mountain—Springs frozen—Willow Bunch—Dangerous descent—Alkali Lake—No water—Big

bluffs—A huge camp fire—Intense cold—Sufferings—
Frostbites—An accident—The mirage—New riding-school
—The cowboy troop—1887—A blizzard—Drills—Blood
Indians—Crees—An Indian march—" Kinneekinick "—
Indian religion—Handshaking—Pipe of peace—Squaws
—A Sioux lady—" Medicine "—Police fired on by Piegans
—Kootenay Indians—Shuswaps 232

CHAPTER XXI.

Wet weather—A sudden order—Off to the Souris—Mud—A
caboose—Broadview—A big spill of whisky—Moosomin
—The Big Pipestone valley—Indians on the trail—
Travoies—A lovely camp—Cannington—Moose Mountain
—Game—Carlyle—Indian deserters—The sun dance—
Initiation of braves—The Souris—Alameda—The frontier 246

CHAPTER XXII.

Life on the Souris—Flies—Mud turtles—A lovely scene—
Thunderstorms and cyclones—A tent scattered—Man lost
—A cloud of mosquitoes—A narrow escape from drown-
ing—Saved by a comrade 262

CHAPTER XXIII.

Off to Wood End—Hill of the Murdered Scout—Crees and
Blackfeet—A storm—Long Creek—A happy valley—Wild
fruit—A Helena girl and culture—Patrols—Wild horses
—Wild hops—Prairie fire—Winter quarters—The Souris
coal-fields—Good-bye 274

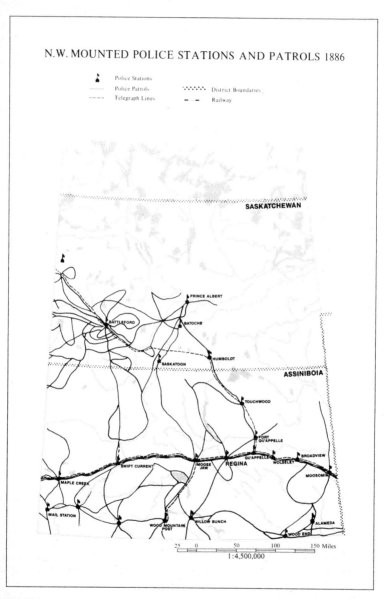

N.W. MOUNTED POLICE STATIONS AND PATROLS 1886

Police Stations
Police Patrols
Telegraph Lines
District Boundaries
Railway

SASKATCHEWAN

PRINCE ALBERT
BATTLEFORD
BATOCHE
HUMBOLDT
SASKATOON
ASSINIBOIA
TOUCHWOOD
FORT QU'APPELLE
QU'APPELLE
BROADVIEW
SWIFT CURRENT
MOOSE JAW
REGINA
WOLSELEY
MOOSOMIN
MAPLE CREEK
MAIL STATION
WOOD MOUNTAIN POST
WILLOW BUNCH
ALAMEDA
WOOD END

25   0   50   100   150 Miles
1:4,500,000

Based on map on page 9 of the *Atlas of Saskatchewan* by J. H.
Richards and K. I. Fung, courtesy Professor J. H. Richards.

Foreword to the Spectra Edition

John Donkin shows us almost four years in the life of a North-West Mounted Police constable. He was a thirty-year-old veteran of the British Army when he signed on for a five-year stint in the force. And he describes a slice of time, 1884–1888, in which the face of the Northwest was being changed forever. The Canadian Pacific Railway had reached Calgary by 1884, and was being pushed, at tremendous cost, through the mountains. At the same time, the Canadian government and the CPR were campaigning for settlers – farmers to till the land – whose presence, it was calculated, would bring profit to the railway and stability to the North-West Territories. Along the rail line towns popped up like mushrooms, each destined, in the eyes of its boosters, to be another Chicago, or perhaps, Winnipeg. All this activity demanded law enforcement: maintaining order in CPR work camps; tracking horse-thieves; seizing smuggled whiskey. The NWMP had been in the Territories just ten years and, by 1884, their numbers had grown to just over five hundred. To use Donkin's figures, this meant that every member had nearly five thousand square miles to patrol. Quite a task!

And if this were not enough, Louis Riel returned to the North-West Territories in 1884. The Red River Rebellion of 1870 had solved nothing for the Métis; the clash of cultures had inflicted wounds that had continued to fester, and Riel's return threatened another upheaval. We see these events—the initial unrest, the rebellion itself, and its tragic end—not in bold brushstrokes on the canvas of history, but in the rumors and speculations of police constables. Through the accounts of other officers, Donkin takes us to the battles at Frog Lake and Cutknife Creek, Duck Lake and Batoche. He shows us, from his own experience, Prince Albert under siege. He details Riel's execution, not from the point of view of one who decided political destinies, but from that of an ordinary policeman who stood guard on the famous prisoner, and who rode patrol on the day of the hanging.

Donkin's account, therefore, is told from the bottom up, so to speak, and it is interesting for precisely that reason. R. Burton Deane, in his *Mounted Police Life in Canada,* writes of the same period as that of Donkin's memoir. But Deane is an officer, and his record is naturally filled with the concerns of an officer: the poor quality of men, the deplorable state of training, the political intrigues of the force. Donkin says little of those things; his account is a useful antidote. When Donkin takes us on border patrol out of Wood Mountain, we see that the most immediate concern is the location of the nearest water, not the latest political maneuver in Ottawa.

Whatever their differences, however, Donkin and Deane write accounts that are alike in one respect: the expressed attitude toward natives and Métis. We may assume that their attitudes were, in their matter-of-fact way, typical of the time. Both men saw themselves as soldiers of the British Empire, with all that that implied. If their opinions are often appallingly racist, that may still be a good thing for us to hear—it's frequently useful to know how far we have come.

Donkin also comments about attempts to farm the Northwest, and he is not optimistic. As a demonstration of the agricultural potential of the West, experimental farms

were established—in defiance of Palliser—on the line west
of Swift Current. By 1886, two years after their
establishment, the experimental farms were counted a
failure. Other experiments were tried in other areas—
Donkin mentions the Bell Farm at Indian Head—some
of which recorded limited success, but all of which,
according to Donkin, were ill-advised. His pessimism
about the future of wheat-growing in the Territories is
based, one suspects, not on some perverse streak of
character, but on his personal struggle with the land, first
as a farmhand near Brandon, and later as a policeman.
Again and again he returns to descriptions of the terrible
loneliness, the breath-taking beauty, the sheer savagery
of the region. His relationship to his surroundings is
paradoxical: a love-hate relationship not unlike that found
in the recorded views of settlers of the time. The urban
boosters were advertising the Northwest in glowing and
extravagant terms: " . . . [in] an illustration of Saskatoon
. . . tall chimneys were emitting volumes of smoke, there
were wharves stacked with merchandise; and huge
steamers, such as adorn the Levees at New Orleans, were
taking in cargo." Donkin saw the real Saskatoon: " . . . six
houses at intervals, and a store." And, as for the matter
of farming on the plains, Donkin saw too many disasters
first-hand: " . . . down came the nipping frost, like a wolf
on the fold, and blighted [the wheat] in a single night."

It was experience of exactly this sort, one suspects,
that colored John Donkin's view of the North-West
Territories. His view was based, not on a vision of what
might be, but on the harsh realities of the emptiness; the
solitude; the shallow, muddy rivers; and the damned,
everlasting weather. A NWMP constable and a farmer
battled the same elements, even if the policeman's wage
was rather more secure.

When Donkin 'purchased' early discharge in 1888, he
left behind a territory that was, in some respects, much

changed. The railway ran all the way to the Pacific Ocean, even if some of the mountain grades were steeper than desirable. Louis Riel was dead, even if his cause was not. More settlers were coming into the Territories, even if their numbers fell short of official hopes. Farming methods were being improved, new strains of wheat were being developed, even if progress was not swift enough to save many farms from disaster.

John Donkin did not live to see later changes in the Northwest: he died in an English workhouse in 1890. One suspects, however, that the vision he took away with him was not one of change and development but rather the one that impressed him more than any other: " . . . the great prairie . . . flat and cheerless like a ghostly sea."

MURRAY MALCOLM

TROOPER

INTRODUCTION

IT is quite a fashionable trip in the tourist season now, to travel from Montreal to Vancouver viâ the Canadian Pacific Railway ; to gaze at the glaciers of the Rockies and the peaks of the Selkirk range ; and perhaps take a run across the Sound to the very English-looking city of Victoria. The majority journey by the beaten track, and their scope of vision is limited by the plate-glass windows of a cosy saloon carriage, or the carved verandah of some Western caravanserai. Many are keen observers and pleasant *raconteurs* of what has actually come within their field of view ; while others, from certain motives, suffer strongly from a self-inflicted strabismus. These former are mostly personal friends of the Governor-General of Canada, while very many more are temporary guests of the mighty potentates who control the destinies of the Canadian Pacific Railway. The tribe of journalistic globe-trotters are special favourites, so long as, by vivid word-painting and artistic pencil, they set forth the wondrous glories of the great North-West.

These chosen of the gods are billeted in luxurious Pulman cars ; the perfect service of the dining-car causes all outward things to be suffused with a rosy light, and unbounded courtesy meets them at every turn. There are even bath-rooms on these trains, and whenever the illustrious stranger pleases to alight at any of the mush-room prairie cities, every official connected with the immense bureaucracy which governs the North-West Territory hastens to do him honour, and act as his *cice-rone*. So, after having been transported across these limitless plains in palaces on bogies, and having been fêted at every halting-place *en route*, they hie them back and add their testimony to the magnificence of the country. No one blames their public-spirited gratitude ; but they have seen nothing of what lies behind the scenes, and they really know nothing of the vast stretch of wild and lonesome land beyond. For, from the 49th parallel of latitude to the great sub-Arctic forest on the left bank of the North Saskatchewan, ranges a *terra incognita* only cut by the ribbon-like line of settlement along the track of the C.P.R. Of this, I declare emphatically, these birds of passage have no knowledge. As well might some social Puritan go into a theatre for the first time : and, having sat through a play in a private box, set up thereafter as an infallible critic of the drama, and an authority on the mysteries of the *coulisses*. A man may go to Bombay in a P. and O. steamer, and yet know nothing of Madagascar. Yet many of these in-vited travellers, after their arrowy flight, send forth their impressions of the unknown with as much dogmatic assertion as the Supreme Pontiff has, when dispensing an encyclical *urbi et orbi*.

I do not think that any one, since Butler wrote his "Great Lone Land," has thrown light on the hidden phases of existence in this vast abode of desolation. The mounted police have been organized since his soli-tary expedition. Indeed he recommended their forma-tion. Therefore I presume to make a new departure and take my indulgent readers away from the world's highway, into strange tracts and scenes of Western life. I shall follow no systematic plan, but simply, in the order they befell, present the things I saw.

They are but the random recollections of a soldier, who had little or no opportunity of taking notes, when in weary bivouac under the comfortless summer's heat, or in icy winter camp. And if the tablets of my memory in places grow but dim, I may call in the aid of other authorities, always being careful to acknowledge my indebtedness.

The Indian *teepe ;* the scattered tents of the mounted police ; or, perhaps, the log-house or sod shanty of some adventurous pioneer, are the only vestiges of human life out in these mighty solitudes. There is the hush of an eternal silence hanging over the far-stretching plains. In early summer, for a brief space, the prairie is green, with shooting threads of gold, and scarlet, and blue, while the odour of wolf-willow and wild-rose floats through the clear air. But, by-and-by, the sun gains power, and scorches, and withers, with a furnace heat ; and through the shimmering haze the grass lies grey and dead. And, under the merciless glare, a great silence broods over all. Is it a wonder that the lonely savage hears the voice of the Manitou in every breath of air in this weird, still desert ? No tree nor bush relieves the aching eye ; there is nothing but the dim, fading ring of the horizon all around. It is truly a strange, haunting silence ;—a hush that may be felt. In winter it is more awful still, covered with one unbroken mantle of pure white ; and stream and sleugh, pond and lake, are locked in the stern grasp of ice. The starved coyoté prowls through the wilderness, and the howling, deathly blizzard revels in demon riot. No buffalo roam these mighty pastures now, a few deer and prairie chicken, and wild duck are all the game.

There is a terrible monotony and sameness in the aspect of this " Great American Desert," as the old maps styled it. You may blindfold a man in places, and take him to another spot 100 miles away; when, on removing his bandage, I would wager he would think he had simply travelled round to his starting-point. But I shall have plenty of opportunity in the course of my narrative to illustrate the scenery through which we pass.

I left Liverpool in the month of April, 1884, by the Dominion Liner *Sarnia;* with no very definite idea as to where my zigzag wanderings would end. On board, there were the usual samples of migratory bipeds, of the human species, that one comes across on an out-going Atlantic steamer.

I heard a good deal regarding Manitoba and the North-West from my *compagnons de voyage*, a few of whom were going out as " premiumed pupils " to farmers. They occasionally produced some extraordinary agreement, which they afterwards found not to be worth the paper upon which it was written, in spite of the penny receipt stamp. I will give the subsequent history of some of these amateur husbandmen, for which I can vouch. I think it will be interesting, and may act as a warning to the gullible. In these pages I shall abstain from all comment when possible, merely stating facts, leaving others to draw the moral.

One was an ex-sergeant of the 9th Lancers, just back from India, after completing his term of service. When he arrived at the rendezvous, Brandon Hills, Manitoba, he was given a potato-shed in which to sleep, by the bucolic professor to whom he was consigned. He forthwith returned to his native county of Banff, sadder and wiser. I believe he, in his righteous wrath, fell foul of the advertising genius who had induced him to emigrate, and the demand for pupils suddenly ceased.

Another example—son of an ex-colonel of the line, joined the mounted police shortly after I did. When I left, he was bugler in A troop.

A third (who displayed most wisdom) went at once from Montreal by a rapid train through the state of Vermont to New York ; and having succeeded in catching that Guion greyhound, the *Alaska*, made a bee-line to Liverpool again.

Two more, with money and brains in an inverse ratio, were pounced upon by the Manitoba representative of " the firm " as very convenient pigeons to pluck, and domesticated with his own saintly family. He was a minister of the gospel, I regret to say. The last time I saw them, they were driving commissariat teams with General Middleton's column, when he relieved us at Prince Albert during the rebellion of 1885.

There was also a son of a Northumbrian vicar, whom I know ; he obtained uncongenial employment, near Winnipeg, hoeing potatoes at fifty cents per diem.

At night, when we of the second class gathered together for our *tabak-parlement*, I had the wonders of the promised land so hammered into me (by these gentle-men who had never been there) that I determined to explore this " wheat-growing oasis " myself. It was here also that I heard first tidings of the corps in which I was afterwards destined to have the honour to serve.

At length, travelling by way of Toronto, Owen Sound, on and across the big lakes by the magnificent new *Algoma* to Port Arthur, I reached Brandon in the middle of May. I hired myself to a farmer, seven miles south-east of the city in the most fertile part of the province. After a few months' trial of the practical teaching of the delights of Virgil's Georgics, I found that the pursuit of husbandry was much too slow for me. So I left the log shanty in the Brandon Hills, one sunny afternoon about the end of August, and betook myself to town.

A day or two afterwards, I was wandering along Rosser Avenue, when I suddenly saw approaching the lithe figure of a scarlet-clad warrior. A cavalry forage cap "on three hairs," two gold-lace chevrons on the arm, a pair of dark-blue riding pants with yellow stripes, long boots faultlessly clean, burnished spurs, a silver-mounted whip and white gauntlets, completed his dress: There was no mistaking the lounging swing and swagger of the "regular." Now, I have a tolerable acquaintance with the Army List, and an average knowledge of the distribution of her Majesty's forces. So I could not make him out. My highly intelligent "boss" out at the farm had informed me, in answer to my inquiries, that the mounted police, in the territories, were clad in "anything and a slouch hat," and he also confided to me that he guessed they were "hard seeds." It was not till later, that the Manitoba Government had to ask for the services of these "hard seeds" to clear their province of horse-thieves, when desperadoes were brandishing revolvers in the streets of Deloraine. This smart cavalryman was quite a conundrum to me. Having served in a cavalry corps at home, my heart warmed to him at once, and I crossed over, saying with Western freedom, "Excuse me, old man, what regiment do you belong to?"

"I belong to the North-West Mounted Police," replied the corporal, smiling.

There was very little either of the half-breed or the "hard seed" about him; and, after some talk, we entered the Grand View Hotel—the best in the city—where he was staying, and over some liquid refreshment exchanged experiences. He was a very gentlemanly fellow, and at one time had held a commission in a Lincolnshire volunteer corps. He was enjoying the mild pleasures of Brandon, on a few days' leave. There is no freemasonry in the world equal to that which exists among soldiers. We were soon immersed in a long talk over " the service," and it ended in my forming the resolution to proceed to Winnipeg, and, if possible, become one of " The Riders of the Plains."

I had experienced quite enough of clod-breaking. I had "broken" thirteen acres of virgin prairie with a team of curse-compelling oxen (a newly coined Homeric epithet) ; I had harrowed and rolled, I had planted potatoes, and made hay ; I had hoed wild buckwheat till my spine was bent ; and had voted it a fraud. It was "not my forte," I was not cut out for a horny handed husbandman, and, having made up my mind to take a turn at soldiering again, I went down to Winnipeg to try my luck.

CHAPTER I

Winnipeg—An unlucky squaw—A contrast—Fort Osborne Barracks
—Accepted—A reminiscence—The ups and downs of life—
Off to Regina—The journey West.

WINNIPEG, in 1871, consisted of a straggling range of
wooden huts ; upon the outskirts of which stood the dingy
teepe of the Indian, and the noisome tent of the half-
breed. It is now a city of nearly 25,000 souls, standing
upon a flat expanse at the junction of the Red River and
the Assineboine. I had seen many bird's-eye views of
Winnipeg in emigration pamphlets ; very florid in
detail, with tramcar lines radiating in all directions along
wide and magnificent streets. There were steamers
speeding over broad rivers, and open spaces laid out as
parks. This may be the happy state of affairs in the
future ; but I was much disappointed in finding nothing
of the sort.

It was in a transition state in 1884 ; the dirt, drink, and
debauchery of the half-breed hovel being cheek by jowl
with a shining structure of brick dedicated to religion.
Main Street, which is now a fine thoroughfare, was then
a perfect *muskeg ;* and I saw an unlucky squaw, with her
pony and Red River cart, firmly embedded in the glu-
tinous compound which did duty as a roadway. I have
had some experience of mud, and once imagined the
Constantinople product could not be beaten ; but for
fixity of tenure I give the palm to the cement-like
mixture of the Canadian North-West. The Red River

cart is a peculiar institution, constructed entirely
of wood, and drawn by an Indian pony. These native
quadrupeds, in the Far West, are called cayeuses, or
shagganappis. When this wondrous rheumatic vehicle
is set in motion the creaking and groaning is most
excruciating ; at one time it was the sole mode of transport across the plains in summer. Place the body upon
runners, and you have the " jumper " sleigh.

Instead of gay passenger craft skimming the far-famed
Red River, I found a couple of steamboats laid up,
owing to the shallowness of the water. The stream is
but a muddy ditch, and the Assineboine is little better.
There were a few lumber-mills along the sides. The
stores and drinking-saloons were principally occupied
by immigrants from Ontario.

I must say I observed a great improvement in the
city on my return in 1888. Main Street is paved with
blocks of wood, buildings of brick and stone everywhere
meet the eye ; the hotels are all that can be desired,
while the new City Hall rears its lofty pinnacles in proud
superiority.

The increase in population shows more clearly the
growth of a city than any other evidence, and the following figures at periods of eight years, prove the marvellous
strides Winnipeg has made ; the 1000 of 1872 had
risen to 6500 in 1880, and to 22,000 in 1888. I may as
well mention here that the city does not stand on the
margin of the huge lake of the same name. It is fully
sixty miles from the shores of that inland sea, which
stretches its desolate waters a length of 240 miles.

It was a lovely morning—clear and slightly frosty—at
the end of September, when I wended my way, past the
ruins of old Fort Garry, towards Fort Osborne. Fort
Garry at one time was the headquarters of the Hudson
Bay Company, and was held by Riel during the first

rebellion, which caused Lord (then Colonel) Wolseley's expedition to the Red River. The borders of the bush along the banks of the two rivers were rich in the russet and scarlet of autumn tints, the blue sky was flecked with fleecy clouds ; and a fresh breeze came scampering from the western prairies, laden with health.

Fort Osborne, in those days, was the only recruiting depôt for the North-West Mounted Police. The force only consisted of 500 men ; and it was not so very easy then to obtain entry into the ranks. The strength of the corps is now 1000 ; and, since the rebellion, Ottawa has been the principal place for obtaining men ; though recruiting parties have at various times made a tour of Ontario. Men who joined in 1884 were obliged to make their own way to the capital of Manitoba ; and had abundance of time to reflect upon the undertaking before them. Now, a recruiting sergeant is not so very particular as to the antecedents of the candidates before him ; and many youths in a chronic state of joviality are shipped to Regina, who imagine that the only duty they have is to ride round the prairie in a general state of independence.

On arriving at the gate of the fort, the first thing that met my eye was a strapping sentry, with his carbine at the " Support," and his revolver in holster at his side. His buttons, spurs, helmet spike, and chain glittered in the sun, his brass cartridges, peeping in even rows from his belt, gleamed with a brilliant lustre ; his white helmet was pipeclayed without a speck ; while his scarlet tunic and long boots were perfect in fit. A small detachment of North-West Mounted Police was stationed here to look after certain stores belonging to the Militia Department. Government House, the residence of the Lieutenant-Governor of Manitoba, was just over the way. The barracks consisted of a series of wooden huts, whitewashed, and standing in a line. On the other side of the square stood the stables. The wooded banks of the Assineboine were behind the stables; and a few artistically painted wooden villas were scattered about the surrounding ground.

On stating my errand, I was told to go across to No. 4 block; and there I found a smart orderly, with spotless gauntlets and riding-whip, sunning himself on a bench in front of the building. He conducted me to the sergeant, a slightly-built man, with a little, fair moustache. I immediately addressed this youthful non-com. as Sergeant-Major, not on diplomatic grounds, but because I observed a gold crown above his triple chevron. In the British Service this is the badge of a troop sergeant-major, but it is worn by every sergeant in the N.W.M.P. I informed him that I wished to join the force, and he, pleasantly, told me that the doctor would not be in attendance till eleven o'clock, and that I could either wait or come back at that hour. As Fort Osborne was some distance from the city, I preferred to remain. So my booted and spurred Mercury led me to the barrack-room, where I was made to feel at home at once. I might have been a returned comrade for all the attentions I received. I was offered many seats, and many plugs of tobacco were produced, with invitations to " have a smoke."

The interior of the room was just the same as any other troopers' quarters from Peshawur to Hong Kong. The floor clean, stove polished, walls white, beds in a row, bedding made up, blankets folded, and kits on shelf, according to regulation pattern, tables down the centre, men employed as usual when off duty ; with jackets off and sleeves rolled up. One engaged in burnishing ; another brushing, and a third daubing his gloves with a wet pipeclay sponge. One trooper with a

black moustache, sitting reading and smoking, but
nearly all "chewing the rag," which is service vernacular
for talking.   The corporal was busy with his enigmatic
"returns," which generally resolve themselves into an
arithmetical puzzle.   They had a pleasant time of it,
these lucky ones.   No drills, short stables, and very
little in the way of duty.   Day and night guard was
the sole trouble.   The guard-mounting and ornamental
work was solely on account of a few obsolete field-pieces,
and the representative of royalty across the way.

There was a very cheery fellow polishing his cartridges, who had been in the Scots Greys, and who
informed me he would rather clean a sword and scab-
bard any day than these.   There are twenty Winchester
and twelve Enfield cartridges in each belt, which is
constructed like a bandolier.   This jovial Yorkshireman
gave me many hints regarding my future, and said I
should meet some jolly fellows at Regina.

At 10 a.m. the sergeant entered and handed me a
printed paper, which he told me to read carefully.   It
contained a number of queries, as to whether I had
served in her Majesty's service, was I married, could I
read and write, was I able to give testimonials as to
character, and was I accustomed to the care and
management of horses.   At eleven o'clock I was marched
into the orderly-room, where an officer, in gold lace,
forage cap and patrol jacket, was seated amid a pile of
papers.   He put a lot of searching questions, eyeing me
keenly the while.   Apparently this inquisitorial exami-
nation was satisfactory, and I signed a paper, in
duplicate, vowing allegiance to the powers that be, and
engaging myself to serve for five years in the North-West
Mounted Police.

I was then introduced to the sanctum of the medico,
who put me through the usual tests as to eyesight, and

examined my architecture generally, while I stood *in puris naturalibus*. During this pretty severe ordeal I observed a paper pinned to the wall above the desk which revealed to me that the previous candidate had been rejected. This made me feel rather nervous as to the result ; but I was relieved to find that I came through, with the magic word " accepted " against my name ; and here also my papers were signed by the doctor, and given me to take back to the orderly-room. After handing in my medical documents, the sergeant informed me I could make myself at home with the men for the remainder of the day, and that I should start the following morning for Regina.

The day passed pleasantly over with jokes, yarns, laughter, and tobacco. The men all seemed to possess a good-humoured spirit of *camaraderie*, and all seemed content. Certainly they were well off, and led a totally different life to the others in the Territories. Many indeed applied for a transfer to head-qnarters, after a spell of this Capua, so that they might have a chance of saving money. Winnipeg and its gaieties were too much for their slender pay. A month's pay—which at the lowest is fifteen dollars, or three pounds—drawn upon a Saturday, would have entirely vanished by the following Monday. The grub at the Fort Osborne barracks was excellent. There was a rattling good dinner of tender beef, mashed potatoes, and rice pudding. But they luckily possessed the services of a female cook, each man subscribing ten cents (fivepence) daily towards the expenses of the mess. The non-coms and men messed together in the barrack-room.

I slept that night once more in the narrow cot of a soldier, taking possession of the bed of a man on guard. I remember, when leaving the old regiment at the Island Bridge barracks in Dublin, the regimental sergeant-major saying to me, on my way to the office for my discharge, " Well, tired of soldiering, eh ? "

"Yes, sir, for a spell," I replied.

But when I doffed the blue and white of the lancer, I certainly never dreamed of joining any band of exiles in such remote quarters as these. So, musing upon the vicissitudes of fortune, I fell asleep, and was awakened about 1 a.m. by a dilapidated arrival from town, who required the services of a sleepy fatigue party from the surrounding beds to remove his clothes. I was soon over once more in the land of nod, and remained there till reveillé.

A defaulter of the previous day was to be my escort to Regina. We made a hasty breakfast of beefsteak, coffee, and bread and butter, and found the transport waggon ready to convey M—— and his baggage and myself to the station. The corporal occupied a seat in front beside the driver, and we took up our perch behind them. We jumped on board the west-bound train at 7.30. The Canadian Pacific Railway was not at that time entirely completed. The trains only ran as far as Calgary, 839 miles west of Winnipeg. It was Fort Calgary then, and merely consisted of the Mounted Police post and a congregation of canvas dwellings. British Columbia was not so easy of access then as it is now. The early French adventurers who first sighted the gleaming summits of the Montagnes des Rochers never imagined that a day would come when the iron horse would rush shrieking through the awful chasms, beneath their ice-clad peaks.

My chum had a cargo of whisky stowed away among his baggage to take to Regina for distribution among " the boys." Each member of the force is expected by his comrades when entering the territory to bring a libation of " old rye " or " bourbon " with him, from the more favoured regions. This is a pretty commentary upon the prohibition law.

The car in which we were seated was peopled with a few Manitoba farmers and Winnipeg grain dealers, and one commercial "gent" in the cigar line. This latter representative of the artistic manufacture of cabbage-leaves attracted my attention from the fact that every cigar he offered for inspection was superior to the preceding one, although he had pronounced each in turn to be the very climax of perfection. The usual newspaper "boy"—*ætat.* thirty—walked through the cars, making periodic visits with peanuts, apples, candies and other indigestible matter at fancy prices. These are fixed with a lofty disregard of the principles of political economy, and seem to be imposed specially to stop the demand.

The country between Port Arthur and Winnipeg, to the east, is muskeg, rock, and forest, gloomy and rough. The scene changes marvellously on crossing the Louise bridge, over the Red River. Here, as one travels westward, the prairie stretches away flat as a billiard-table, far on either side, though in the distance, to the south, you can see the fringe of bush that denotes the windings of the sluggish Assiniboine. The only place to look for timber out here is by the banks of the streams. Log-houses are scattered about at intervals in a sort of skirmishing order, but no pleasant orchard or shady grove adds a tinge of romantic beauty to these lonely western homes. All is bleak, and cheerless, one homestead is the direct counterpart of another. A log-house thatched with straw, a cattle-shed, and corral make up the prairie farm. There are an improved class of houses now, but I am speaking of the general run of pioneer dwellings in 1884.

At Carberry we make a frantic rush across to the

hotel for dinner. There were no sumptuous dining-cars attached to each train in those days, as there are now. On to Brandon again, crossing the Assiniboine by a trestle bridge. Here lies a steamboat which once succeeded in reaching this spot during an exceptional spring flood; but which can never return, save in its original fragments. A few Indian teepes stud the flats by the river.

It was evening when we reached Moosomin, the first station in the North-West Territory. From here to the Rockies, a distance of 700 miles, the train runs through the Great Lone Land. There were only a couple of the Mounted Police stationed here; and this is the extreme eastern limit of their jurisdiction. The train is supposed to be searched for whisky, but a constable or corporal merely promenades with clanking spurs down the aisles of the cars. Freight deposited at the station, however, undergoes a rigid scrutiny. My friend, the corporal, whom I had met in Brandon a month ago, was now stationed here; and he came on board, with blue cloak reaching to his heels, for it was raining. We adjourned to the lavatory (to save scandal) where we each had a sup out of a mysterious bottle.

It was dark when we reached Broadview. Here, in the dining-hall (*Anglicé* refreshment-room) we partook of supper consisting of a tough mallard, tea and buns. For this we paid sixty cents (2s. 6d.) each, police rate. Unfortunate civilians had to stump out fifteen cents more.

Resuming our places on the train again, a Winnipeg banker, with a friend of his from Scotland, joined us in conversation. The stranger,—a gentlemanly man in a light ulster—was going to visit the Bell Farm, near Indian Head. This was one of the show places of the North-West, and was always paraded as one of the seven wonders of the world. It is not mentioned now, in emigration pamphlets, I see. It consisted of 10,000 acres of wheat land, and was a gigantic failure ; it is now being, or has been, sold in small patches of 160 acres each.

Travelling on these trains is dreary work, even now when they run from ocean to ocean. In spite of their sleeping-cars and bath-rooms, in spite of the delicacies of the dining-cars, in spite of the rich upholstering, the polished red and white mahogany and satin-wood, in spite of the adornments of antique brass—they cannot, exceed the speed of twenty miles an hour, even now. It was, if possible, worse in 1884. The engineer "guessed" he didn't care, no more did the conductor. The train was only going that night as far as Moosejaw ; about forty miles west of Regina, and the end of a section. There were only three trains a week further west. So Mr. McA., the banker, produced a pack of cards, and by the struggling light of a wobbling oil-lamp we played whist. Indian Head (where there is a reserve of Assiniboine Indians) was reached eventually, and my chum and I were left alone, till, at length, about 2 a:m. we were set down, in a drizzling rain, upon the desolate platform at Regina.

CHAPTER II

Extent of the North-West Territory—Regina—The barracks—An
expedition—Quarters and comrades.

THE North-West Territories consist of the provisional
districts of Assiniboia, Alberta, Athabasca, and
Saskatchewan. The territory extends from the
boundary of Manitoba on the east, to the summit of
the Rocky Mountains on the west, and from the 49th
parallel of north latitude on the south, to the North
Pole. The area of this immense region is two million
six hundred and sixty-five thousand (2,665,000) square
miles. The total area of the whole of the remaining
portion of Canada is only 885,207 square miles The
total area of Europe is 3,900,000 square miles. The
capital of the whole of the North-West Territory is
Regina. When I say that, in 1884, the chief city of
this region only contained 1000 inhabitants, I may
convey some dim idea to the minds of my readers, of the
surrounding desolation.

There is a station in the town at Regina for a couple
of the police ; a telephone wire connecting it with the
barracks, which are two miles and a half distant to the
west. A corporal and one man are quartered here,
whose principal duty is to meet the various trains and
despatch the various telegrams, verbally, to the barracks,
as they arrive. They also do a considerable amount of
shopping for the officers, who transmit orders by telephone. This building is a frame cottage of two rooms,
with a species of loft upstairs.

We found the corporal meeting the train upon our arrival ; and we followed him across to his shanty.   He was not in a very pleasant humour—*ça va sans dire.*   So M—— went over to one of the hotels, to see if we could secure quarters until breakfast.   His errand was fruitless. The " Assiniboia Agricultural Society "—save the mark ! —was to hold its inaugural show upon the following day, and each hostelry was full.   We sat down in a couple of arm-chairs with adamantine seats, by the stove in the police office, where we nodded in uneasy slumber till day-break.   I was thoroughly weary ; and thanked Heaven I was not some tender chicken, fresh from home, for the first time just taking flight,

> " In busy camps the art to learn
> Of evil natures, hard and stern."

Any homesick youth would have fairly broken down at the dismal scene ; all around outside lay a great muddy expanse, with pools of water, while a soaking rain fell from a leaden sky.   A few unpainted wooden houses opposite, bearing dingy sign-boards, formed Broad Street, as it is known now.   A few more erec- tions of the band-box style of architecture, at right angles to the former, comprised the present South Railway Street.   These houses all stood in open order, with dismal spaces of clay, and puddles intervening. The great prairie stretched away, far as the eye could reach, flat and cheerless like a ghostly sea, the railway lines and telegraph poles running to a vanishing point, far, far in the distance.   A Cree squaw, with painted vermilion cheeks, gaudy blanket drawn over her unkempt head, and bedraggled crimson leggings, was standing at the corner of the Pacific Hotel, looking utterly forlorn, though dull apathy was written on her sullen countenance.   Her tepee was visible across the railway track. These dusky beauties are periodically ordered back to their reserves ; only to reappear again as soon as they fancy the official storm has blown over. It is one of the evils which follow civilization.

We crossed over to the hotel, a big, slate-coloured, wooden-frame building. The solemnity which perennially reigns in a North-West hotel is beyond all words. Long-faced men sit silent around the stove, only varying the grim monotony by an occasional expectoration of tobacco juice. Sometimes they may break out, and engage in the congenial pastime of "swapping lies." The bar dedicated to teetotalism (cider is sold and hop beer) makes a ghastly attempt at conviviality and jocoseness, by having an array of bottles of coloured water and cold tea marshalled upon a series of shelves and labelled, " Old Tom," " Fine Old Rye," Hennessy's "Silver Star," or " Best Jamaica." With what hideous humour do these tantalizing legends taunt the thirsty tenderfoot from " down East."

We performed our ablutions in a tin basin, set upon a rickety chair in the narrow entrance passage, and wiped ourselves upon an antique towel, which seemed to have been recently fished out of the nearest slough. While we were at breakfast, the chief Pieapot drove past the window in a buckboard. This contumacious redskin wore a fur cap adorned with feathers ; his face had been cast in the usual mould which nature uses to produce the Cree ; high cheekbones, flat nose, and small, cunning eyes set closely together. After our meal, comprising tough beefsteak and turbid coffee, we sauntered back to the police quarters. The corporal, after much growling, telephoned to barracks, "Constable —— and a recruit here. Send down a team." Then he went, snarling, to the hotel to breakfast. We lounged about, and smoked the matutinal pipe, till a transport waggon drove up to the door. It was a four-wheeled vehicle, painted ordnance blue, drawn by a couple of fine greys. We took up our position on a seat behind the driver, gathered up M——'s baggage at the railway depôt, and set off through the "streets" of the capital. Through ponds we dashed, splashed from head to foot ; over hills whence we enjoyed an uninterrupted view through bedroom windows ; and down into hollows where we were completely hidden. And this the chief city of a territory nearly two-thirds the size of the whole of Europe !

On our voyage through the town, labouring heavily, we were hailed by a staff-sergeant at Tinning and Hoskin's store. This belaced gentleman wanted a lift, so we waited for him. What a great deal of future benefit I missed, in not knowing, at the time, that he had previously been a non-commissioned officer in the Royal Artillery at a certain northern watering-place, where I had lived. There are many repetitions in real life of Longfellow's Atchafalaya. Just a question or two, given and answered, and we should have become fast friends. I knew his colonel well. I was not aware of this till long afterwards. On driving across the railway line, we met the adjutant, a tall, fine-looking man with a long, yellow moustache, mounted upon a sorrel charger. Here, it was a case of " Eyes right ! " We now caught sight of the barracks in the distance ; the houses clustering like those of a village, with red roofs. The glorious old rag was flying bravely from a flagstaff, and figures on horseback were moving about upon the open ground. One compact body was engaged in field movements, while a few in single file were in the manège There was no covered-in riding-school then. We crossed the Wascana Creek, but it was dry. On the maps it is shown as a river ; but only contains running water for about a fortnight, when the snow melts. Some of the Regina "boomsters" had been recently extolling the many glories of this mysterious stream, which annually vanishes in the summer heat. A savage wit thereupon burst forth in verse, in the columns of the Winnipeg *Sun*, regarding this exaggerated ditch, saying he had beheld all the mighty torrents of the world—

" But of all the famous rivers which our orb terrestrial owns,
   Stands first the Great Wascana, which they term the Pile of Bones;
   Stands first the Great Wascana, fair river of the plains,
   Which bathes august Regina where Viceroy Dewdney reigns.

Wascana; in the Cree language signifies, Pile of Bones. The Hon. Edgar Dewdney was the late Lieut.-Governor of the Territory.

The barracks are built entirely of wood, and are not enclosed, but stand in the centre of the endless plain. They are laid out in the form of a square, about half a mile to the north of the railway line. Scattered around, outside the cantonment, are a few small frame houses, the quarters of the married men or of civilians who obtain employment from the police. All around the inside of the square runs a side-walk of planks, raised a little above the ground, a sort of causeway in fact. The four sides of the barracks correspond with the four cardinal points of the compass. Each block of buildings is at some little distance from the other, to minimize, if possible, the danger in case of fire. New barracks have been erected since, but in 1884 they were merely temporary, portable structures. The corps only consisted of 500 men, as I have said, and only the permanent staff and recruits occupied headquarters. In those days you entered the barracks at the south-east corner, and, on turning to the left, the first block was the officers' mess. You then passed, in succession, the orderly room and commissioner's office, guard-room,

recreation-rooms, sergeant's mess, sergeant-major's
quarters and mess-room, and kitchen at the end. The
flagstaff stood in front of the guard-room. This completed the south side. The whole of the west side
consisted of six frame huts, at intervals, each supposed
to afford accommodation for eleven troopers. At the
north-west corner was a large barrack-room for twenty
men, with the sergeant's quarters attached. Upon the
north side there were offices for the armourer-sergeant
and saddler, with a couple of two-storied houses for
married officers, and the residence of the principal
medical officer. Officers' quarters occupied the remainder
of the square. At the rear of the men's quarters was an
additional space formed by the five troop stables to the
west ; blacksmith's shop and waggon-shed on the south,
and coal-shed and bakehouse to the north. There was
also a lavatory and bath-room behind the men's rooms.
The hospital and quartermaster's store were out on the
prairie to the north. And all around lay the flat
expanse without tree, or bush, or mound to break the
uniform monotony. On clear days, away to the south-
west, might be seen sometimes the dim, low outline of
the Dirt Hills, where grow the trees with a loathsome,
putrid smell. The Indians have a name for the wood,
which is hardly fit to bear translation here. Sometimes
also, to the east, lifted in air by the mirage, could be
discerned a ghostlike line of bush, which clusters like an
oasis upon the slopes of the Qu'Appelle. These islands
of foliage are the remains of a once mighty forest,
reaching south from the Saskatchewan, through the
former serried ranks of which the fire-king has ploughed
his way.

On our arrival, the square was dotted with the usual
figures peculiar to barrack life. Men in fatigue-dress
were loafing around the doorways, and smart orderlies

and non-coms. were hurrying to and fro. There was an extra amount of bustle on this occasion, as an expedition of 100 men were under orders to start for Battleford, a distant post at the confluence of the Battle River with the Saskatchewan. The small column was to take a nine-pounder brass field-piece with them, and, in consequence, all sorts of absurd rumours—the produce of imaginative minds—were floating about. The Indians had risen in the Eagle Hills, said one. Another had certain intelligence that the half-breeds had organized a *razzia* on the Hudson Bay post at Fort Pitt. These canards, I afterwards discovered, were of periodical birth, and were set flying upon very flimsy provocation.

My companion from Winnipeg was warned for this enterprise, as soon as we descended from our chariot. I was taken at once by the orderly sergeant, to the commissioner's office. Colonel Irvine was seated at his table, glancing over my papers, which had been forwarded by mail. He was a slight man, with a keen, grey eye, and reddish beard closely trimmed. His father had been A.D.C. to Lord Gosford, when the latter was Governor-General. He himself had served in the expeditionary force to the Red River. He was one of the most thorough gentlemen whom I have ever had the honour to serve under. After replying to a few brief questions, I was sworn in, and dismissed, having been ordered to report to the sergeant-major.

I found this stalwart specimen of the dragoon in his quarters. He had been formerly in the 2nd Life Guards. He directed me to proceed to No. 8 Barrack-Room, telling me to remain there till further orders. In the afternoon, he said, I should receive a supply of blankets. I was then shown to the large barrack-room at the corner of the square. Every one here was busily engaged in preparing for departure on the morrow. Uniforms were being brushed up ; headropes, helmets, and gauntlets pipeclayed; spurs burnished, and boots polished. There was to be a general parade in the afternoon. I wrote a couple of letters, amid the horrid din, to relatives who probably did not care a rap about my whereabouts. The agony of epistolary composition was materially intensified by the clattering row ; but, *en la guerra como en la guerra*. Only I don't suppose that the booted and moustachioed hidalgo of Alva or the Emperor Charles who gave birth to the above remark ever troubled himself to write from noisy camp or wine-shop.

The kindness of my newly acquired comrades was excessive. I had at least six different offers of paper and stamps.

It was a cold raw day as we went down to the mess-room, when "dinner-up" sounded. This was a large room with a number of tables in rows, a corporal being at the head of each. One of them beckoned me to his table. He was a very nice fellow, and had at one time, been adjutant of an infantry regiment, and had served in South Africa. I found there were several in the ranks who had held commissions at home. We had a very good dinner of roast beef, potatoes, abundance of bread and tea. Tea is always the drink which accompanies dinner. After dinner I returned to the big barrack-room, after visiting the smaller. In one of the latter, I met a man who had been in the 60th Rifles on the Red River Expedition, with Wolseley. While sitting smoking by the stove, there entered a *blasé* individual in civilian dress with a long drooping moustache, who languidly deposited himself on a bed, and proceeded to roll up a cigarette. Then with a drawl, suggestive of Pall Mall, he uttered the following sentiment :—" There's nothing very lively and entertaining about those stables!" He had joined on the previous day, and was now doing duty as stable orderly or stable guard; and having been relieved for his dinner, had come in to take a rest. He looked very much as if he had been born tired. In the Imperial service the stable guards have their meals taken to them, and eat them generally seated on a stable bucket.

The dreaded inspection parade, mounted and dismounted, took place at 3 p.m. The men looked very smart in scarlet tunics with pipe-clayed haversacks and white helmets, the spikes and chin-scales gleaming. A new button had just been issued, bearing a buffalo head surmounted by a crown, and a label with the letters N.W.M.P. Canada. The old buttons only bore a crown. A good number of the men on parade were simply recruits; for, as the authorities were short of men, they were obliged to take every one available. I was assured that, had there been time for me to have received my kit, I should have been included in the gathering. I was subsequently thankful I was not; though I was destined to take part in far harder duty. One Hibernian was in great glee. "Shure! I've only been up foive days an' I'm on active service already." He was called Active Service ever after; and he very soon learnt that was the normal condition of life out here. No swaggering about town, in these parts, with a girl on your arm.

We had "supper" at 6 p.m., after evening stables. This meal consisted of tea, bread, and cold meat. The Government rations are generally sufficient to provide meat three times a day. Your appetite becomes voracious out in the North-West. There was much desultory talk at night in the room;—the usual *causerie* of the *caserne*. The General Orders were read by the orderly sergeant when he called the roll at watch-setting. I found myself "regimentally numbered 1094, posted to 'B' Troop, and taken on the strength of the force." "First Post" sounded at 9.30, "Last Post" at 10, and "Lights Out" at 10.15 p.m. The cook of the sergeants' mess occupied the next bed to mine. He had been to town, and was somewhat convivial, having discovered a particular brand of cider. In fact the sergeant-major had tackled him regarding his condition on his return, and he had replied, "It's a verra remarkable thing, sergeant-major, that a mon canna' get a wee whiff o' a cigar wi'oot bein' told he's drunk."

He was a strange character, and the son of a Scottish divine. He had seen a good deal of service in the "Forty Twas." He kept me awake by confidentially declaring every now and again, in a stage-whisper, that, on the party marching out in the morning, I would "jeest see an arrméd mob!" He was evidently a "wee thing squiffy."

The once familiar sound of the trumpet, or rather bugle here, under the windows announced reveillé at 6 a.m. I did not turn out to stables this morning. Stables are short in the Mounted Police. There is none of that "perpetual grind"— as Lord Wolseley styles it—which characterizes that duty in the Service at home. On the return of the others there were blankets and bedding rolled up in waterproof sheets and pitched into the waggons. The party marched out at 8.30, to the station, proceeding by special train west to Swift Current. From this place would lie before them a toilsome march of more than 200 miles by trail through uninhabited country and across the Eagle Hills to Battleford. They would cross the South Saskatchewan *en route*, a feat which actually occupied them two days. It was a miserable day of sleet and cold; and, when the rear-guard had gone out of the barracks, I was at

once pounced upon and ordered to do " stable orderly."
The barracks were almost deserted, and every available
unit was utilized.   The duties I had to perform were to
keep the stables clean, watch the horses, fill the nose-
bags noon and evening, and remain at the stables till
relieved by the night guard.   Luckily, there were not
many horses left.

CHAPTER III

Organization of N.W.M.P.—General fatigue—Indian Summer—
Cold—Provost guard—Prisoners—Escape of Sioux—The
Broncho—All sorts and conditions of men—Horse-thieves—
Pay—Fever—The irate doctor.

THE organization of the force, in those days, was as
follows. There were five troops, each supposed to
consist of 100 officers, non-commissioned officers and
men. I do not think any of them, with the exception
of " D " Troop, contained their full complement. Each
troop was commanded by a superintendent with the
relative rank of captain, and there were three inspectors
as subalterns. The commissioner and assistant commissioner ranked as lieutenant-colonel and major respec-
tively.

" A " Troop had headquarters at Maple Creek, with a
detachment at Medicine Hut. " B " Troop was
stationed at Regina, and supplied detachments along
the line of railway. " C " Troop held Fort Macleod,
away in the grassy ranching country, among the Bloods
and Peigans, at the foot of the Rockies. " D " Troop
comprised the northern division on the North
Saskatchewan. There were outposts from Battleford at
Prince Albert and Fort Pitt. In the October of 1884,
the hapless Fort Carlton was taken over from the
Hudson Bay Company, and garrisoned by the majority
of the reinforcement which had just left Regina, many
of them never to return. At Calgary, in the Blackfoot
country, and at the then limit of the C.P. Railway, was

" E " Troop, with detached parties up in the mountains where construction was going on. There were also outposts at Edmonton and Fort Saskatchewan ; near to which the river of that name first springs from its glacier bed.

The day following the departure of the Battleford contingent was Saturday, October 4th, and a day of general fatigue. Every one was engaged in cleaning out empty rooms, and there was a general redistribution of quarters. I found myself billeted in No. 5 of the smaller rooms, which actually possessed a couple of corporals. One of these had served in the 6th Carbineers, in Afghanistan and India, and the other was formerly an officer of the Galway Militia. Poor Talbot Lowry ! he was killed at Cut-Knife Creek. Light lie the turf on his head, for a finer fellow never stepped !

This afternoon I drew my kit. I must confess, I do not think that to any other corps in the world do they supply a better outfit—if as good. Not only was the quantity abundant, but the quality was excellent. I do not know anything of the articles supplied to-day. This is a list of my rig out.

2 pairs long riding boots, 7 pairs in 5 years.
1 pair ankle boots, 3 pairs in 5 years.
3 pairs riding breeches (blue, yellow stripe) annually.
1 burnisher.
1 brush, blacking.
1   ,,   polishing.
1   ,,   brass.
1   ,,   cloth.
1 button stick.
3 pairs blankets (10 lbs. each).
1 pair blanket straps.
1   ,,   braces.
1 cloak, cape, and belt (blue cloth).
1 forage cap, annually.
1 fur cap (busby shape, yellow bag).
1 helmet (white) 2 in 5 years.
1 kit bag (like a large valise, waterproof).
1 cup, plate, knife, fork, and spoon.

2 pairs flannel drawers, annually.
1 haversack.
1 rug.
1 buffalo overcoat (not issued now, buffalo extinct).
1 pair gauntlets.
1 ,, mitts (buckskin) annually.
2 pairs moccasins (moose) 7 pairs in 5 years.
1 hold-all with razor, comb, shaving-brush, and sponge.
2 pairs sheets.
2 ,, long stockings (wool).
4 ,, socks (wool).
2 over shirts, flannel.   } Annually.
2 under shirts ,,
1 tunic, scarlet serge.
1 ,, ,, cloth, 3 in 5 years.
1 tuque (red woollen nightcap).
1 waterproof sheet.
1 palliasse and pillow-case.
1 pair overalls (brown duck).
1 jacket.
1 pair steel spurs.
Horse-brush and curry-comb.

We were armed with the Winchester repeating carbine, holding nine rounds ($\cdot$45-75) in the magazine. The Deane and Adams revolver has now been superseded by the Enfield. We rode in the high-peaked Californian saddle made by Main and Winchester in San Francisco. While I am running through a list of dry details, I may as well give the scale of rations per man per diem.

$1\frac{1}{2}$ lbs. beef, or 1 lb. bacon.
$1\frac{1}{2}$ lbs. bread, or $1\frac{1}{4}$ lbs. flour, or $1\frac{1}{4}$ lbs. biscuit.
$\frac{1}{2}$ oz. tea.
$\frac{1}{2}$,, coffee.
$\frac{1}{2}$,, salt.
3 ,, sugar.
1 ,, rice.
$\frac{1}{36}$,, pepper.
1 lb. potatoes, or 2 ozs. dried apples, or 2 ozs. beans.

When out on the prairie, on "active service," these rations are increased one half.

After a few days of biting cold, accompanied by drifting showers of sleet, the Indian summer descended

upon us like a halo of heaven-sent glory. We enjoyed
a fortnight of the most perfect weather. A soft stillness,
with a thin filmy haze of gold, lay upon the slumbering
plain. Nature seemed hushed in prayer, before with-
standing the ice-blasts of the coming winter. Over in
front of the officers' quarters the ladies amused themselves with lawn tennis. But after this beautiful
vision of a magic season the cold period began in earnest,
and increased daily in intensity. We were to experience the most severe winter known since the advent of
settlement. After the 21st of October you could not
expose your ears to the nipping air. Fur caps were taken
into wear; and forage caps consigned to a temporary
burial under the white helmets on the shelf. I found
the routine to be very easy, as I was dismissed drill in
about a week. Owing to the scarcity of duty men it
was impossible to provide a proper barrack guard, so a
provost-guard—as it is called—was mounted instead.
With this guard there is no sentry posted in the daytime. There were a few prisoners, mostly Indians,
confined in the guard-room cells. This was the only
prison in the Territory. The names of some of our
captives were highly edifying and entertaining. "Frog's
Thigh," "Lizard Hips," "Blue Owl," "Cunning Funny,"
"Bear Door," and "Woman-who-sits-during-the-day"
are a few of the poetic epithets. These prisoners were
taken out to work, such as chopping wood and carrying
coal around the barracks at 8.30 a.m. and 1.30 p.m.
They were brought in for their dinner at noon; and
were each locked in a cell at night. A certain number
of troopers were told off daily to attend them as escort,
with loaded arms. This provost guard was a very
trying piece of business, and it "caught" me twice in
three weeks. The non-commissioned officer in charge
of this guard was changed daily at 10 a.m. The four

men comprising the guard remained from Monday at
10 a.m. till the following Monday at the same hour.
You took up your quarters in the guard-room and bid
adieu to society for a week. You were not supposed
to go to your room under any pretext, or to remove any
article of clothing, arms, or accoutrements during your
entire turn of duty. You slept upon the wooden guard-
bed in turn ; being allowed to send to your room for
your blankets, and your cleaning things. There was a
wash-basin in the guard-room, and the prisoners performed the functions of attendants. One jovial little
Cree, whom we called " Fatty," used to clean the boots,
and, with the advantages of tuition, he became a superior
boot-black. The guard-room was connected with the
small prison by two grated wickets. Each one of us
acted as a flying sentry during the night for three hours
each. When "rations" sounded in the afternoon we
took one of the prisoners to the quartermaster's store,
where a supply of tea, sugar, and bread was issued
which we generally indulged in at the witching hour of
midnight. A prisoner was escorted to the troop
kitchen for our meals. When the week was completed,
and other unfortunates took your places, what a blessed
relief it was ! To remove the spur-strap across the
instep and draw off the boots was bliss ! To cast aside
your under-garment of cobwebs and assume a change of
clothing was rapture ! And to stretch your legs between
clean sheets at night was simple ecstasy ! No one who
has not slept in uniform for a week can appreciate the
luxury, though it was only the narrow couch of a soldier.

Two Sioux prisoners escaped very cleverly from the
escort one dark night. He had taken them to the
W.C., and thinking them, like the lad in the ballad,
"lang a comin'," he kicked open the door. He found
them gone, and the prison clothing provided by a

paternal government disdainfully left lying upon the
floor. They were never seen more, and the unfortunate
escort was ordered to fill the place of one of them for
a month. It is supposed they made for the Sioux
camp at Moosejaw, a distance of forty miles. A party
scoured the country as far as the Dirt Hills ; but the
untutored noblemen had left no trail. Shortly after
this, a white man—a horse-thief—had the most
elaborate arrangements made to elope through the
silence of the night. His plan was discovered by the
corporal of the guard, who had sentries posted around
the prison, ready to drop him ; but he must have scented
a rat, as he failed to come up to time. A number of
articles were found secreted in his cell, and he was at
once decorated with a ball and chain, and continued
to wear that uncomfortable piece of jewellery until sent
down to Stony Mountain Penitentiary, in Manitoba, for
two years. All prisoners sentenced to terms exceeding
twelve months are removed thither.

In the early part of November a number of remounts,
young bronchos, were sent down from Calgary by rail.
A party of us were marched down to bring them up to
barracks. The broncho is a cross between the native
cayeuse and the American horse or English thorough-
bred. The majority of saddle-horses in use in the
Mounted Police are of this class. They average about
fifteen hands in height, and this is large enough. Indeed
the standard might be lowered, as the smaller horses
are better coupled. There is another point in their
favour ; in travelling they are much easier on themselves, and require less food. The best bronchos come
from British Columbia and Oregon, as the breeders in
those countries have been using thorough-bred stallions
with the native mares for a much greater length of time
than the breeders in Montana and Alberta.

The entire nonchalance with which a young broncho will regard a railway train is one of those things which no fellow can understand. They have been bred and reared, on horse ranches, far away, amid the waving grass of the lone prairie, and amid the strange silence of these Western plains. The playground of their youth, where they scampered in joyous herds,

"Wild as the wild deer,"

was far distant from the puffing roar of the demon-like machine that glides swiftly along the iron rails. Yet, on their first introduction to this weird object, they will merely raise their winsome heads, and gaze at it with comic impassiveness.

Yet woe to any one who suddenly approaches one of these youthful steeds, in an overcoat of shaggy buffalo skin. They have a shuddering horror of this, and will snort and strike out in abject fear. I once saw a recruit nearly get his brains knocked out, by rushing into the stall of an unbroken broncho, in one of these comfortable but uncouth coverings. The broncho has a bad name, especially among a certain class of American humorists of the Bill Nye order of *littérateurs*. But nowhere is there a more docile animal, if he be properly broken. Of course there are exceptions ; and a bad broncho *is* bad and no mistake. After he has thrown his rider, he will go for the unfortunate being, lying prostrate on the ground, with his teeth. It is from such examples as these that much of the legendary lore surrounding the name of the animal has sprung. Light, active, and wiry, they combine the sterling, serviceable qualities of mustang and thorough-bred.

When we hear of men riding to Macleod and back to Calgary (200 miles) in four days, on ponies scarcely fourteen hands high, and know that they thrive and do

well on prairie grass alone, even although severely
worked, coming out after the hardest summer's work in
the succeeding spring, after rustling all winter for a
living, fat and sound, every one must agree I am .writing
of a notably tough and hardy race of animals.   Such is
the mustang, or cayeuse, or native horse, the exclusive
mount of the Indian.   The bronchos, bred from these,
have immense powers of recuperation and endurance,
and are able to travel long distances without water.   In
1884, the horses in the Mounted Police consisted of a
number of heavy teams from Ontario for transport
requirements.   There was so much trouble and risk in
acclimatizing these that it was resolved to gradually
supply their places with the larger specimens of
bronchos, and the latter are universally driven in harness
now.

Our rough-riding corporal at Regina was a very
pleasant young Englishman.   He nows holds a commission.   He possessed any amount of pluck, and many
a bouncing toss he received in trying to subdue these
fiery untamed youngsters, which we led up to barracks
on a cold, bleak November day, the north wind piercing
fur coat and woollen under-garment.   About a dozen of us
were picked out to ride these "desert-born" steeds.   There
was a pretty extensive circus at first.   In fact one young
chestnut had to be blindfolded before he would allow you
to go near him with the saddle.

" In the full foam of wrath and dread "

the angry colt would struggle and rear in the hands of
his taskmasters.   We were allowed to make our choice of
mounts, and, as we went over to the stables, I thus
soliloquized,—

"Women, pianos, cigars, razors, and horses are all,
more or less, a lottery.   Therefore, I shall go in for
Hobson's choice."

So I pitched upon the first I came to, in the first stall
to the left ; a little mouse-coloured beggar with a quiet,
slumbering eye.   He turned out as tame as one of those
towel-racks which are for hire, in the season, on Scar-
borough Sands.   We used to take them out on the
manège daily, where, at first, several were seized with a
strong desire to explore the surrounding country, and
visit the land of their birth.   After a time they settled
down to the fanciful manœuvres of the school.

After having been about two months in the corps, I
was able to form some idea of the class of comrades
among whom my lot was cast.   I discovered there were
truly "all sorts and conditions of men."   Many I found,
in various troops, were related to English families in
good position.   There were three men at Regina who
had held commissions in the British service.   There
was also an ex-officer of militia, and one of volunteers.
There was an ex-midshipman, son of the Governor of
one of our small Colonial dependencies.   A son of a
major-general, an ex-cadet of the Canadian Royal
Military College at Kingston, a medical student from
Dublin, two ex-troopers of the Scots Greys, a son of a
captain in the line, an Oxford B.A., and several of the
ubiquitous natives of Scotland comprised the mixture.
In addition there were many Canadians belonging to
families of influence, as well as several from the backwoods, who had never seen the light till their fathers
had hewed a way through the bush to a concession
road.   They were none the worse fellows on that
account, though.   There were none of the questionable
characters then, who crept in after the Rebellion, when
recruiting parties went through the slums of Ontario
towns.   Several of our men sported medals won in South
Africa, Egypt, and Afghanistan.   There was one, brother
of a Yorkshire baronet, formerly an officer of a certain

regiment of foot, who as a contortionist and lion-comique was the best amateur I ever knew. There was only an ex-circus clown from Dublin who could beat him. These two would give gratuitous performances nightly, using the barrack-room furniture as acrobatic "properties."

A sergeant and a couple of constables rode into barracks one clear frosty morning, after an eventful trip. Some horses had been stolen from the celebrated Bell Farm, and this non-commissioned officer and his party were detailed to follow the thieves. These of course belonged to the marauding gentry, who have their haunts on the frontiers of Dakota and Montana, and in the wooded fringes of the Missouri. In the bluffs, among the lakes that nestle in the rounded hollows of the Moose Mountain, the sergeant—a smart fellow—took up the trail. Over the sparsely settled prairie, through swamp and coulée, by clumps of poplar balsam, by the tamarac-clad banks of sluggish creeks, over white patches of alkali deposit, and across desert spaces of cactus-plant and sand he followed up the hoof-marks, and ran his quarry to earth in a log shanty, standing in a gloomy thicket, a short distance from Miles City. The thieves were lodged in prison there by the United States Marshal; whence a posse of free and independent citizens hauled them to the nearest convenient place of execution and hanged them. In those days this crime was indulged in to a great extent all along the border. The Moose Mountain district had to be garrisoned by small detachments of redcoats scattered about in the farmers' houses, for these freebooters were the terror of the pioneers. They went about like moving arsenals, armed with the most improved type of weapons. Making unexpected raids upon lonely stables at night, they would drive their booty over the line to wild fastnesses only known to such outlaws. They would even hold up the unprotected settler at the plough, and force him to unhitch his horses. The heinousness of the crime will be understood when the value of a team to the struggling pioneer is taken into consideration. He is cut off from the world, and his principal aid to life is taken from him. Even in Manitoba, where settlement was comparatively thick, the Provincial Government were obliged to ask for the services of the Mounted Police. The Turtle Mountain district was another nest of brigandage.

About the end of November all the scattered detachments were called in, and returned to headquarters. Thus the barracks became pretty well occupied once more. We had a recreation-room, which was very cosy and well looked after, and attached to this was a lending library. One of the buglers had his quarters here, and kept the place in order. Weekly we received *Punch*, the *Illustrated London News, Graphic,* and the *Times ;* also the principal daily Canadian papers. There was a bagatelle-table in the room, and also draught-boards and cards. A large stove gave out ample heat. Pennsylvanian coal was at that time burnt at Regina.

Over on the prairie beside the railway line was a frame building of the bungalow style of architecture, painted white, with a slate-coloured roof of shingles, This was the canteen, the presiding deity being a swarthy civilian from "down East." There was a billiard-table, of uneven tendencies, in the saloon. All sorts of canned goods, such as lobster, sardines, and salmon, were dispensed here at visionary prices. I call them visionary, as they were so seldom realized. Pies of quartz-like solidity and granitic cakes also adorned the counter. There was a flash bar, gorgeous with mirrors, and photographs of American *danseuses* with elephan-

tine legs and busts, surpassing in development the
wildest imagination. These seductive creatures grinned
hideously at you while you imbibed flat cider or hop
beer. These latter beverages were non-intoxicating,
and were not calculated to tickle the palate.

We "ran" a mess in barracks. Each man contributed
ten cents per diem towards messing, and we appointed
a caterer, who laid out the aggregate sum to the best
advantage. Thus, in addition to our rations, we had
milk and butter, and pies, and plum pudding, and other
luxuries. The pay of a trooper on joining was fifty
cents (two shillings) per diem, free from all stoppages.
This was increased annually by five cents, till in the
fifth year of service it amounted to seventy cents. A
man on re-engagement received seventy-five cents as
his daily pay. Certain men for special services received
extra pay at the rate of fifteen cents, while a corporal's
pay was eighty-five cents, or three shillings and
sixpence, daily. During the winter, letters only arrived
at Regina three times a week.

We had a muster parade, at the end of November,
both of horses and men. The sky was overcast, and a
merciless wind swept across the plains, and through the
open square. It is indeed a very rare occurrence to
enjoy a calm day upon the prairie. At night, when I
went to bed, I did not feel very well, and could not get
to sleep. I was hot and feverish, and my mouth was
parched. "Sick call" sounds at 8.30, and, after having
my name put down on the sick report, I was marched
up to the hospital. The doctor stuck a clinical thermometer into the corner of my mouth, and suddenly jerk-
ing it out, laconically ejaculated, "Fever." Thereupon I
was bundled into a large airy ward, the walls of which were
hung with pleasant pictures ; put into bed, given a dose
of calomel, and handed a bundle of illustrated papers.

I shall never take calomel again, if I know it. Balls of
lead seemed to be moving about all over my body, pok-
ing their way all through my interior economy, making
a rush from my mesenteric region, and trying to get out
under my ribs and between my shoulder blades. I com-
plained to the hospital sergeant about this internal disorganization, and he gave me castor oil! Oh, delicious
mixture !

This fever is known all over the world by various
titles, and is just as sweet under any other name. The
Principal Medical Officer, in his annual report, speaks
of it as "endemic fever," and one of the assistant-sur-
geons says it is an anomalous form of fever peculiar to
the tract of country indicated by him. But there is
also recorded the fact that it is of "malarious origin."
In fact it is the typho-malarial scourge ; known as Red
River fever in Manitoba, jungle fever in India, rock
fever at Gib, Maltese fever at the other shop, West
Coast fever among the rotten fens of Africa, and Rocky
Mountain fever in British Columbia. It is of an inter-
mittent type, and the doctor at Regina used to treat it
very successfully by giving fluid extract of eucalyptus
when the thermometer was above 98° ; but when the
fever was off duty he used to ram in quinine, in big
doses. No doubt the causes of this outbreak at Regina
were the poisonous miasma from the standing pools
that represented the course of the mysterious Wascana.
The water for washing purposes was carried to the barracks from the creek, and kept in barrels in the lavatory.

I read in a Government pamphlet, published at Ottawa, the following unblushing assertion :—"There is no
malaria, and there are no diseases arising out of, or
peculiar to, either the climate or territory." The climate is healthy enough, but there is no need to publish
a deliberate mis-statement. This sort of thing only

damages the value of any truths which may appear in emigration literature.

Suddenly there arose a violent storm in matters medical at Regina. A big sacrilege was committed in the eyes of the P.M.O. His sanctuary was desecrated. A young civilian was stricken by fever in the town, and the people with whom he was residing and for whom he had been working, in their inhuman selfishness, turned him to the door. The capital city did not then possess a hospital, and it was decreed by the Colonel, after representations from the Mayor, that the youth should be placed in the police hospital. Thereupon our Æsculapius was roused to fury, and he took to writing protests and despatches all over the shop. He showed his lofty contempt for the *élite* of the capital, by withdrawing his name from the club. He cleared the hospital of police patients, and sent them into a barrack-room. I must say he treated the primary cause of this disturbance with the utmost attention, tenderness, and skill. I was convalescent at the time, and was allowed to roam at large around the wards. When we were removed to our new sanatorium, he ordered me to lie down on a stretcher, and I was thus borne away by a fatigue party of four strapping troopers.

"I would rather walk, sir," I feebly protested.

"You are not to walk, I tell you."

So I reclined upon my litter, amid the jokes of my comrades : "The coroner's waiting, old man ; " "The firing party is ready under old Mahogany," and other ghastly sallies of the same kind of wit. There were about half a dozen of us in this temporary infirmary, and we had a high old time of it. One young fellow was carried in after a slight difference of opinion with a broncho as to which was to have his own way. The quadruped conquered, and the biped was laid by the heels for a spell.

CHAPTER IV

Winter—Volunteers for Saskatchewan—Jumpers and moccasins—
To Qu'Appelle—Intense cold—A model hotel—Tent pegs or
beefsteaks?—A terrible march.

WHEN I was returned as fit for duty, the winter had
set in keenly. I had suffered from a very slight attack,
so that I had not been very long upon the sick-list.
Though the frost had locked the land in its powerful
grasp, and sleugh and creek were bound in solid bands
of ice, there was merely a slight powdering of snow
upon the ground. The buckets of water in the barrack-
rooms for use in case of fire were frozen over, in spite
of the fact that every fire was kept going by the night-
guard. There were two stoves in each of the small
rooms. How can I describe this cold? If I state
simple facts as to its intensity, they do not convey the
least idea of the temperature that seizes upon everything, and almost annihilates existence. If any one
doubts the thermometer readings I give, I refer him to
the meteorological records. One night the thermometer
at our barracks in Regina, in December, 1884, went
down to 58° below zero ; in other words, registered 90°
of frost! This brought a leading article from the
Standard as to the danger to life in such a temperature.
Butler says, in "The Great Lone Land," "40° below
zero means so many things impossible to picture or to
describe, that it would be a hopeless task to enter upon
its delineation. After one has gone through the list of

all those things that freeze ; after one has spoken of the
knife which burns the hand that would touch its blade,
the tea that freezes while it is being drunk, there still
remains a sense of having said nothing ; a sense which
may perhaps be better understood by saying that 40°
below zero means just one thing more than all these
items—it means death, in a period whose duration
would expire in the hours of a winter's daylight, if there
were no fire or means of making it on the track."

We were obliged to turn out on the barrack square to
answer our names at reveillé, before proceeding to
stables. The air nipped with a keenness beyond all
description ; and the orderly corporal struggled
through the long list by the feeble light of a lantern,
while the stars glittered overhead.

It was rumoured, about this time, that a party of
twenty men were to start for Prince Albert, a distant
settlement upon the North Saskatchewan ; and the
report soon took definite shape by the authorities
asking for volunteers. It was not a tempting prospect
—a march of 300 miles over frozen waste in the depth
of a rigorous winter—but I offered and was accepted.

We spent the first week in December in preparation.
Sleighs were purchased, iron tent-pegs were made by
the blacksmith, and a heavy requisition went in to the
Quartermaster's store for camp equipment and rations.
It is impossible to make long journeys in the saddle in
this most excessive cold. Therefore we were each to
drive a jumper, a small sleigh entirely made of wood
with wooden runners. The separate parts of this
fearful and wonderful structure are fastened together
with strips of shaganappi. To this you hitch your
broncho by a light harness. It is part of their necessary
education to learn to draw a jumper.

The biting cold now forbade the use of boots, and

your feet would most assuredly dissolve partnership
with the rest of your body, if you continued to wear
these adjuncts of civilization. Therefore the comfortable Indian moccasin is substituted. People who read
of these articles fail generally to understand exactly
what they are. In "Madcap Violet," one of the
characters asks her, when she is setting off for an
American tour, to snare him a brace of moccasins in
the Rocky Mountains. I suppose William Black meant
to satirise the prevailing ignorance on the subject.

In the days when I was wont to revel in the fascinat-
ing pages of Fenimore Cooper, I used to imagine these
articles of wear consisted of long leggings reaching to
the thigh. Nothing of the sort. We protected our
feet from the dangerous attacks of the frost by first
covering them with two pairs of woollen socks. Over
these we drew a long pair of woollen stockings which
covered our riding pants to the knee. Then we adorned
our feet with moccasins. These are soft, pliable
brogues of dressed deerskin (moose), of a light yellow
colour, and only reach above the ankles. They are
pliant as a glove, and thus there is liberty given to the
foot, so that the circulation remains unimpeded.

After all our preparations were completed, the only
thing to do was to wait for snow. It came with a
vengeance, about the 8th of December. A rude, riotous
wind arose in the north, and went forth in demon
wrath from the desolate shores of the lone Lake
Athabasca, and the far-off icy regions of the musk ox and
reindeer. It swept across the treeless plains, and
whirled the big flakes into heaped masses around the
wooden huts. The vast expanse of prairie was covered
with the storm-rack like a tossing sea ; men struggled
and fought with the blast in crossing the barrack
square, and stumbled and plunged with bent head on

their way to stables. After a day or two of hilarity of this description, the weather suddenly sobered, and all around lay the glittering, crystalline robe, in the still keen air under a brilliant sun.

On Friday, the 12th, our expedition paraded before the Colonel. There was a foot parade at first, in furs ; and then the jumpers were given a spin round the square. Some of the bronchos indulged in various freaks, of a very lively description at first ; but luckily there were no accidents or spills, and they settled down to a steady gait. The intended journey was of a somewhat exceptional character, and in consequence, there were issued to us one extra pair of blankets, a muffler, a driving-whip, and a pair of smoked goggles each : these last were fastened round the head by a string of elastic.

These protective specs are of no earthly use whatever. In fact, your eyes do not require the services of any screen until the sun begins to gain power ; when it beats back from the glassy surface of the melting snow with a blinding glare. A veil of green gauze, or lampblack smeared under the eyes and upon the nose, are much better preventives of conjunctivitis. The buckskin mitts, supplied by Government, only have a forefinger, so as to admit of the carbine being handled. This finger invariably becomes frozen in the extreme cold of mid-winter, if these mitts are worn. Each of us had, therefore, two pairs of mitts without fingers at all. One pair were of wool, knitted, and one pair of unlined buckskin to draw over the former. But the only thing to assure any comfort to the hands in this climate are fur gauntlets, with an ordinary pair of woollen knitted gloves underneath. Thus, if you have occasion to fix a buckle or loose a strap, on removing the outer covering, your fingers are at liberty without exposure.

And it is to be remembered, that to expose the surface of the skin, for a few moments, means a frostbite ; and to touch metal is to bring away the skin. The bits of the horses are of celluloid. When they are not so, the poor animals suffer terribly.

On Saturday morning at eight o'clock, the main party pulled out, under a sergeant ; each jumper was devoted to one man with his kit. A waggon box, on bob sleighs, with a pair of horses, carried the heavy *impedimenta*. The morning was clear, but the thermometer registered 37° below zero, with a breeze. Where the cunning Pieapot has his reserve upon the grassy slopes which dip to the fair valley of the Qu'Appelle, is a dense growth of birch and aspen and poplar. Upon the edge of this bush, about twenty-eight miles from Regina, they were to camp that night, reaching Qu'Appelle on the following day.

As I was detained by special duty, I did not start until Sunday, the 14th December, accompanying the officer and his wife, who travelled to Troy (now Qu'Appelle Station) by train. His servant, with baggage, and myself, were driven to town by a French Canadian teamster in the afternoon. I had my first touch of frostbite on this occasion ; it felt as if a battery of red-hot needles were being applied to the interior lining of my nostril. The train did not pass Regina until midnight, so we patronized the Palmer House for supper ; the *pièce de résistance* was pie, of occult ingredients, handed round by angular damsels, with a pronounced nasal twang, and brief dresses of extensive pattern.

My friend, the bâtman, was a recent pilgrim from London, who had the fixed idea that every one knew all the purlieus of his pet village as accurately as a detective from Scotland Yard. Not to know every obscure region which he introduced into his narrative was to incur his lasting contempt.

On boarding the train, I found every car full of hulking navvies of every nationality, who had been working as construction gangs in the Rocky Mountains, and who were now going east to spend their "little pile," either in Winnipeg or Chicago. We reached Troy Station in about two hours after leaving Regina. Two of the mounted police were stationed at Troy, inhabiting a diminutive hut, which was dignified by the name of barracks. This stood upon a wooded knoll, half a mile from the station, and, after redeeming our respective rolls of bedding (each about 60 lbs in weight), we shouldered these uncouth bundles, and trudged off through the snow under the starlight. The officer and his wife went to the hotel. The two representatives of the law were both out of bed, more wood was banged into the stove, and we spread out our blankets for a few hours' snooze.

There is no undressing here. You must learn to sleep in your clothes when on a journey in out-of-the-way regions of the Wild West. During this trip, I wore my uniform for thirteen days and nights. The two constables here, as indeed at all the out-posts along the Canadian Pacific Railway, take their meals at the principal hotel. On emerging from our shelter, in the morning sunlight, to proceed to the Queen's, the cold was terrible. It went through mitts and buffalo coat, and caught your nose every now and again with a stinging bite that made you wince. This was only a foretaste of what was to come. A man coming fresh from England, is always able to endure the first winter in the North-West better than any of the succeeding ones.

Troy was surrounded on all sides by pleasant trees,

the bare boughs of which wore a coat of sparkling silver this winter's morning, like the mythical branches in some fairy tale. In spite of two stoves in the dining-hall, the Arctic temperature clung around you. The officer and his wife were already seated at one of the small tables, with blue fingers and red noses. The hostess was the most loquacious member of the loquacious sex whom I have ever met. As one of our fellows expressed it, " she would talk the boots off your feet."

The distance from Troy to Fort Qu'Appelle, where the real labour of our march would commence, is eighteen miles. Two constables with sleighs had driven over from the fort, to transport us thither. One of these, stamping about in moccasins, and muffled to the eyes in furs, was waiting at the station, and was kicking up a boisterous shindy because I was not there with the luggage checks. However, we soon bundled the mountain of luggage into the sleigh, and T—— and I took our seats. The keen air seemed to act as a stimulus to our horses, and away they went at a gallop up the village—(I beg pardon, three houses constitute a city)—street. Clumps of willow and poplar—or bluffs— lined the trail on either side, the lace-like tracery of their interwoven branches flashing with myriads of diamonds. The sun shone with a frigid glare from a cloudless sky of steely blue. Mr. T—— sported his goggles, which elicited a question from the old hand who was driving, if he were suffering from myopia, whereupon that verdant youth from far Cockaigne put them aside. I imagine he found the rims a little too hot for him.

We overtook the doctor of the settlement a little way out of town ; he was luxuriating in a closed carriage of strange aspect, the only one I ever saw during my four years' experience of these regions. The scenery continued to present the same features as we sped along ; undulating hillocks, crowned with groves of bushes, and cup-like hollows, in which lay ice-bound, snow-clad lakelets.

Upon the summit of a wind-swept, bleak, and treeless ridge, about nine miles from Troy, stood a solitary farm. This ugly-looking homestead was known as the " halfway house," and it seemed the recognized custom for every one passing to hitch up their horses to a convenient post, enter unceremoniously, take a seat, and spread their legs out to the grateful warmth of the stove. On entering, we found two or three more travellers puffing solemnly at well-seasoned pipes. The settler and his wife did not resent this abrupt invasion ; but, on the contrary, welcomed us with effusive hospitality. Presently came the doctor from his caravan, and quite a flow of lively repartee set in between him and our driver, whom I found to be a well-known character in the force.

Then, as the weather is the one overpowering topic wherever the English language is spoken, bets ensued as to the precise spot to which the spirit had sunk in the thermometer. Jehu said −37° ; and Æsculapius was positive it was −48°. The wager was to be decided by the Fahrenheit thermometer at Smith's hotel, on our arrival at the Fort. After a short rest we buttoned up our heavy coats, muffled up our noses, and set off again to face the music. Past more bush and frozen ponds, with a cutting breeze whose fearful edge you warded off as best you could with uplifted arm and bent head. Our son of Nimshi drove furiously, and we were not long in reaching the edge of the Qu'Appelle valley.

The town lies at the foot of the wooded hills, the

houses clustering by the margin of two fair lakes. It is a charming valley. The trail winds down a very steep descent ; but away dashed our driver at break-neck speed through snowdrifts and over stumps ; while I held on like grim death, with icy hands. The doctor, who was following, remarked afterwards at the hotel, that he was disappointed in not having had an opportunity to earn a fee. Perhaps it was his knowledge of the dare-devil who held the reins, which made him so considerate in following so closely in our rear.

The hotel here is a superior sort of building, and was kept by an Englishman, and furnished in English style with a view to comfort.

The doctor lost his bet as to the temperature, the instrument hanging outside the door showing $-38°$, or $70°$ of frost.

A cutting blast came sweeping down the V-shaped gorge, through which flows the Qu'Appelle river, and laying bare the ice upon the string of lakes. This valley is always considered colder in winter than the surrounding heights. The old fort is on the north side ; and was at one time the headquarters of the Mounted Police. The situation is one of the most romantic in the Territory. There is a flagstaff in front of the police buildings flying a tattered Union Jack. The Hudson Bay Company's store here was at one time one of their principal trading posts between the country of the Assiniboines to the east, and the Crees to the west. Many a wild orgie and scene of bloodshed was witnessed, in the old days when the mighty buffalo roamed these wilds, and glittering beads and gaudy trinkets were traded for the valuable robes, taken from this monarch of the plains. The town also gives a title to a colonial bishopric. At the time of writing, the Hon. Dr. Anson —brother of Lord Lichfield—is the occupant of the See.

There is also an *agricultural* college, under the superin-
tendence of his lordship.

The officer ordered me to have my dinner at the
hotel. He and his wife, his servant, and myself all sat
down together at the same table. This anomalous state
of affairs would not be quite the thing in the British
service ; but such mixing of ranks in social and military
life is quite common out here ; nor is it at all subversive
of discipline. The rank and file of course are of somewhat different material to the average linesman. We
enjoyed a very good dinner ; ministered to by most
attentive and pretty waitresses, in bewitchingly clean
costumes, who deftly handed round the dainty dishes.
All the waiting is done by girls in Canadian hotels.
But there are no barmaids. Society is not sufficiently
educated for them.

After smoking a digestive cigar, presented by the pro-
prietor, we fought our way over to the fort. It was, literally,
a fight against the piercing wind. My recollection of that
day's sufferings stands out in bold relief. Fancy the concentrated essence of cold (the thermometer − 38°) coming
scampering wildly with resistless energy down a narrow
ravine, and across a broad field of ice ! Buffalo coat
with high collar up, the eyes only peeping out above the
muffler ; fur cap well down over the ears ; and double
mitts appeared to be no protection. Ever and again
you had to turn your back to its fury and rest from the
fight.

Arrived at the log buildings under the shelter of the
northern side of the valley, we found the party which
had preceded us from Regina ; packed like herrings in a
barrel, in a small, stuffy apartment. They looked a most
dilapidated crew ; their cheeks and noses were frozen ;
and, as the dye had come off their variegated mufflers,
they would have stricken envy into the soul of any

æsthetic aborigine who wished to excel in a new and artistic style of war-paint.

Several circumstances conspired to detain us in Qu'Appelle for four days. Our stay at the ramshackle old fort was of the most uncomfortable description. We unrolled our blankets at night upon the floor; washing was out of the question, and our grub consisted entirely of greasy bacon salted to the nth power, with hard tack and tea. Tobacco was our only solace; going out to feed and water our horses, our only occupation. The watering-hole, out on the lake, had to be reopened with an axe each time we required it.

It is useless speaking of men indulging in outdoor pastimes in such weather as this. Such cold paralyzes every energy and makes you grumpy and unsociable. We became dirty, unkempt and red-eyed; as though we had been sitting up nightly, on a prolonged " burst."

One of the causes of our delay was a telegram from headquarters ordering us to remain where we were, until the cold snap was over. Had this been carried out we should have adorned society at Qu'Appelle till March. Then we found we were to wait for a sergeant, who had been on leave; and who was bringing up a wife from Manitoba; and the two ladies under our escort were to travel in a covered sleigh, with an abundance of robes of buffalo and rabbit skin. The rabbit-skin robe is white, and pretty in appearance. A rabbit-skin worn inside a moccasin, with the fur against the sole of the foot, is wonderfully warm.

Upon Friday, 19th December, we set out upon our march of 240 miles through the frozen wilderness. I observed Mr. M——'s servant about to deposit a sack, whose contents rattled suspiciously in the sleigh containing our supply of forage. Therefore I spoke.

" Look here, T——, don't put those tent-pegs beside the oats. They'll poke their points through the bag, knock a hole in the corn sacks ; there'll be a leak, and the deuce to pay."

Saith he, looking at me with disdain,—

" Those ain't tent-pegs—they's beefsteaks ! "

So they were, cut ready for use by our commander on the line of march. As a curiosity, I may say that I have seen milk carried in nets. Those of my readers who have spent a winter on the Saskatchewan will bear me out.

The order of our procession was as follows. In front was a transport sleigh and pair of horses, containing tents, camp stoves, and other equipment, as well as our rations. Then came our line of jumpers, each driven by one of us in winter uniform. The officer followed us in a superior sort of jumper, a kind of aristocratic box, with varnished sides and high back, in which he could recline at ease. The canvas-covered sleigh, containing the ladies, drawn by a team, brought up the rear.

The latest specimen of the equine tribe, which had been entrusted to my care, was a black of uncertain temper and ominous name. He was christened Satan. On our way out of the valley, as I was walking along-side fixing my muffler around my face, he took it into his head to bolt at full gallop. He cannoned against every obstacle to his progress, wildly scattering everything like chaff before the wind, distributing my kit into various inaccessible parts of the bush, and smashing the jumper into lucifer matches ; in honour, I suppose, of his namesake. The officer pronounced a benediction ; —nay several benedictions. The anathemas of the Pope, in the Ingoldsby legends, were as the crooning of an infant compared to them.

I helped to gather up the fragments, which we placed in the foremost sleigh. His Satanic majesty was hitched in the team; liberating a little bay mare who was allowed to run behind. Even with the heavy load behind him, and the incline in front, the fiery black was difficult to hold, and this, Sergeant K——, who was driving, confessed. One of the men was riding the officer's charger, a stubborn animal which we nicknamed " Pig." He soon had to leave the saddle, half frozen.

We felt the weather considerably milder on reaching the plateau above, and snow was falling heavily. The thermometer was only 10° below zero, with an easterly wind. The country to the north of the Qu'Appelle valley is fairly well stocked with timber and game. We passed several half-breeds in charge of a long string of jumpers, drawn by their hardy ponies. Each of them wore a long blue overcoat, with *capuchin* or hood, bound round the waist with a gaudy sash, upon the head a tuque or a cap of beaver skin. They were almost as swarthy as their maternal ancestors.

We also passed one or two white freighters, who carried goods from Qu'Appelle to the Saskatchewan at a charge then of four cents per pound. Their sufferings during these winter journeys are intense. One would think the game is not worth the candle, but men must endure bravely to make a living in a climate such as this.

Tall, slender poplars sheltered our trail the entire ten miles which lie between the Fort and Skunk Bluffs. As this was a station on the Prince Albert mail route, there was a house of call kept by one O'Brien. Its comforts, of course, were reserved for our superiors and their wives.

We soon had led our horses into the stable, and

rubbed them down. The pain in my hands, as circulation began to return to the benumbed fingers, was excruciating. Molten lead seemed to be tingling in every vein. We now went to work with our shovels and cleared the snow from a sheltered space in the bluff, where we pitched our tents. Each tent was provided with a small stove. Then we made a raid on the O'Briens' haystack, and placed armfuls of fodder upon the ground inside. We banked up the outside of the curtain with snow, and made fires in the stoves, while our cook had the camp kettle over a blazing pile outside. Some steaming tea, with the usual accompaniment of " rattlesnake pork " and hard-tack, made us feel more comfortable.

This meal we took sitting on our rolls of bedding, under canvas. Each bell-tent felt very cosy that night, Then we unrolled our blankets, crept in beneath them, and lit our pipes. We did not remove any article of our dress, which was as follows : undershirt, next the skin, of knitted wool ; and drawers of the same material ; overshirt of flannel, socks two pairs, stockings one pair, and moccasins ; blue cloth riding pants Cardigan waistcoat, and jacket of scarlet serge. Over these, a brown jacket of duck ; and overalls of the same ; to crown all was a buffalo overcoat and fur cap. At night we substituted a woollen tuque for the latter. We watched our fire in turns during the night until the sergeant sounded reveillé at the unholy hour of 4 a.m. by bawling outside the tents,—

" Now then, boys, turn out and feed your horses."

Oh, the lengthened sigh one heaved on turning out upon the starlit snow ! Half asleep we tumbled over to the stable, and with smarting finger tips gave our bronchos hay and oats. They were only watered twice daily in winter, at 10 a.m. and 4 p.m. Then the everlasting tea, hard-tack, and sowbelly. Try every variation you like on those three words, and you have our daily bill of fare.

After this came the disagreeable labour of striking the tents, loading the sleighs, and harnessing the horses. There was always much growling on leaving camp, and the atmosphere was generally blue with cuss-words. Men grow savage in such cold as this ; especially when there is a march of forty miles ahead. The wind this day was keen, and full in our teeth, as we mounted some bare uplands. Every now and then you had to jump down and run. You cannot smoke, for the juice freezes in the pipe stem. Old Munchausen's yarn about the bugle was not such a gigantic fib after all. Every moment you are exposed to this terrible atmosphere is one of suffering. People have shielded their faces with masks of buffalo hide, and yet have had them frozen. I know very likely there may be a roaring cataract of contra- dictions to these statements, from people who know nothing whatever of the matter. Emigration jugglers will be upon the war-path at once. I am only stating stubborn facts ; and I can appeal to men who have faced the real thing for corroboration. After the sun had risen we made a halt at a sleugh, and cut a hole in the ice to water the horses. In using a bucket for this purpose, in less than five minutes one half the depth of the bucket is solid ice, and the sides are caked with it. In the afternoon we entered the picturesque Touchwood Hills. These abound with game, and many a lovely spot and charming lake nestles amid their winding glens. The sun set in a great flame of crimson and scarlet, orange and amethyst, behind the verge of the great desolate prairie, that stretched away to the west- ward from the foot of these elevations. It was a gorgeous sight, but the sense of gloomy desolation

brought a feeling of sadness and awe. Darkness
hemmed us in, while yet a good way from our intended
destination. We had to trust to the sagacity of our
horses to keep the trail. No sound broke upon the ear
save the crunching of the snow beneath the line of
sleighs.

Suddenly, in turning a corner, I, who was sitting on
the edge of the sleigh-box, kicking my feet together to
keep them from freezing, described a rapid parabola
through the air, and took a lively header into a snow-
drift. I was not missed from my perch of course ; and
when I recovered my scattered senses, it was some time
before I overtook the vanishing jumpers.

Our sergeant was a man who had spent the whole of
his long years of service upon the Saskatchewan, but he
was completely at sea in the darkness. However, we
caught a glimpse of a light twinkling through the
branches which was as welcome as any long-looked-
for harbour light to storm-tossed mariners. I was
suffering intensely from the pain brought on by exposure
in such a cramped position. We soon gladly found
ourselves drawn up in front of the Hudson Bay factor's
house at Touchwood.

These posts are in wild, lonely spots, and generally
consist of a rude collection of log-huts around an open
space. The larger forts boast of a rough wall of
palisades. They possess also a flagstaff upon which
they sometimes sport the Company's flag, which bears
the letters H.B.C. upon a field of flowery device.
Tradition says that a Yankee skipper, sailing the clear
waters of Lake Superior, once upon a time came to
anchor off the mouth of the Kaministiquia. On seeing
this emblem floating proudly above the congregation of
shanties at Fort William, he shut up his glass with a
snap, and ejaculated, "Here Before Christ! Wall,

judging by the look of the hull blamed consarn, I *guess they were !* "

The officer, sergeant, and ladies billeted themselves in the factor's residence, whence the cheerful blaze of a log fire sent a ruddy glare upon the snow outside. The stables were ruinous, great holes gaping through the worn timber of which they were constructed. Here we made our horses as comfortable as we could in such a breezy home. *We* were quartered in a dilapidated, ancient "shack," near the stables, on the edge of a darksome wood. It was weary work, carrying our bedding and grub through the deep drifts. We stumbled, and plunged, and fell again and again. There was a cantonment of redskins and half-breeds in the next-door compartment to us. One tall, blanketed savage came out, and stalked weirdly away, his grey figure appeared ghost-like in the wan glamour of the winter's night. Our temporary resting-place was not inviting. There was no glass in the antique window-frame. The floor had yielded to decay, in places forming many pit-falls for the unwary. The walls were full of yawning holes, admitting every breath of air. We had a wretched night, in spite of our weariness, but after smoking the consolatory calumet, we all fell into an uneasy slumber.

CHAPTER V

The bear—Touchwood Hills—A native gentleman—The great salt
plains—Sixty-two below zero—Played out—A rest—Humboldt
—Timber wolves—Hoodoo—Christmas day.

SHORTLY after midnight a huge black form came
bounding through the rug we had fixed over the
window, landing upon the recumbent form of the
gentleman from Middlesex, who wildly shrieked, "A
bear! a bear!" No doubt, he imagined, in his semi-
somnolent state, that the whole menagerie from the
surrounding bush had turned out to make a night of it.
It was, however, only a train dog of the Huskie breed, in
the service of the fort, who was attracted by the gleam
of our pine logs. He made himself at home, after the
storm of abuse had passed over.

As usual we were roused before dawn, had our
morning meal, and stowed our fry-pans and baggage
into their respective places. Our game bronchos held
up their little heads bravely as we rattled off. We were
to reach the mail station on the Salt Plains that night,
a distance of forty-three miles. The saffron hues of
dawn soon spread and brightened into the morning
splendour of sunrise. We were now in the heart of the
Touchwood Hills—in summer very beautiful with lake
and wood—and the vast plain stretching to the westward. Game is very abundant, but, as it is on an Indian
reserve, fur and feather is sacred to the native gentlemen. Muskowequahn and Day Star are the two chiefs
who hold sway. The whole Indian population amounts

to an aggregrate of five hundred and eighty-three on these reserves.

We were following the mail route by the line of telegraph poles, reaching from the railway to Prince Albert. Of course in winter the trail takes a number of short cuts, which are impossible in summer, and you are enabled by the frost to take cognizance of the fact, that two sides of a triangle are together greater than the third. Sunday, December 21st, was the coldest day on record in the North-West. The thermometer, on the Saskatchewan, registered minus 62° Fahrenheit; or *ninety-four degrees of frost!* As we passed the lonely hut, in which resided the telegraph operator, the mercury was frozen at minus 45°, in the sun.

The atmosphere was clear and bright, but cutting as the keenest steel. We kept up our circulation as well as we could, by running alongside the sleighs; this was no easy task in deep snow, with our weight of furs and underclothing. We passed a weasen-faced old Indian, seated in state in his jumper, with a great rabbit-skin robe around him; his squaw trudged alongside, and kept hammering the cayeuse. We drove by the door of the Indian agent's house, round which were a collection of painted squaws and braves in all the finery of many-coloured blankets. Here our sleighs were piled with a supply of wood, for, right before us, stretching from the foot of the hills, lay the grey expanse of the Great Salt Plains. Dream-like in immensity, there they were; hazy and indistinct; no tree nor bush upon their desert surface. From Wolverine Creek on the West, to where the Red Deer River, of Lake Winipegosis, bends to the Pasquia Hills, they stretch their mournful length, which in the afternoon sunlight of that December Sunday, appeared grim and forbidding. The telegraph poles cross a narrow arm, about forty-five miles from timber to

timber, and we followed their guidance. The sergeant
pointing ahead, said to me,—

" Do you see that ?　No more shelter there, than in
Mid-Atlantic ! "

The grinding of our runners over the frozen snow was
the only sound in that hideous stillness. We were to
make for the log-hut, in which a man was kept at
Government expense, and which was a halting-place for
the mail. The stars sparkled overhead ; and away along
the low horizon they twinkled with deceptive lustre ;
for each one, of the first magnitude, that shone through
the deathly haze was taken to mark our goal. We were
enduring all the pangs of hunger, and a dangerous
drowsiness seemed to seize one, every now and again ;
for the circulation could barely be maintained. I cannot
describe the sensations of that winter night. We were
only a small band in a lone land, fighting in the icy
grasp of a fatal cold. Ninety-four degrees of frost! I
leave it to my readers to imagine what it means. And in
this temperature, in the blackness of a mid-winter night,
we were to pitch tents on a treeless waste ! When, at
length, worn out and silent—painfully silent—we found
our destination, it was with thankful hearts. A dim
light shone through the panes of a small frost-coated
window. We almost ran against the low canvas dwellings of some half-breed freighters who were here encamped. Their train consisted of about 100 ponies.
Had it not been for their welcome aid, I do not see how
we should have managed to rig up our camp. Every
one was completely numbed. As for me, everything
seemed spinning round ; and I should have fallen into
the sleep which knows no waking had I not been able
to secure some warmth and shelter. An incident oc-
cured by which I was permitted to get inside the
mail station. A fine big fellow of ours, from Stirling in

Scotland, had fallen down insensible. We at once pulled him up ; but he was quite delirious. We took him into the hut, which was crowded with a heterogeneous lot of people ; and here some good Samaritan pulled out some forbidden cognac, which was given our comrade in spoonfuls. None had been issued to us for medical purposes. He did not come to his senses for some considerable time. His face, head, and hands were fearfully frozen. On the following morning we were compelled to leave him in these lonely and comfortless quarters ; when he had recovered sufficiently he returned to Regina by stage. I do not think he ever quite got over the shock of that night. Another man was also left behind at this place, too frost-bitten to proceed.

The little room of the station was only twelve feet square ; with two bunks against the far wall, one above the other. In these two women were lying, and a child. One of them was taking her husband's body from Prince Albert to Montreal for interment. A weird journey ! The sleigh in which they travelled was covered with canvas, and had a stove. There were a few white freighters in here also. This mail station stands on a slight eminence, about twenty-seven miles from the north edge of the plains. Pierre, Jean, Ba'tiste and Company had lent a willing hand, and soon our tents rose beside those of the dusky Metis. A third member of our party was so thoroughly benumbed that two of us, kneeling beside him in the tent, had to chafe him for some time. The ladies of our party stood it bravely. We simply turned our horses loose, to rustle for themselves. They found sufficient forage in a stack of hay which stood alongside ; and when morning broke they were all grouped around it, as fresh as paint.

We did not turn out till daylight on this occasion, and

we were a set of haggard-looking objects, as we gazed
into each other's dull and bloodshot eyes. I managed
to get some breakfast at the mail station. I told
McLeod to charge any sum he pleased. He only
charged fifty cents ; but I would have willingly paid
him five dollars, had he asked it, for the greasy bacon,
black tea and slap-jack.   The civilians had all folded

> " Their tents like the Arabs,
> And as silently stole away,"

long before dawn.   It was determined by the officer to
leave the men on the sick-list where they were ; and
we were to proceed to the " Edge of the Plain," as the
outer fringe of bush to the northward was termed.
When we had gained this shelter, we were to camp for
a rest, as we were all pretty well played out. My left
heel had been frost-bitten during the night, in spite of
all covering. We broke camp and pushed ahead about
ten o'clock. We got across this infernal desert by half-
past three in the afternoon, and pitched our tents in a
lovely grove of poplar. We soon had our stoves going,
made ourselves comfortable, and forgot the tribulations
of the previous day. How we enjoyed our supper this
evening, as the crimson blush of sunset glowed through
the branches to the west ! Then pipes were lit, and
songs trolled out by manly throats. " The Midship-
mite," " Ehren on the Rhine," and the well-worn camp
song known as the " Spanish Cavalier."
   Our horses were picketed among the trees in a
sheltered spot ; and the sergeant fed them at night. It
is a pity there are so few non-coms. like him. He was
a smart-looking fellow, with keen features and bright
yellow moustache. Having been on leave, he was wearing a long coat of raccoon skin. He had spent ten
years in exile in the wilds of Saskatchewan. The usual

coyoté came prowling around at night, but his respect
for his own skin kept him at a distance. He is a
cowardly beast, and only wanted to lift our rations.
We heard the bells of some freighters passing about
midnight. These men travel at all hours, only making
a halt when they consider it necessary for their cattle.
Each of their horses wears a bell, as they leave them
entirely to their own devices when they camp. We
were all very much the better for our splendid rest ; and
when the considerate bearer of the triple chevron awoke
us at 5 a.m., he also imparted the cheerful intelligence
that our horses were fed and the kettle boiling. He
had done all this himself. More power to your elbow,
Harry K——, wherever you may be ! But there is one
very good thing in the North-West Mounted Police,
officers and non-commissioned officers alike share the
hardships of the men ; and all join together in lending
a hand when out upon the plains. This day we had a
pleasant and short march of twenty-five miles to Humboldt, through woods full of prairie chicken. These
birds roost on trees, and don't show the least alarm at
the approach of a vehicle. Thus you can always secure
a shot at them from a buck-board. We were now
approaching the habitat of the ptarmigan, plenty of
which are to be had on the North Saskatchewan.

Humboldt is another mail station, and at that time
consisted of a couple of log-huts, in one of which dwelt
the telegraph operator. In some of the more out-of-
the-way places, the winter exile of these men is terrible
beyond expression. They become victims to a most
depressing *ennui*. There was a Dundee Scotsman, in
charge here, who informed me that he had killed five
timber wolves in the adjoining bush. The timber wolf
is a different animal from the pusillanimous coyoté.
The former *will* attack a man ; whereas the latter

contents himself with squatting on his haunches, and gazing from a reasonably safe distance. We took up our lodgings for the night in the mail hut, which would have held our small party in comfort ; but a squad of unsavoury freighters landed at dusk, and we all occupied the floor, in layers, like sardines. A range of long, low stables stood between the two houses, and into the dim recesses of this building our teamster was mysteriously invited by a huge civilian in an ancient buffalo coat, and long stockings of felt. This bearded habitant of the wilds opened his shaggy capote and produced a black bottle of well-known shape.

"This is some of the genuine stingo you bet." But the whisky *was frozen!* So much for the contraband nectar of the Territories. And our man departed into the silence of the night, tearfully. On the following day we were treated to an icy wind from the north-west which searched through your very bones. A stretch of desolate rolling prairie lay upon our way, its billowy hillocks presenting a breadth of fifteen miles. We passed by two dogs standing frozen in their tracks. At two o'clock in the afternoon the sun shone out gloriously upon thicket, and lake, and the distant range of the Birch Hills. We had crossed our last patch of prairie, and here before us was the mail station of Hoodoo ; amid clumps of birch that fringe a number of pretty little lakes.

The acme of dirt and discomfort was exhibited in the interior of the house at this place ; and we reversed our usual plan with regard to our arrangements for sleeping quarters. We pitched two tents for our married superiors, and inhabited H.M. Post-office ourselves. It was a most abominable hole in which to spend a Christmas Eve ; but as usual we made ourselves as merry as we could. The worst of it was, the *chargé-*

d'affaires at this post—an Ontario backwoodsman—
would persist in singing execrable ditties of a very
depressing type, till he was summarily shut up. Then
he began a fearfully amorous yarn of still more melancholy import, to the libretto of which we added a chorus
of groans.

It was a strange Christmas Eve, and as we smoked
our pipes before going to sleep, we thought of all the
doings at home. At least I know my mind wandered
far away to a certain cosy room, where the holly
berries would be shining scarlet over the fireplace; to
the dear valley wrapt in its mantle of snow; the dark
firs under the grand old hills; the village church with
snow-clad roof; and all the seasonable mirth of my
beloved borderland. And I thought too of my
comrades, and envied them, in distant barracks across
the frozen plains.

We slept upon the floor as well as we were able.
A disreputable crowd we looked on the following
morning! Our fur coats were ornamented with hay
seeds and straws. Our chins, noses, and cheeks were
raw with frostbites, and smeared with vasseline. One
man was dyed purple; another blue, and a third was
brown. A beard of a fortnight's growth did not add
to the many fascinations of our appearance. The
ladies entered the hovel to wish us all a very Merry
Christmas; and we seemed to afford considerable
merriment to them. We all blushed like a lot of idiotic
school-boys; and such was our plight on Christmas
Day.

CHAPTER VI

Leave Hoodoo—Manitchinass Hill—A splendid view—Our Christmas   dinner—Batoche—The   South   Saskatchewan—Duck
Lake—Fort Carlton.

THE light from the rising sun was darting through the
feathery sprays of birch and aspen as we bid adieu to
Hoodoo.   It was a tearless farewell.   The name of this
spot is suggestive of the soft, sad cooing of the wood-
pigeon, but the recollection of its torments conjures up language of a very unparliamentary character.   I remember
how keenly I felt the hardship of being unable to smoke
this morning.   It was cold, but it was a morning filled
with a golden gleam that flooded lake and bush and
plain.   Away to the north-east the snowy contour of the
Birch Hills merged into the pale blue of the cloudless
sky.   The air was still, as though nature herself was
dead.   A solemn hush lay on brake, and stream, on
mountain and on lake.   The snow lay mysterious in its
whiteness, smooth and in places ribbed like the hard
sea-sand.   I can never forget the view this day from the
summit of the Manitchinass Hill; a limitless plain
with round groves of trees, fading away into the viewless
distance.   There it lay spread out in all its vast majesty,
like an ice-bound ocean with myriads upon myriads of
rounded islands.   And through this, the dark line of the
South Saskatchewan wound its length.   What a sense
of measureless immensity steals upon the senses in such
a scene !   This day—Christmas—we made our noon
camp upon the bosom of a romantic lake.   Its circular

surface lay wrapt in virgin snow, in a bowl-like hollow.
Giant-rocks stood sentinel around its margin. Above
these, tall trees, with heavy boughs of dark green, spread
their gloom, adding a picturesque contrast to the dazzling whiteness all around. There was of course no
roast beef or plum-pudding to send up their savoury
odour before us on this festive occasion. The usual
stereotyped regulation bacon was hauled from its bag,
in a frozen block. Scattered members of our party
went along the shores with axes, and brought sturdy
boughs of dried pine to add to the fire, which was
sending its blue smoke-wreaths up on high. A square-
cut hole was made alongside, and, as the clear water
bubbled through the crystal sides, camp kettles were
quickly filled. As we were standing around our
crackling faggots, suddenly a sleigh and pair of horses
appeared, which dashed wildly down the opposite incline
and glided along the frozen level. Another sleigh followed
immediately after the first. The brown buffalo coats with
brass buttons, the black sealskin caps with yellow busby-
bags soon showed the men to be police. A wild cheer
rang through the forest aisles in welcome and was echoed
back from rock and bank. Down sprang the drivers
and stamped their feet as they reported to our commander. Who would care to stand stiffly at "attention" in
such a cold as this ? The magic of the telegraph wire
had told the garrison in far-off Fort Carlton of our
approach, and the commanding officer had sent on these
sleighs to our assistance. Questions were rapidly asked and
answered, news exchanged, and yarns spun. No doubt
the two stalwart drivers (one has since died of malaria)
missed the warmth of the mess-room at Carlton and the
rich Christmas fare provided there to-day ; but they
laughed heartily as they joined us in drinking our
strong tea, and munching our tasteless biscuits.

Cooking utensils, plates, and cups were rattled into the dirty sack, and chucked into the sleigh. The two Fort Carlton men were sent ahead to Batoche, having relieved us of some of our heavy baggage. Then, with spirits revived, we emerged from the basin of the lake upon the high ground to the north, and sped on through a dense growth of tangled bush. Poplar, willow, and birch hemmed in the narrow trail. The sky became clouded and leaden hued, as we went down the gentle slopes, among the woods that shroud the approaches to the south branch of that noble river that flows through 1300 miles of prairie, forest, swamps, and rushing rapids into Lake Winnipeg. Behind a screen of leafless twigs peeped a few half-breed huts, as we neared Batoche. As this Metis settlement has been rendered famous by being the birthplace of Riel's second rebellion, which culminated in General Middleton's three days' fight against the rebels at this very spot, I shall have something to say about it further on. Scattered houses are half hidden in trees above the river. Some are built of frame, and others of log. Many are dingy, others are resplendent in paint. There is a Catholic church here, and the residence of M. Batoche is a many-windowed house painted a pale green. The nucleus of the settlement consists of a cluster, where stand the blacksmith's shop, post office, and hotel of Philippe Garnot. This gentleman, a dark, pale-faced person with straight hair, was subsequently sentenced to seven years' Government hospitality, for having acted as secretary to Louis Riel. Our horses were led into his stable, and we carried our bedding into this uninviting hostelry. Our sergeant had been stationed at Batoche during the previous summer, to shadow Riel, who had commenced his inflammatory tactics even then. Many of these half-breeds had served under his greasy banner, before, at Fort Garry. The inhabitants of this place are all French Canadians and "breeds." It was like being in some old-world Norman village, listening to their quaint jargon. They use the same antique phrases introduced into the wilds by their forefathers, who came out in the service of La Compagnie de la Nouvelle France. As this was the holiday season, the officer very kindly sent word that we were to be provided with everything we wished for, at his expense. Monsieur Garnot's cuisine was not of the Brillat Savarin type. We were fain to be content with steak and rice pudding.

At night, the carpenter of this village commune came to pay a visit of ceremony to our host, and Solomon in all his glory was not arrayed like unto him. He was refulgent in lavender trousers, and brilliant scarlet scarf. Had it not been for the dingy moccasins, he was fitted to adorn the Closerie de Lilas on a gala night. It seemed such a pitiful waste of sweetness on the desert air of these regions. A loft with bare-peaked roof formed our dormitory, and upon the boarded floor of this we laid out our blankets. Philippe and his *confrère* were indulging in the usual warmth of Gallic argument underneath, and this roaring cataract of patois did not soothe us into repose. "Sacrée—monjoo !" yelled out an irate peeler from Cork, "will you dry up down there?" And the stream of talk below was forthwith dammed.

Next morning we harnessed up, after breakfast, and soon looked down from the lofty bank upon the broad band of the majestic river. The sides of the South Saskatchewan here rise abruptly, clothed with a rich growth of timber. At this time there was a steel cable stretched from shore to shore for the use of the summer ferry. It was destroyed during the rebellion. I should think the width of the stream is about 200 yards. Little did we dream how many were to lose their lives at this very place before another winter, and how the hurtling missiles of the field-piece were to crash through the leafy screen of the primeval forest. Far away in the country of the Blackfeet, among the rolling foot-hills at the base of the Rocky Mountains, flow the Bow and Belly Rivers; and at the confluence of their waters, near to Grassy Lake, they become the mighty river which joins its sister at the Forks, about thirty miles east from Prince Albert, and about 800 miles from its southern source. From the Forks, the combined waters flow through dense forest and cedar swamps to Cedar Lake, and thence, dashing by the Grand Rapids, into Lake Winnipeg. During the bustle of landing at Quebec, beset on every side by touts of every description, I found a pamphlet thrust into my hand, by a clerical-looking man in seedy dress. This paper-backed volume professed to show the glorious future which awaited any one who took up land near the South Saskatchewan, under the ægis of the Temperance Colonization Company. There was even an illustration of Saskatoon ; above the title of " A North-West City." Tall chimneys were emitting volumes of smoke, there were wharves stocked with merchandise ; and huge steamers, such as adorn the Levées at New Orleans, were taking in cargo. Subsequently I found Saskatoon to consist of six houses at intervals, and a store. It is near the Sioux reserve under White Cap, about sixty miles south of Batoche. Flat-bottomed steam barges, drawing two feet of water, can make one journey down the South Branch in the season. White Cap did penance for taking up arms during the rebellion, along with the other red gentry. Having crossed the river in our sleighs, we mounted the steep ascent, and passed Walter's and Baker's store, where Riel made his first " requisition." The renowned Gabriel Dumont, Riel's lieutenant nominally, had a saloon at this time at Batoche,—a small, low-roofed log erection plastered with mud. In this smoky den French billiards were played, nauseous hop-beer imbibed, and much violent sedition talked by the half-breed *habitués*. Gabriel escaped, after the fight at Batoche, and for some time placed his talents at the disposal of Buffalo Bill, who exhibited him.

Undulating ground, studded with clumps of trees, met our eyes on all sides as we drove along. About five miles north of Batoche we skirted the edge of Duck Lake. Here was shed the first blood during the rebellion, in March, 1885. This pretty sheet of water is about seven miles in length, and upon the southern shore was the trading-post of Messrs Hughes. The mail station and telegraph office were both in the same cluster of white-washed log buildings. Mr. Tompkins, the telegraph clerk here, became a captive of Monsieur Riel's bow and spear ; and inhabited a foul cellar in noisome darkness, for a couple of months. A snake fence ran along the side of the trail, behind it a few ponies were pawing away among the snow for food.

The reserves of Beardy and One Arrow—both Crees of the plains—circled around the northern end of the lake. One Arrow was sent into seclusion after his capture in June, 1885. Old Beardy, however, with the crafty duplicity of the guileless dusky, managed cleverly to bamboozle General Middleton, and got off very cheaply by having his medal taken from him. The latter old sinner now has the entire reserve ; but the number of his tribe is reduced to 143. One Arrow, in a wondrous blanket and head-dress of fox-skin, the ears of which stood up fantastically, shouted a welcome to us as we sped rapidly along. He gesticulated with the appearance of much glee, and yelled out, "How ! How ! " most effusively. His squaw, or one of them, was alongside. Dense bush once more enshrouded us after passing the reserve. We were now nearing Fort Carlton, and, on gaining the edge of the valley, we met two sleighs, one containing the captain, the sergeant-major occupying the other. Fort Carlton is (or was, for it no longer exists) situated on a flat open space on the right bank of the North Saskatchewan. The further side rises in gently rounded hills of marvellous fertility and beauty. But the fort is surrounded on all sides by densely wooded heights, down whose precipitous slopes a narrow trail wound round its zigzag way. It was, at one time, a highly important post of the Hudson Bay Company. It then stood in the heart of the Cree and Blackfoot war country. The strategic position was execrable ; it did not require the teaching of after-events to prove this. Why the Dominion Government paid a fabulous sum to garrison it with red-coats, is another of those perplexing problems which no fellow can understand. We rattled down the break-neck road merrily ; through the great wide gateway of the fort into the square. The notes of the bugle rang out the very moment we turned the corner, and all hands bundled out on a general fatigue, to look after our horses and baggage. Each one of us was summarily hurried off into the mess-room. This was a long, wide, low-ceilinged apartment, cosy and warm, its clean, whitewashed walls decorated with trophies of arms. What a feed we sat down to enjoy at the long table, with its snowy cloth ! roast pork and green peas! The Hudson Bay stores are now generally provided with many luxuries, as well as goods of the best English manufacture. There is a discount of twenty per cent. generously conceded to the police. We then were given plum pudding *ad libitum*, with "lashings" of tea and milk! Our mental grace, after this meal, was a spontaneous doxology.

The call for "Evening Stables" sounded at half-past four. The long string of horses—about sixty—were led down to the North Saskatchewan to water. It was a long cold walk in the starlight, with a lantern flashing here and there, and a keen breeze coming sweeping down the frozen reaches of the river.

Now, before our arrival, great and glad tidings had gone forth among the dusky neighbours of the red-coated "Samogoniss," the name by which we were known among the Crees. It had been told in cabin and in teepe, that on this night a dance was to be given at the fort ; and, at the appointed hour, Cree Indians and Metis, male and female, came trooping into the mess-room, from which the tables had been cleared. We were in all the splendour of scarlet tunics, shining boots, and burnished spurs. Our officers, in all the bravery of mess uniform, sat upon chairs at the head of the room. The two ladies whom we had escorted, also occupied seats in the place of honour ; and were the only white women present. Two dark-skinned Metis fiddlers provided the music. The programme was limited to the Red River Jig. How wildly excited grew the swarthy dancers, as the discordant notes of the rasping violin followed each other quicker and quicker! How they whooped, as they pounded the floor in their moccasined feet! How passionately in earnest they appeared as they bobbed about opposite to each other! And when one of the *vis-à-vis* became exhausted, another enthusiast was at once ready to spring into the gap. Gallons of tea and coffee were handed out from the troop kitchen over the refreshment counter ; and

there was an endless supply of cigarettes, provided by
the hosts, and indulged in by both sexes without dis-
tinction. Mountains of pies and piles of sugary sweet-
meats were passed around. The squaws and half-breed
women, four deep, were squatted upon the floor. You
would hand a dusky beauty a plate of cake, and you
vainly imagined the native lady would pass it on to the
detachment in her rear. *Pas si bête!* With one fell
sweep the contents were deposited in the maiden's lap
and then she, with a gleam of her pearly teeth, handed
you the vessel back.

At eleven o'clock my eyes refused to keep open any
longer, in spite of all the seductions of music, dancing,
and swarthy beauty. So I quietly mounted the stairs to
the barrack-room and went off to bed. In the " wee
sma' hours ayont the twal' " I was awakened by a stout
voice underneath, singing—

> " Patsey go moind the infant,
> Patsey go moind the choild;
> Go cover him wid yer overcoat,
> For fear he should go woild,"

with a rich accent that brought forth memories of the
mountains of Connemara ; and to this Hibernian
refrain regarding connubial duties, I tumbled off to
sleep again. The unwelcome sound of *reveillé* broke
in upon my slumbers at half-past six in the morning,
and at seven we were all out in the starlight, on the
icy square, answering to the roll-call. Then to stables,
marched in sections, and dismissed to our duties of
cleaning out the stalls and grooming. All this is no
joke with the thermometer right away below zero, and
the iron bands on the handle of shovel and manure-fork
burning your finger tips. A big rush at once followed
upon " dismiss " sounding, to the lavatory, where basins
and hot water were secured by the first arrivals. Fish

and game, in the shape of prairie chicken, beef and pork, preserves and pies were the delicacies that met my astonished eyes at breakfast. Of course around such a place as Carlton a great many supplies for the larder were secured by the fowling-piece and rifle ; and the Indians brought in fish and ptarmigan, which they traded for tobacco and tea. But in all my service I never saw things done to such perfection as in the D troop mess at Carlton. This being Saturday morning, there was cleaning out of barrack-rooms at 8.30, and a general fatigue at 9. I was told off to " buck " wood ; which mysterious occupation consists simply in sawing up cordwood, with a bucksaw, into lengths adjustable to the size of the stove. After mid-day stables we had the afternoon to ourselves. Some indulged in the luxury of a novel, lying upon their beds ; others went out shooting ; while a few passed away the time among some Indian teepes in the bush.

The revelation was now made public that, of the whole party who had volunteered at Regina to proceed to Prince Albert, only the officer's servant and myself were really destined for that settlement. The remainder were to strengthen the Carlton contingent. Our friend Riel had been holding Home Rule meetings of an effervescing type at Batoche ; and, as it was feared he might cause some trouble, it was deemed advisable to have a strong force in hand ready for any emergency. I have reason to believe that strong representations were sent to headquarters as to the expediency of arresting this hero of Red River notoriety. Carlton is fifty miles from Prince Albert, and the latter place is forty-five miles from Batoche. A distance of only ten miles intervened between Batoche and Carlton. My comrades accepted their new lot with stoical indifference. Duty was very light here. They could go out and

shoot in the snow-clad woods, and enjoy the half-breed
dances in the adobe houses around. These " breeds," as
we called them, are truly a light-hearted, volatile race.
What stories do they tell of the old happy hunting
days, when the mighty buffalo roamed these wilds in
countless herds.

There are two species of the class. Both are descended
from the Indian on the maternal side, but their paternal
descent springs from two different stems. The Scotch
half-breeds inherit the loyalty and type of feature and
clan names of the hardy highlanders and Orkneymen
who embraced a life of terrible exile, far from their
native glens, in the pay of the Honourable Company of
Merchant Adventurers trading from England into Hudson
Bay. The Metis claim their male ancestry from the gallant
Frenchmen and *habitans* of Lower Canada, who intrepidly
penetrated into these remote regions when La Compagnie de la Nouvelle France was formed, to bring back
the rich furs of mink and marten and beaver for the
beauties who graced the terraces of Versailles. The
latter organization received its death-blow when the
thunder of Wolfe's guns was heard on the Heights of
Abraham. The North-West Fur Company then took
its place, but was merged in the Hudson Bay Company
after 1815. And the latter ruled this immense tract
with the powers of a paternal despot.

Much card-playing went on among the men at Carlton. Here, in this lonely fort, amid all the rigours of a
long northern winter, a vast frozen wilderness between
them and civilization, is it to be wondered at that the
excitement of gambling held sway ? Wrapped up in
furs, with moccasins on feet, the hardy troopers took
their horses a short exercise ride daily, among the bluffs
of slender birch and poplar which overhung the steep
banks of the river. And the great Saskatchewan, wrapt

in its white robe of winter, lay slumbering in the icy
stillness ; while the wan sunlight shone on forest and
lakelet and solemn plain. All nature was silent, save
when the twitter of the snow-birds, or the whirr of the
prarie chicken broke the mysterious hush.

Sunday the 28th shone with the splendour of turquoise
sky, glittering landscape, and glorious sun. It was
intensely cold when we pulled out for Prince Albert at
two o'clock in the afternoon. The verandah and gables
and quaint windows of the brightly painted officers'
quarters, with the feathery bush climbing the slopes
behind, resembled some pretty Alpine scene with its old-
world *châlet*. Our officer and his wife reclined amid a
pile of buffalo robes in a double sleigh. I perched
myself beside the driver, while another sleigh carried the
servant and baggage. A corporal, proceeding to Prince
Albert on leave, brought up the rear in a jumper. How
I envied that blue-eyed, light-haired non-com. ! His
time would expire in the following September, and he
would hie him back to his native island, where the
Atlantic surge beats against the Outer Hebrides. A
sorrowful sigh escaped me as I thought of the five dreary
years ahead !

The sun sank in matchless magnificence, and night
overshadowed us, before we reached " The Pines." This
is the very frontier of settlement. Away beyond, to
the north, begins the mighty sub-arctic forest, studded
here and there with gem-like lakes, their waters clear as
those of some fabled spring. It is the home of the
sullen Chipweyan and the bear. At very rare intervals
stand the remote forts of the H.B. Co.

Our drive through this moonlit, winding aisle was
dreary, the weird shadows of the black trunks were cast
across the trail, and in the gruesome recesses the snow
was drifted thickly into heaps, overhung by the black

pall of the interlacing boughs. The uneven road, covered with stumps, caused the sleigh to roll and pitch, like a boat on the dancing waves, and the crunching of the snow beneath the runners was the only sound that startled the everlasting stillness. The buffalo robes were powerless to prevent the weary, painful aching in one's knees. At length, on emerging from this sepulchral chiaroscuro into the brilliant reflection of the moonbeams on the open, we espied a solitary half-breed shack upon our right. Here we inquired which was the correct trail to Cameron's, as the Glasgow Scotsman was named at whose house we were to put up for the night.

In the course of an hour's travel by lofty bluffs, we halted beside a comfortable-looking homestead, surrounded by outbuildings, and shadowed by an immense haystack. Everything here was clean and neat, in striking contrast to that which we had hitherto seen on our line of march. A lamp shed its mellow rays over a white tablecloth laden with good things, and a soft carpet covered the floor. A well-polished stove sent defiance to the outer air. The "best bedroom" was at the disposal of Mr. and Mrs. M., Mac——, the corporal, and I lay down our blankets on a carpeted landing, and slept the sleep of the just, after a good-night pipe in the kitchen.

CHAPTER VII

Carlton to Prince Albert—Frozen wheat—A digression—A splendid grazing country—"Johnnie Saskatchewan's" palace—Brick barracks—Freedom of social life—A look round.

WE were aroused by the sleepy " boss," in a *negligé* sort of costume, bearing a candle, who informed us, between yawns, that it was five o'clock, and that it was "gey cauld!" One always sleeps with the blankets drawn over the head. After being fortified with some beefsteak and hot coffee, we set off upon the final stage of our toilsome trip, just as the dawn was flushing the Eastern sky. Now the country grew more open, and farms studded the landscape. Some acres of frozen wheat, standing uncut alongside the trail, did not pose as a very favourable witness to the climate of this fertile belt. The autumn's sun had gilded the ears with ripeness, when—snap!—down came the nipping frost, like the wolf on the fold, and blighted it with ruin in a single night. The Ontario Jews of Scotch extraction, who rig the land-market in Winnipeg, will doubtless endeavour to explain away these little facts.

I am induced to make the above remark by the following circumstance. A private statement of mine to a friend, that I had been under canvas when the temperature was 62° below zero, found its way into print in England. Thereupon the howl that went up from the descendants of Ananias and Sapphira, who have gathered together in Winnipeg, was heartrending. A comrade of mine sent me a cutting from *Winnipeg*

Siftings, in which the gentlemanly and accomplished editor stigmatized me as a liar. I was strongly urged to reply, as every one in Regina knew my statement to be true. But I was away, out on the prairies, at the time; and when I returned, *Winnipeg Siftings* was defunct, the editor having been obliged to abscond. He was threatened with an action for libel by Mr. Hugh Macdonald—son of the Canadian Premier—and also with an application of rawhide by the irate relative of a slandered lady. I merely make this digression to show from what class these random contradictions come; and I repeat my positive declaration regarding the temperature on the night of Sunday, December 21st, 1884.

A man who had resided for forty years on the Saskatchewan, informed me that he had only known wheat escape frost five times during the whole of that lengthened period. Why will those responsible for emigration indicate localities as wheat-growing, when they are nothing of the sort? Wheat is the perpetual symbol of a new El Dorado. The zone of the Saskatchewan valley is a magnificent grazing country:—why not hold it up as such?

We were now entering the white settlements around Prince Albert. A large building, painted white, with wide verandah, greeted us from an enclosure on our right. This was the Bishop's Palace. The late celebrated Dr. Maclean, sacrilegiously known as "Johnnie Saskatchewan," resided there in those days. In the days of the old rebellion at Fort Garry this prelate, then a simple parson, had the task of preparing sundry of Riel's prisoners for death. On our left lay the deep, silent valley of the North Saskatchewan. More wooden houses, painted white, peeped out from a network of bush in a hollow amphitheatre before us.

"This is Prince Albert," said the burly Prussian driving.

"Then by Jove, I'll walk," I replied. There seemed no circulation in my nether limbs at all. The two sleighs passed on ahead leaving me on foot. The corporal, in his jumper, presently overtook me, his eyebrows and wraps white with a powdery frost.

"Hello! what's up?"

"I'm going to walk, that is all."

"Jump in, old man; you have six miles to go yet."

This was the unpalatable truth which I had to swallow, for the town of Prince Albert stretches its broken length, like a disjointed snake, fully the above distance. There is about almost half a mile between each house in the "suburbs" for, in the days of "the boom," the minds of men had dreamed a magnificent dream which was never destined to emerge into reality. We passed along the main street, fronting the river, with houses rich in paint alongside dingy stores, by hotels and blacksmiths' shops, and by dreary open spaces. Two huge black stove pipes stood up against the bright blue sky and the lower line of the dark forest on the opposite shore. This was the steamboat *North-West* laid up in winter quarters. Then came the huge straggling buildings of the H.B. Co., with its surrounding cluster of tiny, trim, ornate cottages, shining in green and lavender paint. Here also was the inevitable flagstaff. Then more scattered houses and sparse bushes under a razor-like ridge of upland. Suddenly, while I was wrapt in thoughts of bears, and snow-shoes, and dog sleds, and all the sports of the wild North Land, we swept round the corner of a two-storied edifice of brick, and came to an abrupt stoppage before the door. Over this was a wooden balcony, decorated with many rabbits in their light fur, hanging in strings, reminding one of a game-dealer's establishment. Whitewashed log-huts, few in number, occupied the wide level in front of the barracks, while the towering form of an ugly mill overhung the shelving bank of the river. And, to the south, a fringe of spear-like trees pierced the horizon.

Presently a mob of troopers came tumbling down the bare, narrow staircase, and took possession of horse and sleigh. I went up as directed, with aching limbs, into a long, well-lighted, plastered and whitewashed barrack-room, with lofty ceiling.

I at once made for the stove, and endeavoured to infuse some heat into my chilled bones, feeling as if it would take two years in the tropics to warm me.

There was one constable at the far end of the room, when I entered, who came up to me with offers of every kindness, and the fullest expression of sympathy.

My comrades of the corps were more like a band of brothers than merely a chance medley of individual atoms, thrown together to serve a stated term, and then to fly apart again. This feeling is doubtless fostered in a great measure by the fact, that we were in exile together, and in danger often by ourselves, far from any extraneous aid. So the sense of interdependence became dominant. We were a type after General Lord Wolseley's own heart, inasmuch as we nurtured a most thorough contempt for civilians. This was wrong no doubt, as we should all have to drift into civil life ourselves, by-and-by. I know, at present, that I myself nurse a feeling far from contempt for my publishers, for instance. The far-away, isolated posts we held, begot a sensation of loneliness, which only obtained relief in mutual confidences and sympathetic actions. Hence also the affection for the canine tribe that reigned in the breasts of all of us. The veriest mongrel and pariah was sure of a home in barracks, if he pleaded with mute eyes of sorrow, and tail reversed. And I myself can speak of the tacit understanding that exists, on the lone prairie, between man and horse.

Thus was that fifteen days' march from Regina brought to a close. We had left headquarters on the 14th, and we reached Prince Albert on December 29th. Our tribulations and hardships have been passed over lightly, because my pen is too feeble to describe them adequately; but every minute of exposure in that intense cold was one of pain. If it did not catch our nose, it was in our feet. If our knees felt all right, you may be sure it tingled in our fingers. Many in Regina, when the thermometer fell with such a startling drop (it was — 58° there), were of opinion that we should not be able to complete the journey. The majority of us were new to the country, simply "tenderfeet." It was one of the most severe ever taken by men in the force, because it must be remembered, that this winter was unparalleled in its severity. The Arctic climate, in winter, is the one drawback to this magnificent land. Out-door work is impossible, and freighting or lumber cutting are the only occupations which can be indulged in by the idle farmer. Even our sentries have to dispense with their carbines as the metal would freeze their hands. Men grow old before their time. A worn look comes into the features ploughed with furrows by the piercing air—

> "As if the man had fixed his face,
> In many a solitary place,
> Against the wind and open sky."

It is impossible to hold yourself erect, you must shield your head in your high fur collar, while your heavy clothing weighs you down. So that, in spring, there is an annual period of "setting up" drill, devoted in a great measure, to what is known in the red book as extension notions.

With the first warm breath of the vernal season, a transformation scene takes place over all the land. Forage caps are stuck jauntily on three hairs. Scarlet jackets are bright against the budding green, leaves are rustling in a wealth of foliage in three days from their birth, birds of brilliant plumage flash in the sunshine, and the prairie blossoms with embroidery of flower and waving grass. The luscious perfume of wolf-willow and wild rose, and all the healthy ozone of this sunset land, comes scampering on the western breeze. And a load seems lifted from the shoulders of mankind.

My first night was spent in a tour of inspection, under the guidance of Corporal Mac— from Carlton. As a matter of course, the streets of these western cities were unlighted in those days. Calgary now boasts of the electric light. I found that the side-walks of Prince Albert came to an abrupt conclusion, every ten yards or so, above a deep abyss, and great caution was requisite in navigating the public promenades after dark. There were a couple of saloons in the principal thoroughfare, where the most villainous hop beer was retailed at ten cents a glass, and billiard-balls of uncertain colour knocked about upon rickety tables. In all western towns, you generally find the chief politician, seated on a keg of molasses, in one of these establishments, holding forth to an audience of open-mouthed settlers, who express their adherence to his views by muttering "You bet !" and "Thet's so!" A man must wager his life or his "sweet socks," on any *questio vexata* here. "Bet yer life !" or "bet yer sweet socks !" is the strongest affirmative in support of an assertion. Your boots are also a commodity in the speculative market· With regard to the free and easy habits of society, in these remote settlements, I may state that I have seen the leading barrister in Prince Albert, sitting in his shirt-sleeves on the side-walk (in summer), talking to an officer of police !

My new chums I found to be a very jovial crew all round. One of them had been formerly an officer in the 17th Foot, and A.D.C. to a certain general in India. He showed me correspondence, which proved the fact. Two other constables were sons of English officers, while the father of another was Minister of Public Works in the Quebec Government. The whole of our detach-ment consisted of one officer and twenty non-com-missioned officers and men. The subaltern, who was transferred to a fresh station, handed over his command on December 31st.

CHAPTER VIII

1885—Inspection—Our surroundings—Clear Sky Land—Rabbits and lynx—Easy routine—A whisky desperado—Precious snow —North-west liquor law—Curling—Skating—Dog trains— An Indian swell—Mother Smoke—Night picquet—A night scene—Night thoughts.

NEW-YEAR'S DAY, 1885,—most memorable year upon the Saskatchewan,—came upon us in all the splendour of glorious sun, glittering snow-scape, and intense frost. The thermometer was −49°, with an air as still as death.

Major Crozier—a tall, fine-looking man, the very *beau-ideal* of a soldier—had arrived from Battleford (160 miles west) to inspect us. He was in command of the whole Northern Division. We had a short parade in the snow in front of the quarters ; and our kits were laid out on the beds upstairs. He promoted our corporal to the rank of sergeant ; and expressed himself pleased with all he saw.

Before we come to the stirring time of the rebellion, I should like to say something about winter life, far away in this lonely settlement. The barracks of the detachment, built of brick, were originally intended for an hotel. They were situated on the extreme eastern verge of Prince Albert ; in the suburb that is known by the scriptural name of Goshen. There is only the width of the roadway between the building and the river, which here forms almost a lake, with bays, and promontories, and islands. The primeval forest rose on the opposite shore. Scattered houses dotted the flat expanse around ; and the ridge clothed with timber bounded the horizon to the east and south. The Hudson Bay Post was about half-a-mile to the westward. The weather continued clear and bright, but with a terrible cold. Strange to say, I did not feel it, here, so much as I subsequently have done on the prairie with a higher temperature. The thermometer averaged — 40° for six weeks. But this was my first winter ; and consequently I was better enabled to withstand it. The stillness of the atmosphere here is intense ; and strangely clear. You can hear sounds at an immense distance. It was once my luck to witness two waterspouts and a thunderstorm at work in the gut of Gibraltar.

"There's always some sort of weather here," said the mate.

Such is the case on the open prairie ; there is always wind ; a perpetual vibration of the air. We had a succession of lovely days. The sun shone with dazzling brilliancy upon the sparkling snow ; the broad river lay silent, and robed in white ; the Great Forest on the northern bank, stood dark and still. Amid its sombre boughs the smoke from a few lodges of Teton Sioux curled up into the crystal air. A few snow-birds hopped about the ground. There was a large island not far off, which swarmed with rabbits. These we snared, or shot, and they were a welcome addition to our mess. Our balcony was always draped with frozen bunnies. Of course, I need hardly say that this species do not burrow, as ours do. The rabbits in the Territories are almost totally exterminated, every seven years, by throat disease. And at the same period there is a corresponding decrease of lynx. For the guidance of sportsmen of the future, I beg to state that the next visitation of this kind will take place in 1894.

The routine at this outpost was very easy. In fact

the two short months we enjoyed previous to the outbreak were very pleasant, in spite of the terrible isolation.
The settlement girls used to drive their showy cutters
down past our quarters daily ; and the skating rink
was the big attraction at night. We only had eleven
horses in our stables ; and these did not take up much
of our time. Twice daily a hole on the Saskatchewan
was cut open with our axes, and thither we rode our
steeds to water. One of them was always at the
disposal of any one who wished to ride into the town.
There were no parades, and little fatigue duty, except
when the manure was drawn away on Saturday.
One or two expeditions went out after whisky ; and
we captured one notorious gentleman, who had
intimated his intention of "doing for" any one who
came to take him. Like most gasconading outlaws he
simply did nothing at all ; but accepted his fate with
sensible resignation. Whisky hunting is not popular
in the corps ; and a man who persistently prosecutes
for this offence is looked upon with contempt. But
large traders of contraband liquor may expect no mercy ;
and a man who supplies an Indian with intoxicating
drink, will, if discovered, catch it pretty severely.
The Lieutenant-Governor of the North-West Territory
has the power to grant periodical permits, to enable
people to have a certain quantity of liquor in their
possession for domestic or medicinal use. By the
exercise of his prerogative, the present Lieutenant-
Governor, Mr. Royal, has allowed the sale of beer containing alcohol to the maximum of 4 per cent. The
Commissioner of the North-West Mounted Police, in
his annual report for 1887, says :—

"The enforcement of the North-West prohibitory law
is more difficult than ever, the sympathy of many of the
settlers being generally against us in this matter. Large

quantities of liquor have been seized and spilt, but a great deal more illicit liquor has undoubtedly been used under the cloak of the permit system. Liquor is run into the country in every conceivable manner, in barrels of sugar, salt, and as ginger ale, and even in neatly constructed imitation eggs ; and respectable people, who otherwise are honest, will resort to every device to evade the liquor laws, and when caught they generally have the quantity covered by their permits. It is really curious the length of time some holders of permits can keep their liquor.

" The permit system should be done away with in the first place, if the law is to be enforced ; and the law itself should be cleared of the technicalities that have enabled so many to escape punishment this last year.

" The importation and manufacture of a good article of lager beer, under stringent Inland Revenue regulations, would, in my opinion, greatly assist the satisfactory settlement of this vexed question. Nearly all the opprobrium that has been cast upon the Police, gene-rally, and my management in particular, can be directly traced to public sentiment on the attempt to enforce this law.

" Although it has been stated by parties interested in free liquor, that great facilities for drunkenness occur, I can say that there has been no crime of any consequence during the year in this country attributable to whisky, and that the towns and villages throughout the Territories are as quiet and orderly and free from outrages as any place of the same size in the world, which is saying a great deal when it is taken into consideration that we have the usual amount of unsettled population common to all new and frontier countries."

When any whisky which had been confiscated at Prince Albert was spilled, and any of the natives witnessed the operation, the half-breeds and Indians would reverently gather up the precious snow and devour it eagerly.

Prince Albert consists of a long, straggling settlement, stretching along the right bank of the North Branch, beginning at a distance of thirty miles from the Forks of the Saskatchewan. A trail passes from the town through a country rich in grassy hollows, lakelets, and clumps of trees, to the Hudson Bay Ferry on the South Branch, about twelve miles distant. There is a considerable population of Scotch half-breeds on the outskirts, and the first germ of this colony was a Presbyterian mission. The women are excellent laundresses, though their charges would strike astonishment into the minds of the female professors of the art at home. The uniform settled rate is ten cents for each article that passes through their hands, whether it be a sheet or a pocket handkerchief. A large lumber-mill now stands here, and logs are rafted down the stream. The residence of the Hon. L. Clarke, the Chief Factor of the Hudson Bay Company, was a many-gabled house of painted frame-work, with a wide verandah, standing in an enclosure, which could scarcely by any stretch of courtesy be termed "grounds." Near to this, by the river, rose the glittering tin spire of the church, attached to the Convent and the Roman Catholic Mission. A long straggling street of wooden stores fronted the wide Saskatchewan, which at this point is studded with lovely islands. The Presbyterian Church and manse were built of brick ; there is a theological college in connection with the Church of England. The skating rink was in the centre of the town, and a band frequently discoursed music to the gliding throng. Wherever you find Scotchmen, you are sure of a curling club, unless you are frizzling under the torrid zone. As the Caledonian element was very strong here, there were

two clubs, one in the town and the other at Goshen.
After any exciting match, the winning team would
drive round the settlement in sleighs, with brooms at
" the carry," and give periodic whoops. The Hudson
Bay Store displayed a varied assortment of English
goods, ranging from electro-plated silver ware down to
G.B.D. briar pipes. Some of the latter were assessed
at as much as five dollars. Many of the " moccasin
aristocracy "—as we dubbed the French half-breeds, in
barrack parlance—lived in huts for the winter, on the
north side of the river, a quarter which was named
Chicago. When the warmth of spring enabled them to
emerge from their foul-smelling dens, they migrated in
canoes, with tent and teepe, to the open spaces in the
town, and went in for mild labour, such as a little wood-
chopping, for the citizens. There was also a camp of
thirty lodges of Téton Sioux, in a glade of the forest on
the northern side. As they were simply refugees from
the United States, after the Custer massacre, they were
not treaty Indians. That is to say, they received
nothing from the Dominion Government in consideration of lands surrendered by them. They were consequently in winter often on the very verge of famine.
After a donation of scraps from the barrack-kitchen, they
would indulge in a pow-wow of wild hilarity, and the
beating of the tom-tom, mingled with piercing yells
would sound across the snow-robed river far into the
night, and their strange forms would be seen dancing
round the ruddy camp-fire. The tradesmen of Prince
Albert were principally from Ontario, who had been
lured to speculate here by the imagined course of the
Canadian Pacific line. They were not a pleasant class
of people by any means, and did not compare favour-
ably with the civilians of other posts. At the skating-
rink were frequent carnival nights, when the band would

play, and every one appear in fancy dress. I have seen some very good and costly costumes here, and some very ingenious ones also. One stout party, I remember, personated Bottled Beer, and the familiar red triangle shielded his portly stomach. There was, of course, generally a flaming Mephistopheles, and the inevitable young lady dressed as Night. Unlike a European masquerade, the Red Indian was conspicuous by his absence. There was no romance about him here. The musicians generally struck up rattling tunes, under a wooden shed, where a stove gave the necessary warmth. The skaters whirled round and round upon the ice, under the sparkling stars; for there was no roof but that of heaven, and the enclosure was surrounded with a tall palisading.

It was at Prince Albert that I first beheld a train of dogs. These animals are harnessed by a padded collar to a light flat sleigh, of skins stretched across a frame of thin wood, called a toboggan. A dog is supposed to be capable of drawing 100 lbs. Each train consists of from four to six of these useful quadrupeds. They travel almost incredible distances, with deerskin boots as a protection to the feet. One frozen fish each, at the end of the day, is their regulation allowance of food. A half-breed drives them, running alongside with ready whip. With many a loud and vehement *sacré-é-é*, he unmercifully leathers his panting charge. They have been educated to the use of strange oaths and Metis blasphemy from puppyhood. One glorious February afternoon, I was riding along the bank of the Saskatchewan. Down the broad frozen reach of the river were speeding three trains of dogs with laden sleds. Suddenly, there came upon my ears, a most unearthly wail. The driver, in blue capote and scarlet sash, was castigating a refractory bow-wow in the front team, and thereupon every other dog in the whole menagerie struck work, and, squatting on his haunches, gave voice to these most hideous lamentations, in sympathy. It was ludicrous beyond measure.

In winter, when the rigid grasp of ice has locked in its stern embrace lake and stream, and the canoe and boat are useless, this is the only mode of transport in the far regions north of the Saskatchewan from the desolate shores of Athabasca to James' Bay. When a Chipweyan from the Peace River made his appearance at Prince Albert, his astonishment was great, on first casting his eyes upon a horse. He considered that the "medicine" of the white man must be great, when it could evolve such a gigantic breed of dogs! We had many bears also around the settlement.

The red-coats were always welcome to the many dances which the Scotch half-breeds gave in their houses at the west end. Some of our fellows were regular *habitués* of these assemblies. The white people gave no entertainments, and we did not take the initiative in the matter here. We were generally celebrated for the hops which we gave, all over the Territories. The Hudson Bay store was the principal rendezvous of the Indians. One pompous chief was always on view there, like one of Madame Tussaud's inanimate celebrities. He was a stately being, with a melancholy expression of countenance, and always reminded me of Fennimore Cooper's Chingachook. He had a square emblem, worked in beads, upon his breast, like unto the phylactery of a Pharisee. The ground-work was of blue, and upon this a black bull's head. He wore his blanket with dignity; as the Roman senator is supposed to have habitually worn his toga. The crimson leggings and moccasins of this aristocratic savage were a marvel. He carried a tomahawk (blunt), and a calumet. His stoical reserve was wonderful to behold, for the Indian in reality is no stoic. I should like to have bought that specimen of a dying race. I believe he was known in the councils of his nation and the family circle, as " the Crow."

A sleigh in winter, and a four-in-hand stage in summer, brought us the mail, weekly, from Troy. The fare for the whole distance of 240 miles was twenty-five dollars. As the mail stations were closed in summer on this route, the passengers were obliged to provide their own grub, and camp out nightly.

An ancient half-breed of the female gender, a gem of the first water, assisted by her daughter, of an uncertain age, visited the barracks weekly, and, by combining their forces, used to scrub out our quarters in a day ; for the " moccasin aristocracy " do not love to work.   It was impossible to guess the age of this unlovely hag ; for she was wrinkled and seamed and blear-eyed, and her skin was as dry as that of Rameses I, in his case in the Bloomsbury district.   She was known amongst us by the *sobriquet* of Mother Smoke ; both on account of her inordinate predilection for tobacco, and because, owing to a chronic kleptomania, she used to secrete in the mysterious folds of her garment every decent pipe she could " snaffle."   Therefore, on Saturdays, all cherished briars and well-coloured clays were carefully " cached " from the evil eye of this weird sister.   Sophie —*la fille*—was a heavy-featured, sulky-looking " breed," with as much virtue as the rest, and as taciturn as the Hyde Park statue of Achilles.   Joe, our French Canadian cook, was, I think, first favourite with this dusky Lalage, and our caterer (an Englishman), who entered for the same stakes, was nowhere. Consequently, the diplomatic relations between mess-waiter and cook were slightly strained. Joe one day confided to me the fact that,—

"Q. is mad vit Sophie, because she not lofe him."

Old Smoke—*madame la mère*—had also an insatiable appetite for fiery liquids. I verily believe she would have thrived on mustang liniment, the fierce potency of which may be algebraically expressed by x. She would have done anything for a bottle of pain-killer, which is a forbidden fluid to the copper-hued subjects of her Majesty. One day I gave this pre-adamite fossil about a wine-glassful of sulphuric ether—*neat!* She had pointed with interrogatory grimaces at the bottle, which was standing beside my cleaning things. She swallowed my libation unmoved, then gave a satisfied grunt, rubbed gleefully her mesenteric region, and uttered the one word *me-wa-sin;* which is Cree for "good," with emphatic content. I merely recite this fact to illustrate the habitual longing for intoxicants in the soul of the natives and the armour-plated nature of their stomachs.

Our night picquet at this outpost was not severe by any means. Each turn for duty arrived every eighth night. The first relief went to the guard-room at 6.30 p.m., taking his blankets and a book. He had previously lighted a fire in the stove, and could amuse himself as it suited his taste ; but of course could not indulge in a nap, unless he wished to become a fixture there for a month. He was supposed to visit the stables every half-hour ; and also keep the fires going in the quarters. Half an hour after midnight he called the second relief, who in turn, roused the barracks at 6.30 a.m. We had no bugler here at that time. The second relief was exempt from all parades, until evening stables at 4.30 p.m. How brilliant were these midnight skies on that far-off Saskatchewan! The stars, the waving arch of the mysterious aurora, with its myriad hues and the immaculate robe of snow beneath—all hushed

in a weird silence, save when, in the intense frost, the
giant trees in the great sub-arctic forest would crack
and rend.   Wrapped in furs though one always was, the
cold was too great to admit of much meditation in the
open air.   But the mysterious stillness brought strange
fancies ; often one's thoughts flashed across the vast
space between the lonely sentry and home.   Across the
frozen prairie, far over the Kitchi Gami (Lake Superior),
away beyond the pines—over the sleeping cities and
misty ocean—a phantom view would rise before me of a
certain bonnie glen, hidden in my own romantic borderland ; the clustering village houses, the purple slopes and
rugged crags ;   the waving bracken and the tasselled
firs ;   and the grey ruins above the brown waters of the
brawling trout-stream.

CHAPTER IX

An unwelcome prisoner—Riel busy—Seditious meetings—Threats
—The Metis—Louis David Riel—A prophet—A council of
State—The provisional government—A new religion—Red
tape—Urgent despatches—Carlton strengthened—A convenient eclipse—Arrival of arms—The volunteers—Scouts—A
man who wanted gore—A meddling official—The rebellion
inaugurated—Officials imprisoned—A Batoche farce—Arrival
of Colonel Irvine—Frostbite—Snow blindness.

THE days glided on in monotonous succession, and
towards the end of February the weather showed some
few signs of increasing mildness. The windows of our
rooms were coated with a cake of frost, which still
remained opaque in spite of the warmth within. The
sky continued cloudless, and the whiteness still lay
unblemished over the land. We had one solitary
prisoner now, whose presence necessitated the mounting
of a continual guard, so that our captive was by no
means a welcome guest. He was daily used in wood-
cutting, which saved us some fatigue duty. This man
had been receiving wages at the rate of six dollars
(twenty-four shillings) *per diem*, as driver of the engine
at the H.B. Company's flour-mill, yet he preferred enduring two months' confinement to paying the value of a
miserable mongrel dog—the property of a neighbour—
which he had shot.

Meanwhile, Riel had been steadily at work in all
directions, sounding the dispositions of the Indians, and
promising untold wealth and glory to his own beloved
Metis. This, of course, stripped of ornate imagery, meant

unlimited facilities for plunder, and drink, and debauchery. He had emissaries among the Blackfeet, but Crowfoot was too old a bird to be caught. Poundmaker and his tribe of Stonies, among the Eagle Hills, were (like a Tipperary Irishman) always ready for a row.

In the beginning of March, strange rumours came in, as to the doings of "the French," for by this title were the Metis invariably known to the white settlers. This vague Gallic nationality had been holding meetings at Batoche and St. Laurent, and fulminating threats towards every representative of law and order. Their political leanings and animosities were summed up in the historic dictum of that son of Erin who declared, "Oi'm agin the Government, *anyway !*" They had sold their land on the margin of the Red River, on the advent of settlement, in the days of the Winnipeg "boom," and had migrated to their present holdings, when there were still buffalo among the grassy hills and wide parks that stretch along the course of the "Kissas-katchewan." Some had crossed Lake Winnipeg in boats and made their way up stream from Cedar Lake. Others had gathered their Lares and Penates into Red River carts, and had toiled over the great plains, hunting by the way. They were to receive their share of land up here, they stated, and the Government was slow in granting their demands ; so of course they would make things particularly lively, if that Government did not stump out. And they reasoned, probably, the powers that be would give them an additional bribe to remain quiet. That really, in plain language, was the essence of all the protests, and despatches to Ottawa, and long-winded harangues at the scattered log shanties and in the school-rooms of the villages.

It is no use here entering into a long disquisition as

to what should have been done, or what ought not to have taken place. I do not wish to pose as a very knowing individual. I have neither space nor inclination, and it does not become one serving in the ranks, to criticize his superiors. I have only to recount facts.

Louis David Riel—saint and martyr in the French-Canadian calendar—was the prime agitator, having with him about a dozen other spirits more wicked than himself, such as Garnot, Maxime Lepine, Gabriel Dumont, and the renegade Jackson.

Jackson was the son of a Yorkshireman, and ambitious. Gabriel Dumont was an expert shot, and a mighty hunter; and, in addition, was that which Ferdinand Mendez Pinto was said to be,—a liar of the first magnitude. As for Riel, he was, in my humble opinion, a fanatic, who having begun by taking in others, ended by deluding himself. His previous Red River escapade, when he fled on hearing of the arrival of the 60th Rifles under Wolseley, had been no warning to him. He had been educated for the priesthood, and therefore no one could say he was deficient in average intelligence.

I venture to think the Canadian Government were wrong in ever permitting this firebrand to return from exile. But they were still more to blame in ever paying him an "indemnity." I don't want to attempt a psychological analysis of this man's character, though—as will be seen subsequently—I had abundance of special opportunity to study him. I verily believe he imagined he was created to be the saviour of the half-breeds, and the founder of a new nation that was to be established between the Saskatchewan, and the Missouri. His visionary schemes had taken such a grasp upon his superstitious mind, that he had worked himself into a full belief of their feasibility.

This little Napoleon, as he was styled by his former

Red River admirers, had once more come over from his exile in the United States, and had taken up his abode in 1884, near Batoche. Some said that he had made the territory of Montana too hot to hold him, and, if so, his warmth-kindling capabilities must have been of no mean order, for Montana is a perfect hotbed of the hardest of "hard seeds." At least, it was in those days. Every second man you met on the Upper Missouri and the Yellowstone was at one time an outlaw. However, he had landed amongst the excitable Metis of the Saskatchewan, many of whom had been under him before.

Now, these ignorant half-castes inherit all the love of dramatic incident, all the grotesque affection for stage effect, which is the characteristic of both their Gallic and redskin ancestors.

By wily scheming and an unlimited flow of sophistry, and gas, M. Riel prepared the minds of the whole French settlement, around St. Laurent and Batoche, to receive his doctrine. He was a prophet, he told them, and had enjoyed visions of the saints and revelations from on high. The same old game from Mohammed to the Mahdi! All this time, he was being watched, and reports went down from Fort Carlton to Regina regarding his movements. It is whispered that these documents were relegated at once to the seclusion of a pigeon-hole in the headquarters orderly-room. Thus having laid the foundation of his sovereignty, the "dictator" proceeded to form a "Council of State" and a "Provisional Government." He also entrusted Garnot with the formation of a Cabinet, and went in for all the mock solemnity of a real state. He had a staff of secretaries, and, of course, he himself was the President of the new republic. He even took the church to himself, and repudiated the authority of Rome. Père

André poured out the vials of his wrath with many anathemas, but this did not disturb Riel's serenity in the least. He had been sent by Heaven to create a new church. It was a pity such a broad farce was destined to end in such grim reality !

Everything now was approaching a crisis. Indeed we of the rank and file used to talk in quite a familiar way, in the barrack-room, of the coming rebellion as a matter of course. We even had the date fixed. I remember our corporal singing out from his bed, "Well, boys, old Riel will be starting in on the 18th." (The speaker had his thigh broken by a shot, at Duck Lake, on the 26th.) A civilian—an Englishman—who had been a guest for some little time of our commanding officer, came over to take his leave of me in the early part of March. "Good-bye, old man," he said ; " I want to get through before this rebellion begins."

It was therefore openly spoken of, yet the Government pretended that it came upon them like a bolt from the blue ! Nothing was done, and no arrests were made because every one in authority on the Saskatchewan was tied up in red tape.

Matters had grown manifestly worse since the third of March, on which day Riel had ordered the half-breeds to attend a meeting at Batoche under arms. Those who came he kept there as a garrison and would not permit to return to their homes. As prophet and chief priest of his new religion he had baptized Jackson (whose brother had a drug store at Prince Albert), and in honour of the occasion had held a mighty feast. On the 16th of March, Major Crozier came over from Fort Carlton to confer with the principal citizens as to the serious turn which affairs had taken, and to form a corps of volunteers. He also had an interview with Père André, whom he requested to use his influence in the way of

mediation. This reverend father always reminded me
of those mendicant priests of the Greek church whom
one sees hanging around the wharves at Galata. He
wore a lofty cap of beaver, and a greasy cassock very
much the worse for wear. In addition he sported an
uncared-for beard of iron-grey. His reverence could
not undertake to act as peacemaker, because the little
Napoleon had set up a rival establishment of his own,
and had intimated metaphorically that he did not
care a snap for the whole College of Cardinals.
After the major had held a council of war with the
officer commanding here, and others, he took his departure for Fort Carlton to await the outbreak of the
émeute. Urgent telegrams and despatches had already
been sent to Regina and Ottawa, and the garrison at
Carlton had been secretly strengthened. A party had
arrived there from Battleford under cover of night,
bringing with them one gun, a brass nine-pounder.

A partial eclipse of the sun was visible over the whole
of Northern America on the date of Major Crozier's
visit. The weather had suddenly grown very much
more springlike in character; indeed on the 15th we
had been treated to a shower of rain. On the day
of the eclipse Riel was displaying his eloquence to
a blanketed and painted gathering of Indians, for
many tribes had sent warriors to attend the summons of
this red-bearded chief who was to inaugurate a new era
of unlimited grub and tobacco for the red man. The
education of this crafty imitator of other like adventurers
had given him an immense superiority over his followers,
but never had it stood him in such good stead as now.
The almanack had heralded to all the world the approach
of the coming shadow over the face of the god of day.
In the most telling part of his address, Riel informed
these benighted savages that in order to sanctify his

words to them, the Great Spirit would throw a darkness
over the sun. And the superstitious aborigines squatting
in a circle were stricken with a great awe, when the
eclipse began, and forthwith Monsieur Louis David Riel
was the embodiment of big medicine to them. A man
who was so thoroughly *en rapport* with the Manitou
must be believed in and obeyed implicitly.

On the night following, a supply of snider rifles and
ammunition arrived at our barracks for the Prince
Albert volunteers. They were conveyed in, under a
heavy mounted escort in charge of a sergeant, doing
the fifty miles in eight hours. We were roused from
our beds, and turned out in the darkness where the
steaming horses and tired troopers were standing drawn
up in front of the doorway. We carried the rifles, and
rolled the kegs of cartridges into our mess-room.
Sentries were at once posted around the barracks. Joe
McKay, our best and most famous scout, accompanied
this party. He wore a fur cap and a buckskin jacket
richly adorned with fringes and bead-work. A few
scouts and interpreters are attached to each troop,
receiving an allowance of rations and quarters, with pay
at the rate of seventy-five dollars per month. Joe was
a Scotch half-breed, the whole of whose family had
been, or were, valued servants in the employ of the H.B.
Company. He was a good-looking young fellow with dark
complexion, active in build, and strongly knit together.

He was always courteous and gentlemanly in manner.
After attending to their horses and the wants of the
inner man, the members of the escort unrolled their
blankets upon the floor of the mess-room and lay down
to rest. I happened to look in upon the recumbent
figures, as they were stretched in various attitudes under
the struggling light of a single oil lamp. All were
engaged in smoking and indulging in a desultory fire

of remarks regarding the "French." I heard Joe, in reply to some one who asked for a match, say loudly as he handed over the required article, "What I want is *gore !* I've been kept out of bed for four nights by those black sons of ——, and I want gore !"

He eventually got it, for he emptied his revolver at Duck Lake into the chief "Star Blanket," completely perforating that feathered and painted individual. The Carlton party departed on the morning of the 18th, taking with them a corporal and seven men.

The sum of history is made up of very trifling incidents, when one goes behind the scenes; and I believe an ingenious Frenchman once wrote a treatise on the influence of the *cuisine* upon diplomacy. A battle has been lost, or a kingdom dismembered because, say, a *salmis de faisan truffes* has disagreed with a certain illustrious personage. Thus, a few thoughtless words, hastily spoken, in this case, brought the simmering Metis volcano into active eruption. I have never seen an allusion to this little matter in print, because, in the North-West, it does not do to throw too strong a light upon certain people. But, about this time, the "Hon." Lawrence Clarke was returning from Eastern Canada, and on his way to his painted wooden villa, he was obliged to pass Batoche. He was here asked by the rebel leader what reply the Government intended to despatch to his "Bill of Rights," and if there were a probability of the half-breeds' demands being granted soon.

"The reply will be 500 mounted police," said his Factorship, and drove on. Now, up to this, I believe Riel had been playing a game of bluff. He had been hanging back for a bribe ; but he now resolved to go ahead. He would burn his boats with theatrical accompaniments, and on the 18th the final act of the

drama was begun. His Metis "troops" cut the telegraph wires at Batoche, seized upon a quantity of freight
destined for the H.B. Company sacked the store of Messrs.
Walters and Baker at Batoche, and imprisoned Hannafin,
the clerk. The establishment of Kerr Brothers at
St. Laurent was also raided, the Indian agent, Lash,
Astley the surveyor, Tompkins the telegraph operator,
and other Government officials, were taken prisoners.
On the receipt of these tidings vedettes and scouts were
thrown out in all directions around Prince Albert.
Couriers arrived through the night from Carlton with
cipher despatches ; a picquet was posted to watch
the trail at the forks of the road, where it diverges
towards Batoche ; the muster-roll of the Prince Albert
volunteers had been instantaneously filled up. These
citizen soldiers, under Colonel Sproat, paraded in front
of our barracks, and each man was marched through
into our mess-room, where a rifle and sword-bayonet
was issued to him. A Téton Sioux, a magnificent
specimen of the Indian, who had been the principal
recipient of our bounty from the kitchen, showed his
fidelity on this occasion by parading, on the flank, in
full war-paint. The majority of these newly fledged
militaires were fine-looking, hardy men, destined in a
few days to prove their pluck and, some of them, to
consecrate the soil with their blood.

Our officer was now continually receiving orders at
all hours of the day and night. Groups of excited
citizens gathered in stores, and on the street, eagerly
canvassing the latest intelligence. The mail-driver had
been obliged to return, and had luckily managed to
bring back his bags. A message was sent to Colonel
Irvine, who had set out with a strong force from Regina,
warning him to avoid Batoche, where an ambuscade was
laid for him. This was carried on snow-shoes by an

intrepid Englishman named Gordon, who went direct
across country, and traversing the trackless wilds,
prairies, lake, and bush, found the colonel and his column
crossing the desolate Salt Plains. Major Crozier had
written for reinforcements from Prince Albert, and, on the
20th, forty of the volunteers, under Captains Moore and
Young, departed in sleighs. We had a cordon of sentries
all around the Government reserve, upon which the barracks were situated. Of course, as the mail had ceased
to run, we were now completely cut off from the outer
world. From the 18th of March until May 12th we were
unable to receive or send a scrap of correspondence.
Nor, in all this time, did we see a newspaper. The most
absurd yarns were evolved from the inner consciousness
of every *quidnunc.* At the corner of the roadway
leading up to the Presbyterian Church, and on the
street facing the river, was a millinery establishment.
Here were a trio of damsels, presided over by an antique
maiden who employed them in the recondite mysteries
of female dress. These young ladies, I know, used
nightly to retire to rest attired in the most bewitching
of blanket costumes, with knowing tuques on their
dainty heads, and revolvers stuck in their gorgeous
sashes ! The days glided slowly on at Prince Albert,
while the following scene was being enacted at the
theatre of Batoche. If such serious issues had not been
involved, one could style it a screaming farce.

Riel had sent a letter couched in magniloquent language, demanding the immediate surrender of Fort
Carlton with its garrison, the latter to have " all the
usages of war." This came to the hands of Major
Crozier through Mr. Mitchell, who was the owner of a
store at Duck Lake. The major at once sent Thomas
McKay, a fine, bluff specimen of the English half-breed
who was supposed to possess much influence in these

parts, to the assembled brigands on the South Branch, in order to persuade them to disperse. Mitchell and he arrived at Walters and Baker's store on the north side of the river, early on the morning of the 21st. Here they were met with all the formality of a German Grand Duchy. A guard was in waiting to escort them across the river to the Council Chamber, which Riel had established in the Catholic Church. There was, apparently, a good deal of Cromwell about him, in his manner of using ecclesiastical buildings. This description simply follows McKay's sworn account of the interview, and clearly demonstrates the fact that this miniature Napoleon was fully determined on the shedding of blood. Had he not ordered Thomas Scott to execution years ago, and nothing had been done to him ? Mitchell introduced Major Crozier's ambassador, who was at once promised protection as the bearer of correspondence. The same had been previously guaranteed to Mr. Mitchell. After these preliminaries had been gone through, McKay remarked, " There seems to be great excitement here, Mr. Riel ? "

" Oh, no," replied the latter ; " there is no excitement at all. It is simply that the people are trying to redress their grievances, as they had asked repeatedly for their rights."

Thereupon McKay quietly hinted that a resort to arms was a somewhat dangerous proceeding. The budding dictator rejoined that he had been waiting fifteen long years, that his people had been imposed upon, and that it was time now that the *pauvres Métis* should have what they asked for. McKay ventured to dispute his wisdom, and advised him to adopt more lawful measures. Riel then accused McKay of having neglected the half-breeds. But the latter told him that he had certainly taken an interest in them, his stake in the country being the same as theirs, and that, time and again, he had so advised them. He also retorted that Riel himself must have neglected them a very long time, although he professed such a deep interest in the matter. Riel jumped up in great agitation, gesticulating wildly.

"You do not know what we are after. It is blood, blood; we want blood; it is a war of extermination. Everybody that is against us is to be driven out of the country. There are two curses in the country—the Government and the Hudson Bay Company." He then wheeled round upon McKay with a tirade of furious abuse. He told him he was a traitor to his (M. Louis Riel's) Government; that he was a speculator and a scoundrel, a robber and a thief. He finally ended this display of Billingsgate oratory, by declaring it was blood, and the first blood they wanted was his. There were some small dishes upon the table; for the Council of State often deliberated over their national *bouillon*. Riel grabbed a spoon; and, tragically holding it up to McKay's face, he pointed to it. "You have no blood, you are a traitor to your people, all your blood is frozen, and all the little blood you have will be there in five minutes."

To this threatening harangue, McKay replied, "If you think you are benefiting your cause by taking my blood, you are quite welcome to it."

Thereupon this petty despot waxed exceeding wroth. At once, he wished to put McKay on trial for his life; and called incoherently upon the members of his council and his people. Philippe Garnot (of the Restaurant Batoche) went over to the table with a sheet of paper. Gabriel Dumont, the War Minister and Commander-in-Chief, took his seat upon a keg of molasses. The solemn court-martial had begun! Riel was the first witness himself, and stated that McKay was a liar. Then he

flew off at a tangent and began to address the crowd.
Emmanuel Champagne next rose, and spoke in McKay's
favour. Then McKay—who a few minutes before had
been guaranteed safe conduct—told the people who had
come in that Riel was threatening his life ; and added,
" If you think by taking my life, you will benefit your
cause, you are welcome to do so."

Champagne denied that any one wished anything of
the kind ; they wanted to redress their wrongs in a con-
stitutional way. Riel then got up abruptly, muttered something about a committee meeting upstairs, and went off the
scene. McKay addressed the unkempt, motley assemblage
for some time. Riel came down at intervals, and popped
his head through the doorway. He informed them that
the committee was being disturbed in its deliberations
by the noise. When McKay had finished his speech, he
asked for some refreshment, as he was pretty hungry.
After he had eaten, he lay down upon a pile of blankets
in the corner until Mitchell was ready. As soon as the
latter appeared, they prepared to leave for Fort Carlton.
Riel also presently entered and apologized to McKay.
He said he had no desire to harm him, and that it was
not too late for him to join the true cause of the half-
breeds. He entertained great respect for Mr. McKay.
This was Major Crozier's last opportunity of averting
bloodshed, and that, unless he surrendered Fort Carlton
an attack would be made at noon.

We, in Prince Albert, were now daily expecting the
arrival of Colonel Irvine. On the afternoon of the 24th
three of us went down to Captain Moore's house to bring
up a band of native ponies for use on vedette duty and
for scouting purposes. We were extremely short of
horse-flesh at the barracks. We found the little wiry,
shaggy cayeuses in a large corral beside a wood of
poplars, and we each selected one, mounted our choice

without saddle or bridle, and drove the others up before
us, over the dirty snow. The sun had now gained the
ascendency in the daytime ; but the frost was bitterly
keen at night.   On our return, I was told off for night
picquet.   Just at guard-mounting a couple of scouts
came galloping in, wild with haste, bearing tidings that
Colonel Irvine, with 150 men, was at the Hudson Bay
crossing on the North Branch.   These irregular horsemen were drawn from the ranks of the civilians, and
were got up in all sorts of fantastic garbs, suggestive of
stage bandits.   Immense revolvers were in their belts,
and Winchester carbines slung horizontally across the
saddle-bow.   I was on sentry between the barracks and
the stables, when I heard the far-away roaring sound
made by the sleigh runners over the hardened trail.   It
increased in volume, coming nearer and nearer ; for of
course, there was an immensely long string of transport
sleighs.   Then came faint cheering, which also gathered
strength as the column neared us.   The populace were
frantically enthusiastic ; every place of vantage was
crowded with yelling throngs.   All would be at an end
now, folk imagined, Riel arrested, and the current of
life flow smoothly once again.   *L'homme propose, mais
Dieu dispose :* the whole Dominion of Canada was yet to
ring with tales of massacre and bloodshed.   Presently
the advance-guard, in fur coats with carbines at "the
carry," swept round the corner.   " On the outer flank
—right form !   Eyes right !   Dress !   Eyes front !"
Then a sergeant rode up to me to ask for information
regarding the stables.

It was now growing dark ; but every window in our
quarters had been illuminated, by order, so as to throw
a flood of light upon the wide, open space in front.   The
long array of sleighs was drawn up in double lines.
The rear-guard followed, through the gloom.   Then the

parade was dismissed by the colonel, and a scene of bustle and confusion ensued. Lanterns went dancing about in all directions. The march had been hurried and trying. All were bronzed with the sun and wind ; and the majority were more or less frost-bitten. One young fellow was carried into the barracks with both feet a huge black mass ; and his toes had afterwards to be amputated. He had persisted in remaining in the sleigh, and wearing boots, probably too lazy to run alongside, and he was now paying the penalty of his own folly. But snow-blindness had done its work : one sergeant had to be led by the hand,—he was totally blind. There were also a corporal and a dozen men on the sick-list, suffering in a lesser degree.

The mess-room resembled one of those lodging-houses which Mr. Samuel Weller, junior, describes so graphically, and which were characteristic of his earlier reminiscences. And after the unshaved and unwashed troopers had been refreshed with tea and meat, all their toils and hardships were forgotten, and the light heart of the soldier rose buoyant as it is wont. Pipes were lit, and sitting around against the walls, on rolls of bedding, songs were joyfully given out. But by-and-by weariness conquered, a rude bed was shaken down, and one by one dropped off into slumber.

CHAPTER X

Colonel Irvine departs—The fight at Duck Lake.

GREAT soft flakes of snow, whirling and eddying against a leaden background, and gently falling on the slushy ground. This was the picture presented on the morning of the 25th. The day was spent in re-fitting the expedition. Canards of various hues were flying around. One was to the effect that the French were just outside the town,—behind the ridge! The men suffering from snow-blindness were secluded in a darkened room, and veils of green gauze were served out to the remainder. The ground outside was simply a quagmire. The baggage had been abandoned at Humboldt in order to expedite their movements, leaving them in a sorry plight. Socks and other articles had to be purchased before they started for Fort Carlton. Their kits were destined to have a pretty rough experience, and when eventually they did arrive, in May, after running the gauntlet of the rebels in the steamboat *Northcote*, the perforating process had been so effective that everything was useless from bullet-holes. In the afternoon the men were ordered to take as much rest as possible, but the excitement was too keen, and the prevailing noise too loud to permit of any sleep. General orders were read at 5 p.m. "Lights out" was to take effect at eight o'clock, and reveillé on this occasion was to sound one hour before midnight.

Time sped on somehow, and Colonel Irvine's party

marched out in the brilliant starlight, for Fort Carlton. Some of our detachment were taken with them, but one smart sergeant was left. I had been unluckily promoted (or otherwise) to the staff, and was forced to remain here " in cold obstruction." Our garrison was now reduced to eight mounted police, all told. This day was devoted to cleaning up *débris*, and Madame Smoke came " on fatigue." A picquet of volunteers occupied our mess-room as a guard-room this night. At midnight a courier came flying in with important despatches to our officer. Ominous whisperings took place when our men were roused from bed. The officer then came in and informed us that a fight had taken place at Duck Lake, and that the mounted police and volunteers had been obliged to retreat. Three of our men were killed and nine of the Prince Albert volunteers : thirty-five had been wounded. By this time the news was flashing over many a wire, and stirring the whole Dominion from the Bay of Fundy to the Straits of San Juan de Fuca.

After the diplomatic visit of Messrs. Mitchell and McKay to the Batoche " Government," affairs at Fort Carlton remained for a few days *in statu quo*, as Major Crozier was awaiting anxiously the arrival of Colonel Irvine before striking a decisive blow. A good deal of forage, and a large quantity of provisions were stored in the log-houses, which belonged to Mr. Mitchell, on the wooded shore of Duck Lake. In order, if possible, to save them from falling into the grasp of the rebels, Major Crozier determined to have them carried away into a place of safety. Therefore on the morning of the 26th at four o'clock, when the stars were twinkling on the men of Colonel Irvine's command, as they threaded the dense bush *en route* to Carlton, the major ordered Sergeant Stewart to take a small detachment with a dozen sleighs, and remove the goods in question. Four mounted men were thrown forward as an advance-guard. With their fur collars well up over their ears in the keen frosty air, and carbines ready at the "advance," they warily moved forward, every sense on the alert, through the tall bluffs of aspen and willow that lined the trail. The patriots around the fort had once or twice been fired upon, and one ambitious redskin—a Cree, had endeavoured to throw a lasso over the head of an angry Scotsman.

The road wound in and out, over steep hillocks and through deep hollows filled with yielding sticky snow. Stewart and his sleighs followed some distance in rear. When about a mile and a half from Duck Lake, the advance-guard were seen returning at full gallop, with a number of half-breeds in pursuit. The sleighs were immediately halted and drawn up in line, and McKay, who was with them, stepped out to await the coming of the enemy. About forty Metis, mounted on ponies, with rifles of every calibre and pattern, from the long buffalo gun of the prairie to the short Winchester, galloped up. They were a long-haired and wild-looking crowd. Some were clad in suits of buckskin, and others wore cloth capotes. Gabriel Dumont was at their head in a state of frantic excitement. No doubt this reminded him somewhat of the brave days of old, when the buffalo were on the plains, and he fought for his friends, the Crees, against the painted hordes of Blackfeet. He jumped off his long-tailed horse, with many a patois oath, and deliberately loaded his rifle. Then he cocked it, and walking up to McKay with a look of savage ferocity on his ugly face, and the foam of rage on his matted beard, threatened to blow out his brains. McKay suggested that, as two could play at that interesting and absorbing pastime, it would be advisable for M. Dumont to moderate his language. The latter then sputtered forth a torrent of incoherent words, the gist of which was that Sergeant Stewart's whole party was to surrender. This very obliging offer was scornfully refused. Some of these Batoche brigands then jumped into the sleigh boxes and attempted to snatch the reins, but the police teamsters were too many for them. The renowned Gabriel then fired his rifle over their heads. As each man of the party was pretty well broken in to stand fire of this description, it did not have the intimidating effect expected. Thereupon the sleighs. were permitted to return to Carlton, but without having secured the provisions or forage.

On the first appearance of these swarthy bandits Stewart had despatched one of his party to the fort, with the intelligence that he had met with resistance and that he required support. About three miles from Carlton the returning detachment met Major Crozier on his way to vindicate the law with every available man of his command, about one hundred, officers and men, and one gun. A mounted orderly had been sent to Colonel Irvine with a despatch, indicating that he had marched out to support some teams, and that in all probability help would be needed. Sergeant Stewart's detachment was ordered to return again, and the whole column, consisting of 100 police and volunteers, advanced along the trail leading towards Duck Lake, When crossing Beardy's reserve, the advance-guard reported a log-house, standing in the bluffs, to be full of Crees in their war-paint. Beardy had joined the insurgents.

Here the major fell into a great error by taking his men past this house. At the point where the events of the morning had transpired the advance-guard were again observed returning and stated that a large force of rebels were advancing. One of our men had been fired upon, and had received a bullet in his saddle. The sun was shining brightly, with full strength, upon the melting snow, which was deep and sticky upon both sides of the trail. The sleighs were drawn up in line across the road, the horses taken out and led to the rear. The ground here dipped into a narrow basin between two ridges, and a rail fence ran out of the woods upon the right flank. The house spoken of lay at the further end of this. It was a wretched position, lying in an exposed hollow and surrounded on three sides by scrubby bush, behind which the Indian loves to fight. Joe McKay, our scout, was riding beside Major Crozier. The latter said, "I will hold a parley with them, before attempting to advance."

Part of the rebels now appeared on the ridge ahead. A few were mounted, but the greater number were on foot. Star Blanket, in full panoply of feathers and vermilion, came down to where the major -was standing. The parley began, but the major noticed that the half-breeds and painted savages were creeping round behind the bushes on both flanks, and beginning to surround him. He at once gave the order to fire. Bullets now rained thick as hail. Puffs of smoke came from every point of the bluffs, and from behind every snow-clad hillock ; the fire was murderous. Star Blanket endeavoured to snatch away McKay's rifle, and the latter emptied the contents of his revolver into him. Not a word was spoken, only the whistling "ping" of the bullets and the rattle of the musketry broke the stillness. Men lay down in the sloppy snow, and took steady aim at whatever was visible. Poor Gibson was shot dead, as he was handing out ammunition for the gun. One of the horses attached to this was killed. This useless piece of artillery was loaded ready for action, and might have been of service at first, but

Major Crozier was standing in the line of fire. The depth of snow, and the fact that it was upon wheels rendered it utterly unserviceable. Before the major got out of the way, the rebels who were in front had disappeared out of danger. He turned round angrily and exclaimed, "Why don't you fire? I am only one man."

Captain Morton took his volunteers away to the right flank, where, from the house only seventy-five yards' distant, a deadly fusillade was maintained. The ambuscade was so complete that he did not know of its existence. His men were open to the concentrated volley of the Crees. Disastrous as the skirmish was, it only lasted twenty minutes. The Indian war-whoop could now be heard ringing in fiendish triumph through the woods. Amid the pauses of the dropping fire the groans of the wounded and dying were piteous in their comrades' ears. The dingy snow was crimson in places. Dr. Millar's instrument-case was struck by a bullet. When Arnold, of the police, fell, he said, "Tell the boys I died game."

Corporal Gilchrist, of ours, who had his thigh broken, exclaimed "Don't leave me for those black devils to scalp."

Constable Garrett was shot through the neck and died that night. Thus, three of our men were killed, and nine of the Prince Albert volunteers. Among the latter was Captain Morton. The number of wounded, was thirty-five, a startling percentage!

The skulking system of tactics, so dear to the heart of the redskin, was throughout adopted by the rebels. One of the mounted police kept pegging away for some time at an Indian head-dress and blanket which appeared above the snow, the owner of which was ten yards away, deliberately picking off his victim. There was no possibility of an advance owing to the state of the ground and the density of the undergrowth. The police were sheltered by the breastwork of sleighs in some measure. Six of the rebels were known to have been killed, and Gabriel Dumont received a severe scalp-wound. Riel himself was never · visible : he went about among his men bearing a crucifix, and exhorting them with much florid eloquence, to make short work of the redcoats. The greatest mistake of Major Crozier was in holding a parley. The treacherous leader of the insurgents, with low cunning, took advantage of this to send his forces round in extended order under cover of the buttes, and nearly succeeded in surrounding and capturing the whole party.

The major ordered his men to retire before it was too late. The horses were placed in the sleighs under fire ; and the retreat was managed in a most orderly manner. The dead had to be abandoned. One wounded Englishman was left unnoticed : when the Indians came upon him, they were for clubbing him to death ; he put up his hands to shield his face, and they broke his knuckles. Some half-breeds intervened, and saved his life. The dastardly Crees perpetrated all sorts of indignities upon the bodies, and battered in the faces of the brave men who had died to protect their hearths and homes. Captain Moore, as he was mounting into a sleigh, had his leg shattered with a bullet, and it eventually had to be amputated.

In the afternoon, about four o'clock, as the setting sun was flooding the lone valley of the Saskatchewan with its golden rays, and the windows of the fort were flashing back its brightness, the little force so sadly broken, and bringing dying and wounded in their midst, descended the wooded slopes to Carlton. Colonel Irvine and his command arrived an hour later.

Major Crozier, from past experience in dealing with disaffected redskins, was not prepared for such an encounter as this had been. He imagined that a display of moral force would have the same salutary effect which had hitherto resulted. The Indian population of this wild and limitless region had been held in cheek by five hundred mounted police ; who had combined the elements of both civil and military Government. The law had been well and fairly administered. It had been the same for the redskin as the white settler. The former saw this, and in consequence respected its representatives.

Times without number, a handful of troopers had entered Indian camps, and, by coolness and nerve, had taken away their prisoners from the midst of the feathered braves, without bloodshed. This had happened on Poundmaker's reserve in 1884, while he and all his tribe were standing around with menacing gestures, in full war-paint, with loaded weapons. The ability of the police in handling the natives had frequently elicited admiration from American officers ; who had to despatch a regiment for the capture of a murderer or a whisky trader, and never accomplished it without the loss of life.

There were fully thirty thousand Indians scattered about the Territories ; and the danger which now presented itself was that the whole of these nomadic tribes would rise and massacre and burn without compunction. Settlements would be laid waste, and the budding promise of future prosperity be blighted. Major Crozier was led into the unfortunate trap, while smarting under the repeated insults hurled at him by Riel. The latter now sent his runners to all the tribes, even at a distance of hundreds of miles ; to the Assiniboines and Sioux on the boundary of Manitoba ; to the Chipweyans in the far north ; and to the Blackfeet, Piegans, Sarcees, and Bloods away beside the Rockies.

Poundmaker and Big Bear, around Battleford and Fort Pitt, did not need much coaxing, but jumped at the chance of murder, plunder, and debauchery. Big Bear was an old and seasoned sinner of the first water. Mistawasis near Carlton, Chicastafasin (another Star Blanket) at Snake Plains, Moosomin and others left their reserves to escape being drawn into the trouble. Crowfoot, head-chief of the Blackfeet, sent a loyal letter to the Lieutenant-Governor and remained staunch to the Great Mother throughout.

The spirit of the whole Canadian people rose at once on receipt of the tidings of the Duck Lake affair. Every province was in arms, and an expedition of 3000 men, under Major-General Middleton was at once despatched to relieve the beleaguered garrisons at Fort Pitt, Battleford, and Prince Albert. The utmost enthusiam was shown over all the land. The streets of Montreal, Toronto, and Winnipeg, of Halifax and Quebec, and many a backwoods town, were filled with martial music as " the boys " marched away. Ladies' Aid Societies were formed for the relief of the wounded ; and the ubiquitous newspaper correspondent pocketed his note-book and hied him to the once Lone Land.

CHAPTER XI

Prince Albert after the fight—Settlers summoned together—Church
fortified—Scenes within the stockade—Exalted warriors—
Inside the church—A sortie for grub—A flutter in the dove-cot
—The burning of Fort Carlton—A retreat—An excited Scots-
man and an astonished parade—A false alarm—Inaction—
Colonel Irvine.

As soon as the news of the Duck Lake catastrophe
reached Prince Albert, measures of defence were immediately taken. There was no knowing how soon the
exultant bands of the "Dictator" might sweep down
upon the unprotected town. The despatch ordered
our officer to warn all the surrounding settlers and
summon them to a place of rendezvous. Steps were to
be taken to fortify a central place of retreat. The
Presbyterian church and manse were pitched upon as
the most commodious and convenient for the purpose,
and a stockade of cordwood, nine feet high, was erected
around them. This was finished between 1 a.m. and
daylight. The civilians worked splendidly. Many a
house was mourning, and many a tearful eye was seen
upon the streets. It was a day of unparalleled brilliancy.
The warm sun beat down from a cloudless sky; the
snow was giving way in places to frothy pools, and here
and there a brown patch of earth showed through the
ragged robe of winter.

We were engaged in taking cartridges, and ice, and
necessary stores of all descriptions, into the improvised
citadel in the centre of the town; and sleighs kept

plying backward and forward between the church and
and barracks. Sleigh-loads of women and children
came hurrying in from the Carrot River district ; and
from many a lonely homestead, hidden away among the
bluffs. Every house in the town itself was very soon
vacant, the inhabitants all taking sanctuary in the church
precincts. We abandoned the barracks at noon ; the
sergeant and I being the last to leave. I carried the
Union Jack under my regimental fur coat. We left
everything else behind us as they were ; locking all the
doors. The scene inside the stockade was one of the
most uncomfortable that can be imagined. The
entrance was narrow, and blocked with curious members
of the fair sex, straining their necks as though they
expected to see the enemy walk calmly up and ring the
bell.

The mud was almost unfathomable, and of the
consistency of " coaguline," or any of the other
compounds, with impossible names, which are advertised
for the healing of broken china. Our horses sank to
their hocks, and could hardly extricate their feet. On
the top of the cordwood rampart, on each side, were
four civilian sentries, with fixed bayonets and lofty
bearing, pacing rapidly from point to point, and looking
like warders of the middle ages expecting a challenge
trumpet to blow beyond the moat beneath. They were
about as much use there as the wooden soldiers which
delight the martial-minded youngster. Vedettes were
posted on every hill ; and many people were still
congregated outside " the walls." But these proud
defenders marched erect and defiant, little conscious of
the merriment they were causing to the few initiated.
However, it evidently afforded them satisfaction, and did
no harm to any one else.

A zealous sergeant of volunteers was marching and

countermarching a squad behind the church. Every
open window of the large brick manse was filled with
anxious women's faces, the eyes of many being dim
with tears. A man with field-glasses, scanning every
inch of the horizon, was perched upon the flat roof.
There was much noise of hammering and the clatter of
falling boards. Lumber was being hauled in, and a
long, covered species of barrack was being rapidly run
up. The enclosure was filled with sleighs, and a restless, surging throng. At the entrance-door of the
church was a large square tent, containing a cooking
range, at which a detachment of male cooks were at
work preparing the everlasting bacon for the refugees.
A Gargantuan feed of beans was bubbling and bobbing
in two huge boilers. The interior of the ecclesiastical
edifice was simply a vast nursery of noisy children and
screaming females. Infants were squalling, and a
sound as of loud applause occasionally announced that
some mutinous youngster was receiving condign casti-
gation. Some were "ministering" to the young fellow
of ours whose feet were frozen, and who was laid on a
sort of daïs near the pulpit. Two long tables, covered
with plates, cups, knives, and forks, stretched the entire
length of "the kirk," with benches on each side. Here
the hungry ones were demolishing a varied assortment
of viands. It was a strange sight. Some were apparently unable to restrain their risible faculties over
the whole picnic. Some Scotch half-breed girls were of
this number. One strong man was weeping piteously
for the loss of his brother in the recent fight. There
were the faces of men and women worn with anxiety
and dread. Stalwart settlers lounged about with determined looks. On going out again, I found the sleighs
were pouring in from every quarter. There was my
old friend, the hostess of the caravanserai between here

and Carlton, calling sturdily, "Where is ma mon?
Ha'e ony o' ye seen ma mon, Jock?" in the broadest of
"braid Scots."

The strategic position of a certain house was not
deemed the correct thing, in professional eyes, and it
was ordered to be pulled to pieces. This was some
work for us. Nolin—one of Riel's Government—had
come in and surrendered. He was not placed in durance
vile; and I was ordered to attend on him in his walks
abroad. He was a stout man, about six feet in height,
with flabby, unprepossessing features. We took the
guard on the gate over from the volunteers this evening.
I was utterly worn out from work, excitement, and
want of sleep for sixty-two hours! I placed nine
cartridges in the magazine of my Winchester, and lay
down with it in my hand. The Rev. Messrs. Wright
and Hilton, English clergymen, were on either side of
me; if they should ever see these pages, they will
remember.

I slept the sleep of the just, for material and spiritual
support was very handy. I arose stiff and unrefreshed,
from my comfortless couch of hard boards, amid the
mephitic atmosphere of this overcrowded house of
prayer. Of course it was quite impossible to wash.
Food had, literally, to be fought for.

The sergeant and I discussed the situation. The
result of our deliberations was that we asked for and
obtained leave to make a reconnoissance in the direction
of the barracks. Ostensibly, this was put down to our
zeal to see if the Téton Sioux were quiet, and everything all right down there. In reality, we had registered
a vow to enjoy a "square meal" at any cost. No one
was visible as we rode down the deserted street. On
the summit of the ridge we could observe our vedettes
pacing along, against the sky-line. A solitary employé

of the Hudson Bay Company, who had been left in charge, unbarred the ponderous door of the store at our summons. From this extremely obliging person we purchased quite a quantity of edible luxuries, which we took with us on our steeds to barracks. Having stabled the horses, we unlocked the door. Everything remained undisturbed, and the great empty building re-echoed to the clank of our spurs and the strange sound of our voices. We lit a fire in the mess-room, and soon enjoyed a rattling feed, after which we returned to the stockade and reported everything all correct.

On entering the stockade a gentleman with a black beard clutched me wildly by the arm, and pointed frantically to a moving speck on the horizon. Murmurs were heard among the crowd, and nervous women kept telling each other that "it" was the "French." Scouts were seen to be galloping in the direction indicated by the hysterical store-keeper. I believe "it" turned out to be one of Riel's scouts, who was chased for some distance.

Disquieting rumours filled the air this afternoon, and one of our fellows told me that bad news had been received from Carlton. About four o'clock the look-out, on the roof of the minister's residence, signalled that he had some communication to make. It was to the effect that two mounted policemen were visible on the trail to the westward, advancing very slowly in the direction of the town. Their horses had the appearance of being jaded and played out. There was an immediate flutter in the dove-cot, every coign of vantage was occupied, and an eager crowd awaited their coming. In a little while they rode up to the gate of the stockade, and the people pressed upon them on every side. Their bronchos were completely tired out with long and hard riding, and the men were worn and haggard. They seemed to droop in the saddle, and rubbed their bloodshot eyes, sore from the brilliant reflection of the sun. They dismounted stiffly, and made their report, handing despatches from their wallets to our officer. Fort Carlton had been burnt to the ground—a heap of charred ashes—and the main body, with Colonel Irvine and Major Crozier, were an hour's march in their rear. We took charge of their horses, and they soon brightened up under the cheering influence of some much-needed refreshment. Then they told their tale.

After the events of Thursday, it had been decided to evacuate Fort Carlton. From its strategic position it was quite untenable. Colonel Irvine had determined to concentrate his forces at Prince Albert for the defence of this populous district, and to await the action of the Dominion Government. This was thought to be more prudent than to risk defeat. The protection of the settlers was the principal object, and already their lives and property were considered to be in great danger.

This was decisively arranged on the evening of Friday, the 27th. The fort was in a miserably exposed situation. Sharpshooters, stationed in the overhanging bush, could easily pick off any one attempting to cross the square. I am astonished that Riel did not march upon Prince Albert in the interval, and devastate the entire settlement. There was nothing whatever to prevent his making a rapid sweep upon the defenceless town. His intelligence department was incomparably better than ours at that time. In other respects, no doubt, he was weaker than we imagined him to be.

On Friday evening the men at Fort Carlton were told that they could go into the Hudson Bay store and help themselves. They were given *carte blanche*, and the whole place was looted. Suits of clothing,

underclothing, blankets, tobacco, pipes, and even perfumes, were taken possession of. There was no respect
of rank. One plethoric bearer of the triple chevron,
whom we called "Daddy," was fain to content himself
with a bottle of bergamot and some of Fry's chocolate.
Barrels and bags of flour and biscuit, and big packages
of bacon, in sacking, were taken out and saturated with
coal-oil, to prevent their being of any service to the
rebels. Tins of preserves, of lobsters, of sardines,and
boxes of fancy biscuits were carried off to the rooms ;
and there was a general picnic on the beds. At midnight the "alarm" rang out in the frosty darkness.

A strange ruddy light flamed from the sergeant-
major's quarters, and a thick smoke arose that obscured
the twinkling stars. This was above the archway and
next the hospital. The buildings had taken fire, and a
frightful scene ensued. Bugle-calls were sounding,
officers hurrying around with hoarse words of command,
and the men, half-asleep, were bewildered. Volunteers
and red-coats were mixed up indiscriminately. The
wounded were removed at once, down the narrow stairs,
out of danger into the cold outside, suffering the most
excruciating agony. Our corporal, with his shattered
thigh, gave vent to the most heartrending cries. Some
who were engaged in the humane work of rescue were
terribly burned about the face.—Poor Gilchrist ! I
helped to carry his wounded form from the sleigh at
Prince Albert, and nine months afterwards I assisted to
put his lifeless clay into the coffin at Regina.—The
horses were infected with the prevailing excitement, and
it was no easy task saddling them, while the transport
teams were hastily harnessed up. Every atom of baggage,
kits, bedding, and "plunder" were left behind. Everything had to be abandoned ; cherished letters from
loved ones far away, and photos, and private papers.

Women and children (friendly half-breed refugees) were placed in the sleighs, crying and shrieking. The whole fort, every building on every side of the square, was now a lurid blaze, which shed its vivid light on the broad snow-clad river, on dark trees and lofty slopes. The last sleigh and the mounted rear-guard just managed to escape from this fiery furnace in time. The groans of the wounded, the jingle of the horses' trappings, the crackling roar of the flames, and the deep voices of command all mingled in one bewildering sound. The place burned like tinder. Then commenced a hurried and a trying march. The summit of the precipitous heights had to be gained, by a narrow trail winding among thick bush. This path seemed designed as a splendid ambuscade,—a regular trap for massacre. Every moment the weird war-whoop of the savage might peal from the impenetrable gloom. Below the struggling troops, the scene was one of infinite grandeur, baffling the word-painter's skill. Riel once more missed his chance of annihilating his detested foes. The men were completely knocked up, from constant patrols, picquets, guards, marching and fighting, and fell asleep in the saddle or on the sleighs. The " Pines " (dreaded by all) was traversed by the long, thin column in grim silence, where a handful of Metis or Indians could have butchered every man. Every one breathed more freely once through this dark and gloomy defile. So, Prince Albert was once more reached by about five o'clock on Saturday evening. Loud cheers came from the citizens on the stockade ; and women, with eyes full of tears, cheered feebly too. The wounded waved out signs of greeting, from where they lay covered in the sleighs ; and many a woman's kiss—sweet and long—welcomed a dear one home. Our troopers sat in the saddle, their lined faces bent down with fatigue ; too much done up to sit erect, when "halt!" sounded on the bugle. The brass field-piece was in the centre of the line. The wounded were distributed at once among the private houses. "D" troop was stationed in the completed shed, within the palisade; "B" troop was marched down to Goshen. We of the old detachment were ordered to our former quarters. The civil population were informed that they might return to their respective homes; but were to reassemble at the church upon the bell tolling. No one was destined to enjoy much rest this night, as will be seen presently. A Metis prisoner had been brought in from Carlton, and he and Nolin were taken down to barracks with us. I had the honour to escort these two unsavoury gentlemen of the new nationality. The latest addition was about twenty years of age, and had attempted to commit suicide in his cell at Carlton. All the way down, this dingy youth kept asking Blight, "Ah, serg-eant! just von leetle bul-let you give me? von leetle bul-let, serg-eant?" His very mild request was refused, with a smiling shake of the head.

Any satisfactory solution of the food question down at the barracks was out of the question, therefore a chum and I made our way to a boarding-house kept by a very clean, tidy, Scotch half-breed woman, who was married to a man from Suffolk. Several very respectable ci-vilians used to patronize this establishment, and some were seated, pegging away at the pile of solids on the table, when we entered. We were taking our first cup of tea when the others rose hurriedly, made a rush for their rifles, and vanished through the doorway. Our buxom hostess—fair, fat, and forty, with big blue eyes—entered with the stereotyped information that "the French" were coming; and that the church bell was ringing for the people to gather. I am afraid I muttered "bosh;" for excessive familiarity had made me learn to despise this continual cry of "wolf!" We quietly finished our meal, and went out. A man who lived opposite was loading his sleigh with household goods, and as soon as his ancestral clock had been deposited upon the top, he lashed out at his horses and started off at a panic speed. As we turned the corner of our quarters we suddenly came upon a full parade, on foot, the colonel addressing the men. I made a rush and secured my arms. On going down the supernumerary rank a sergeant told me to fall in on the left; which unnecessary order I complied with. Then, without warning, rang out the "wild courser's hoofs of fear," and a frenzied figure, mounted on a black cayeuse, shot wildly past the building, and nearly came charging through the astonished ranks.

"Turn oot! Turn oot! Th' Indians are on us! Gie us a rifle, ane o' ye chaps," he yelled out frantically, and without a pause, in the richest Doric. He was an employé of the H.B. Company, and hailed from the pleasant little town of Kelso, on the Tweed. This apparition nearly demoralized the whole parade with laughter.

"Steady, men!" said the colonel, though his own risible faculties were hardly under control.

Owing to the alarm we were kept on the *qui-vive* till morning, when it turned out to be the exaggerated idea of some hasty brain. Some scouts at the forks of the road had observed a large party of Indians in war-paint advancing. They were, in reality, on their way to Batoche; but without waiting to watch the direction of their line of march, these civilian scouts at once jumped to the conclusion that they were Riel's advance-guard, and setting spurs to their horses flew into Prince Albert with the news of an approaching attack.

Now ensued a period of soulless inaction, every one

waiting in Micawber-like expectation of something turning up. To us of the rank and file this unsatisfactory state of suspense was trying. Why we did not march out, and attack the rebels, was the daily—nay, hourly—subject of speculation. All things are plain now, but then, of course, one saw darkly. There were so many wheels within wheels at Prince Albert, so many conflicting interests at stake, that I presume any offensive movement was not deemed expedient. I have a very high opinion of Colonel Irvine, and a good deal of mud has been thrown at him by people who deal in that commodity, because he remained shut up in this town. I am glad to be able to wield even a feeble pen in his favour, though it is merely the record of a trooper in the ranks. His sensitive regard for the feelings of others let him be swayed too easily by men who never allowed themselves to be actuated by any like motive. He was a man who I verily believe thought no wrong of any one, and he was utterly unfitted to deal with the unscrupulous citizens around him. His courage no one can call in question. He has spoken in his own defence ; but this gentlemanly respect of his for others has led him to remain silent on many cardinal points of controversy. I deem myself happy to have the opportunity to stick up (in however humble a way) for my old chief.

CHAPTER XII

Dreary days—Defence organized—Strange weapons of war—
Patriots—An arrival—Bad news—Battleford burnt—A fighting
rig—Dead disfigured—Fighting corrals—Rumours—A sortie
and a countermarch—Ice breaks up—Frog Lake massacre—
Retreat from Fort Pitt—Leave barracks—Fish Creek—A
Jingo Bishop—The Zoo—Battle of Batoche.

IT would be of little interest to my patient reader to
tell him the petty details of each miserable day of dull
monotony, of the leaden-hued skies with driving snow,
or of the merciless sun beating down from the cloudless
vault above ; of the gradual death of winter and of the
struggling birth of spring ; of the restless longing for
news from home ; of the eternal wish for some movement to be made ; of the daily lies which were put in
circulation ; of the harassing patrols.

The days were literally spent in vain wondering as to
what was coming next, and nothing arose to break the
sluggish stream of existence into a merry, babbling rapid.
We in Prince Albert, at that time, knew absolutely nothing
whatever of what was transpiring in the outer world.

It was long after this that we heard of the relief
columns ; and of the excitement in the Dominion. For
eight long weeks we did not see a newspaper or a letter.
An organized system of defence was now published.
No one was allowed to leave the town or go beyond
the lines without a pass. Mr. Hayter Reid, of the Indian
Department, was appointed brigade-major. The brigade
office was in a disused beer saloon. All able-bodied

men were to bear arms in the ranks of the volunteers,
or their families would be denied the privilege of drawing
rations. The town was placarded with general orders :
civilians were to remain indoors after 8 p.m. Mr.
Lawrence Clarke was selected to act as quartermaster.
The volunteers were divided into four companies, and
the whole were under the command of Colonel Sproat,
a gentleman whose martial ardour was of the fiercest
description. He beamed with satisfaction when saluted.
I regret to say that No. 4 company of the gallant
colonel's infantry was armed with weapons of a very
heterogeneous order. They varied from shot-guns of an
antique and nondescript pattern, down to the useful, but
unornamental club. One hundred and twenty men
mounted guard nightly. Outlying picquets and
vedettes were posted. There were inlying picquets
along the river's bank, and a service of scouts, which,
after being weeded of the uncertain element, were to be
depended upon.

We found the different barrack-guards, and orderlies.
Patrol was the most dangerous and trying duty. At seven
o'clock, each evening, a body of men were turned out,
mounted on bronchos, or native ponies. We were to
ride completely round the settlement ; and this was anything but a pleasing task, in all weathers, and in the
murky darkness, when every thicket in the outskirts
might hold a prowling redskin. We were sixteen hours
in the saddle at a stretch, before being relieved for
breakfast ; after this we continued the patrol again till
night.

A friendly half-breed, who had managed to penetrate
the rebel lines, came in one morning from Battleford.
He was a great hulking fellow in a ragged cap of beaver
skin, and a greasy overcoat, bound round his waist with
a seedy sash. This garment had done duty as a night-

gown in many a solitary camp in the wilderness, and borne the brunt of many a wintry storm. His moccasins were soaked with muddy wet, and threatened instant dissolution, but the idea of boots is repulsive, somehow, to the native mind. He bore tidings of sad disaster, but brought us no intelligence of the doings in Canada. Poundmaker had let loose his hordes from among the wooded coulées of the Eagle Hills ; Tremont, Payne, and Smart had been foully murdered by the Stonies ; and a career of pillage and bloodshed had been begun. They had sacked the village of Battleford, and gutted the Hudson Bay stores, and had then burnt the whole, indulging in wild orgies and dances around the flames. After appropriating the contents of the various trading posts, they had clad themselves fantastically in tall hats, and gaudy shirts, with refulgent scarves.

The garrison was shut up within the fort, where 600 townspeople had taken refuge.

There was no news of the little band of Mounted Police at Fort Pitt, under the command of Inspector Dickens—son of the celebrated novelist.

We luckily had abundance of supplies in Prince Albert. As our scarlet uniform was too conspicuous and utterly unadapted for active service, we were served out with a fighting rig, improvised from every clothing establishment in the town. This consisted of a black slouch hat with red puggarree, a brown Norfolk jacket of duck, moleskin riding pants, a brown canvas bandolier holding forty rounds of extra ammunition, and a brown haversack. This was a serviceable garb, but not showy, and a contrast to our red and yellow. Each of us appeared a cross between a Montana desperado, and a Sardinian chasseur. When wearing our long blue cloaks, we resembled the students of a Catholic ecclesiastical seminary. Nothing exciting occurred to enliven the tedium of the leaden-footed days. There were constant parades and drills, whenever the state of the weather permitted. Shortly after the commencement of the siege, we had sent out a flag of truce to recover and bring in the dead from Duck Lake. The bodies were unmolested, but the features were horribly disfigured, from the fiendish revenge of the Indians. When the snow had quite disappeared, and wheeled vehicles came into use once more, we were daily instructed in the formation and defence of "fighting corrals." These improvised entrenchments are to the great plains of the far North-West, what the laager is to the veldts of South Africa, and the zareba to the burning sands of Egypt. Our waggons were drawn up in a circle, the poles inward, and roped together. The horses were tied up inside, and the ambulance, bearing the red cross, placed· in the centre. Picquets and vedettes were thrown out all around this.

All this time our headquarter staff were in receipt of reliable information, but no fragment of this was imparted to us. The scouts were bound to the strictest secrecy. On April 13th, General Middleton, with his relief column, had reached Humboldt. From this place Messrs. McDowell and Bedson ran the blockade of the rebel outposts, on horseback, and entered Prince Albert. They communicated with Colonel Irvine, and rode back in safety. We knew nothing of this until afterwards. On April 18th, Lord Melgund, with Boulton's scouts, captured three Sioux of Whitecap's band, on the South Branch. Sunday, the 19th, was a day of warm and brilliant sunshine. We made a sortie that afternoon, and proceeded as far as Scott's farm, on a lofty height, surrounded by undulating woodlands about twelve miles from town. There were about 150 Mounted Police of all ranks, and a long string of transport waggons.

The farm buildings were of the usual type peculiar to this region,—a low log-house, rudely thatched with straw, the sides plastered with mud, an enclosure of dilapidated railings, a small haystack, a pile of manure, and a few roughly-made sheds for the cattle. The whole was surrounded by a large patch of coarse grass, while the forest trended away to the edge of the deep Saskatchewan valley. The place was quite deserted, save for a couple of young, half-tame black bears, who, with comic indifference, were prowling round and performing acrobatic feats on the telegraph poles and trunks of the pine-trees. They were cunningly deaf to all our blandishments. The evening was lovely, and from our eminence we could see the sun setting in a gorgeous blaze of prismatic light. Far away stretched the unbroken forest, along the verge of the dark ravine through which flowed the lone and majestic river. The blue smoke from our camp fires rose straight into the still air of the evening. Pipes were indulged in as we lay on the ground inside our fighting corral, and conjectures were hazarded as to our intended destination. We fully expected to move on to Batoche, but silently we mounted and rode away at 1 a.m., and—countermarched ! There was bitter disappointment as we again entered the sleeping town, and passed the picquets. The mystery of this abortive piece of strategy has yet to be solved ; but no doubt urgent reasons prompted the retrograde movement. The ice, across the river, broke up upon the 21st, and in two days the mighty Saskatchewan was careering down in waves of muddy foam. The breaking up of ice on Canadian streams is a welcome sight. The great masses come whirling and grinding in a rapid rush, hurling themselves in riot against the sloping shores. The green buds burst forth as if by magic, the birds sing joyfully among the boughs, the grass springs fresh on the prairie, the wild flowers bloom, and summer comes tripping on the scene with joyous laugh. But far away on the lone waters of Lake Winnipeg the last sign of ice does not disappear till June, for the frost god makes a stubborn fight before he relaxes his hold.

Frog Lake is a lovely sheet of water lying amid groves of trees and surrounded by beautiful meadows. It is about thirty miles from Fort Pitt, and some ten miles from the Saskatchewan. Here a corporal and five men of the Mounted Police had been stationed during the winter. After the fight at Duck Lake, Inspector Dickens recalled his men from this outpost, and also advised the whites to come into the fort. There was a church and village, but on every side were treacherous redskins under that old scoundrel Big Bear. On the receipt of tidings that hostilities had broken out, they at once went on the war-path in all the hideousness of semi-nudity and paint. From first demanding stores they proceeded to make prisoners. Then on the 2nd of April, while the people were in church, commenced that horrible scene of riot and bloodshed, known as the Frog Lake Massacre. Gowanlock and Delaney were the first victims to the rifles of the savages. Fathers Farfand and Marchand, the two courageous priests, were killed also. The remainder, including the tenderly reared ladies of this remote settlement, were marched off captives. Quinn, Gilchrist, and Dill were then brutally shot, the latter being chased by Indians on horseback. Williscroft was slain by Little Bear. The church and every house was burnt to the ground.

Some kind-hearted half-breed prisoners purchased Mrs. Gowanlock and Mrs. Delaney from the Indians, and took them to their families, and tenderly guarded them during the remainder of their captivity. Fort Pitt was then summoned to surrender. Here Mr. Maclean, the Hudson Bay officer, was treacherously made prisoner during a parley. Big Bear guaranteed that if the fort were delivered, he would protect the families. Thereupon Maclean wrote for his wife and children to come to the Indian camp, and counselled the others to do the same. Cowan and Loasby, of the Police, who were out scouting, were shot on returning. Loasby escaped within the palisades; but Cowan was killed as he lay wounded. His heart was cut out and stuck upon a pole; he was most terribly mutilated also by these incarnate fiends. On April 15th the post was abandoned. A few extracts from the diary of Corporal Sleigh, who was killed at Cut-Knife Creek, will give a graphic picture of the escape of the detachment.

April 15.—Mr. Maclean at noon went on hill to parley. Three scouts came galloping through towards Pitt. Constable Cowan shot dead, Loasby badly wounded, and horse killed. Shots fired from loopholes; two Indians killed. Quinn missing, and two wounded. Mr Maclean and François Dufresne taken prisoners Mr. Maclean wrote down to his wife to come out and give herself up, and all the Hudson Bay Company's employés to do the same. The Hudson's Bay employées, twenty-two in number, gave themselves up to Big Bear. Impossible to hold fort now, so we had to gracefully retire across the river in scow, and camped for night, not forgetting to bring colours along. Nearly swamped crossing, river being rough, and scow leaking badly. General idea prevailing that we would be attacked going down river. Took Loasby along. Thus ended the siege of Fort Pitt.

April 16.—Up at 4.30, after passing a wretched night Snowing fast, and very windy. Several men frost-bitten. Clothing frozen on our backs. Had some narrow escapes from ice jams. Camped at nine for dinner. Resumed trip at noon.

April 18.—Started at 7 a.m. Day dull and cold. Much ice running.

April 19, Sunday.—Left Slap Jack Island at 7.13 a.m. Ran for five hours. Camped on Beaver Island, number 35. Ran on three hours, and camped on Pine Island for night.

April 20.—Here all day. Barricaded the scow. Inspected arms. Rough-looking parade. Wounded man better.

April 21.—Left island at 7 a.m. 11 a.m. hailed interpreter Joseph Alexander, and two policemen on South bank. They had despatches for us. They reported Battleford safe, and troops expected daily. Ran all day and stopped on Small Island for the night. River falling rapidly. Struck on sand-bars. All slept on board scow. Two men on picquet.

April 22.—Started at 5.45 a.m., and reached Battleford at 9 a.m. Garrison turned out and presented arms. Police band played us into fort. Enthusiastic greeting. Ladies gave us a grand dinner.

Fort Pitt, of course, was thoroughly looted, the squaws being foremost in the fight for annexation. Big Bear then moved off into the wild morasses of the North. It is astonishing how his thirty prisoners, many of them tender children, could have been dragged from camp to camp, from April 16th to May 28th, and yet escape outrage and death. This was owing to some Wood Crees who had been forced to join Big Bear, unwillingly. They are very much superior to the Indians of the plains.

On the 23rd of April there was a general parade at Prince Albert, when men were picked out for service at the front, if it were found necessary to co-operate with the relieving column. I was happy to find myself, among the elect. On the following day we all, with the exception of a small detachment, moved into camp near the church. Rifle-pits were constructed on the side of the town most open to the attack.

On this day—April 24th—General Middleton's advance was checked by the rebels at Fish Creek. He sustained a loss of ten killed and forty-two wounded. The General himself received a bullet through his cap from the rifle of Gabriel Dumont. His aide-de-camp Captain Wise, had his horse shot under him, and was wounded in the foot.

About this time stray scraps of information began to perforate through the official net of reticence. Daily we expected to be led out against the enemy. Camp rumours, however, are never to be relied upon. One of the volunteers was shot, accidentally, by one of his comrades, as he lay asleep. He awoke with a broken thigh,—rather an abrupt and unsatisfactory method of rousing a man. The worthy Bishop used to hold service every Sunday within the stockade. He took his stand beneath the shadow of the flagstaff, and with many a proud gesture towards the Union Jack, which floated bravely above him, he would preach the most deliciously Jingo sermons, and deliver many a stately sentence with reference to that " great and glorious emblem of a mighty empire." His periods were adorned with many a rolling adjective in the strongest accent of the granite city, Aberdeen. We always finished by singing, at his request, "that magnificent anthem ' God save the Queen.' "

A large empty store had been taken for the accommodation of the half-breed women and children, and this paradise of houris we called the " Zoo." Dusky beauties and wrinkled hags were to be seen, in every stage of *déshabillé* lounging out of the open windows at all hours. I never penetrated the mysterious recesses of this zenana ; but it must have been a frightful abode of female warfare and liberty of speech. The tents looked white and clean against the emerald of the springing verdure. (Kissaskatchewan, by the way, signifies rapid flowing.) The sky was blue, and flecked and ribbed with fleecy clouds. The sunshine was warm and pleasant, and the many islands lay like gems on the molten gold of the broad waters.

About the 9th of May, the officers were observed in frequent consultation, and there was much galloping in and out of scouts. The guards were doubled and more frequently visited, and extra picquets were posted along the river's bank. On the 12th a sudden order was given for the ambulance and some waggons to be sent over to the South Branch at once. The steamer *Northcote* had run the gauntlet of the rebels at Batoche, and three of those on board had been wounded ; and she had brought an eight weeks' mail ! No words can tell of the wild rejoicing that went through the tents !

The ambulance very soon returned, and the wounded men held quite a levée. Mr. Pringle, of the Medical Staff, had been shot in the shoulder, and Mr. Vinen, of the Transport Department, had a flesh wound in the thigh. One of the steamboat hands still carried a bullet in his ankle. The mail was distributed as rapidly as possible, and most welcome it was. The kits of " B." Troop arrived also, in a highly demoralized condition. The bags had been used to fortify the boat, and, consequently the contents had been mercilessly riddled with bullets.

"Never mind, lads, the Government will have to stump up for this," was the consolatory cry.

On the 14th arrived full tidings of the general defeat

of the rebels, at Batoche, after four days' hard fighting. The loss on our side was eight killed and forty-six wounded. The Catholic priest gave the following list of the enemy's losses:—1st day, 4 killed and 5 wounded; 2nd day, 2 wounded ; 3rd day, 3 wounded ; 4th day, 47 killed 163 wounded. Total, 51 killed and 173 wounded.

It had been found impossible to shell the rebels from their ingeniously constructed rifle-pits ; and they were carried in a general charge, with rattling cheers. The prisoners were released, unharmed, save for the terrible mental agony they had endured. The defeat was a regular *sauve qui peut.* Gabriel Dumont escaped to Montana. Riel was found wandering in the woods and captured by two scouts, Armstrong and Howrie, on the afternoon of the 15th. He was sent under a strong guard to Regina, viâ the South Saskatchewan and Medicine Hat. Riel's diary came into the possession of Major Jarvis, who commanded the Winnipeg Field Battery, and who afterwards obtained a commission in the Mounted Police. According to this semi-mystical effusion, which mixed up religion and riot, prayer and pillage, murder and meditation, in sweet confusion, the Sioux squaws were to receive the white women of Prince Albert as their own private prisoners, and the dusky ladies were to torture them according to their own pleasing fancies. The red-coats—*nous autres enfans perdus*—were to be utterly exterminated, and no quarter offered. The rebel prisoners were brought into Prince Albert on the 21st, by some of us, who had proceeded to Batoche to receive them. One Indian was literally pea-green with terror. They were all lodged temporarily in the church.

CHAPTER XIII

Battle of Cut-Knife Creek—Painted horses—Capture of transport
—General Middleton enters Prince Albert—" Gophers "—An
invidious comparison—Martial music—Saskatchewan steamers
—Departure of troops—A strange coincidence—Pursuit of Big
Bear—Hot weather—Mosquitoes—Fish—Big Bear captured—
Return of Green Lake column.

THE chief, Poundmaker, after thoroughly looting and
burning Battleford, withdrew his braves into the Eagle
Hills, where they indulged in feasting and merry-
making over their spoil. They pitched their camp at a
place known as Cut-Knife Hill, above a creek of the
same name, where the Crees had gained a victory, some
few years previously, over the Sarcees. Thus, they
knew every advantageous point of the position which
they occupied. Colonel Otter, with his column, had
reached Battleford on April 25th ; and on May 2nd he
engaged these Indians, with the Mounted Police,
Queen's Own Rifles (Canadians), a battery of Royal
Canadian Artillery, "C" Company of regular (Canadian)
Infantry, the Ottawa sharpshooters, and Battleford
Rifles. To give my readers some idea of the general
method of Indian tactics all through this rebellion, I
take the following description of this engagement from
Major Boulton's " North-West Rebellions."

"The rattle of musketry and fusillade of the Gatling
were soon heard, and the startled Indians opened fire
upon the advancing line. (Colonel Herchmer, with
Mounted Police in skirmishing order.) The guns and
the Gatling were brought promptly into action ; and,

as in the battle of Batoche, the Indians made a determined charge to try and capture them, dreading the
destructiveness of their fire, which they were powerless
to silence. They advanced, holding their blankets in
front of them, running in a zigzag manner to puzzle
our riflemen. Major Short called for volunteers to
protect his guns, and made a gallant charge upon the
advancing enemy, which caused them to fall back. In
this charge Corporal Sleigh, of the Mounted Police,
who had passed safely through the Fort Pitt danger,
was killed, and Lieutenant Pelletier and Sergeants
Gaffney and Ward were wounded. Major Short
received a bullet through his forage cap, coolly remark-
ing, 'It's a new one, too.' This charge was made
before the remainder of the column had got into
position.

"The Indians, who now came pouring out of their
encampment, were not long in taking up the positions
they had thoroughly studied, in anticipation of a prairie
fight. . . . The Queen's Own were extended along
the crest of the gully to the left to protect that flank;
"C" Company and the Ottawa Sharpshooters were
extended to protect the right flank; the Battleford
Rifles protected the rear, while the Mounted Police and
the Artillery attacked the front. Not many minutes
had elapsed before Colonel Otter perceived he was
being attacked on all sides, the enemy, under cover of
the gully through which the column had approached,
having even gone round and menaced his rear. . . .
Their thrilling war-cries, intermingled with the roar
of the guns and the rattle of small arms, made the
scene a peculiarly impressive one, and likely to strike
terror into the hearts of raw and inexperienced troops.

"Death was dealing destruction all around. As soon
as one flank was attacked and repulsed, another flank

came under fire, and the rear was menaced. But the Indians gained no advantage, and got as good as they gave, although the clever way in which they are accustomed to take cover made it difficult for our troops to get a fair shot at them.

" Colonel Otter, an hour after the action opened, finding that his rear was in danger, instructed the Battleford Rifles to clear the enemy from that position —a work which they admirably performed under Captain Nash and Lieutenant Marigold.

" The artillery supported the various corps, from time to time, by shelling the enemy, occasionally dropping a shell into their encampment some fifteen hundred yards away. . . . Colonel Otter, surrounded as he was by these precipitous gullies filled with savages, did not change his original intention of coming out to make a reconnaissance, to punish the turbulent tribes, and then to retire. He maintained the fight, which may very properly be termed an unequal one, until noon, when he determined to withdraw and return to Battleford with his tired troops."

So far, Major Boulton. The Indians made a desperate rush when they observed the troops retreating ; but the sweeping fire of the guns and Gatling held them back. Thus the little force was enabled to form up upon the open prairie, where the Indian will not attack, and return to Battleford.

Corporals Sleigh and Lowry, and trumpeter Burke, of the Mounted Police, were among the killed. Poor Talbot Lowry I mourn as a friend ! One of our fellows informed me that the redskins had their horses painted in this engagement. Major Boulton is about the fairest of those scribes who have taken up the pen, after laying down the sword, in order to blazon forth the deeds of the Canadian Militia. But he does not mention in his account of this action, that, had it not been for the Mounted Police, one of the guns would undoubtedly have fallen into the hands of the Indians.

After the battle at Cut-Knife, Poundmaker captured a whole transport train. The sixteen teamsters would have been shot by the warlike Stonies had it not been for the presence of some half-breeds. They were afterwards released, when Poundmaker had made up his mind to surrender.

On May 20th General Middleton's column marched into Prince Albert, arriving about noon, having performed the last eighteen miles that morning, with only half an hour's rest. The scarlet of their tunics was a dingy purple with exposure to all the storm and sunshine of their march, and the smoke and work of battle. Their war-worn features were bronzed with weather and over this "shadowed livery of the burnished sun," the dust of the trail had spread a coat of black. With their old forage caps and swarthy faces, they resembled Sepoys of the time of John Company. Their uniforms were out of date, about the time of the Crimean War. It is a pity these Canadian militiamen spoilt the good work they had done by never-failing bluster. But for pure and unadulterated brag I will back the lower-class Canuck against the world. The Yankee is a very sucking dove compared to his northern neighbour. I regret to say we had donned our purple and fine linen as a compliment to the arrival of our comrades in arms. But our brilliant scarlet had the same effect upon the General as a rag of the same colour generally has upon a male member of the bovine species.

"Look at my men, sir," he said to our Colonel, "look at the colour of their uniforms, sir!"

Of course, as Sir Frederick Middleton is a G.C.M.G., a C.B., and a Major-General, I must speak of him with bated breath. But I wish mildly to state that our Colonel was not such a fool as to permit his men to do all the worst work of a campaign in review order.

An immense transport train followed the infantry. This, of course, is a necessity in such a country as this. Civilians were hired for this duty with their teams ; being paid at the rate of ten dollars (2*l*.) per diem, with forage and rations thrown in.

Boulton's scouts and the Intelligence Corps, who formed the rear-guard, were a fine body of young fellows, the majority being old countrymen. They wore slouch hats and the general garb of the western plains, and were armed with repeating rifles.

General Middleton had dubbed the mounted police in Prince Albert, "gophers." This is an animal of the ground-squirrel type, who burrows on the prairie, and who retreats to its hole on any approach of danger. This wonderful feat of intellectual ingenuity on the part of their commander had taken immensely with the rural Canadians under him, who could only understand a simile that related to the soil. The gentlemanly and accomplished members of the Midland Battalion, for instance, thought it the very highest order of wit ; and one of them, to show his appreciation of it, just mentioned it casually as our troop sergeant-major happened to pass down their lines on the evening of their arrival. He had been under Burnaby in the Blues, and was a first-rate man with the gloves.

"Did you make that remark to me, young fellow ? " he asked. " Because if any of you want satisfaction, I will take you all, one after the other."

The invitation was declined in silence by these backwoods braves, and their sergeant-major afterwards offered an apology. We got on splendidly with the 90th Battalion from Winnipeg, who wore the dark green

of the 60th Rifles. They were a rattling good lot of
fellows. We volunteered *en masse* to accompany the
General on his departure up the river ; but our services
were declined. I verily think that had we been permitted, and an engagement had taken place, not one of
us would have come out alive. We were all smarting
under the keenest sense of marked and stubborn in-
justice. Just one word, and then I am done with those
self-complacent warriors, the Midland Battalion. Mind,
I don't deny their pluck ;—that they inherit and cannot
help. But I want to show that they are not the flower
of the armies of the earth, as they vainly imagine.

I have seen the Prussian in *pickelhaube* loafing about
the cities of the Fatherland ; and I have been amused
in Amsterdam, watching the Dutch conscripts, like a
school of boys, playing at soldiers. I have also observed
—at a safe distance—the extraordinary gyrations of the
Belgian sentries in the Place de la Monnaie at Brussels.
I have studied the manœuvres of a whole French army
of observation, at Bayonne. It has been my lot to
follow, for a time, the fortunes of the Carlists among the
rugged passes of the Pyrenees. I have stood in a street
of Stamboul while the Sultan went to mosque, and a
regiment of wiry Turks, who had fought at Plevna,
presented arms. Also have I envied the nonchalance of
the sentinel in front of the arsenal facing the Bosphorus
on one blazing day ; slouching along with one hand in
the pocket of his baggy pants, and his rifle at a sort of
inverted slope, his bayonet pointing to the ground in his
rear. I have seen Tommy Atkins in many lands in the
glory of scarlet and white ; so that a sort of *civis
Romanus sum* feeling went through one with a glow.
" The boys " of Uncle Sam have also passed before me.
To crown all, I have visited the Canadian militia-man
" at home," in camp, at Gananoque—I refer to the

rural battalions—and I must confess that for dirt and general slovenliness and demoralization, they, in their own elegant language, "take the cake."

General Middleton pitched his camp upon a level plateau, near the residence of Mr. Lawrence Clark. What a luxury it was to us poor exiles to hear the bands discoursing the latest tunes at night while the headquarters staff were at dinner. There was an enclosure roped off; and on the outside were gathered the military, and the rank, and beauty, white and dusky, of the Prince Albert settlement. Every one was there. The broad river looked lovely in the evening light ; the green islands with their rich foliage mirrored in its still bosom. A small bear was tied in front of the General's tent. At the first signal of the drum this shaggy little ball of cinnamon-hued fur would stand upon his hind-legs, and dance wildly till the last note of the music had died away.

During his stay here the General held a pow-wow with the Indian chiefs in this neighbourhood. They came to his tent in all the glory of war-dress. Those who had remained loyal—Mistawasis and the rest—he rewarded with tea and tobacco. Beardy was degraded from his rank of chieftainship, and his medal, stamped with the counterfeit presentment of the erstwhile First Gentleman in Europe, was taken away.

The steamers were now in the river. The flotilla consisted of the *North-west*, *Northcote*, and *Marquis*. They are all flat-bottomed boats, or twin scows, and only draw two feet of water. They have often to be warped over the shifting sand-bars which form so serious a drawback to navigation on this river. Owing to the melting of the snow and ice among the towering glacier peaks at its source, the Saskatchewan continues still to flow with ample stream in the blazing heat of the short torrid summer. But in the early autumn it dwindles down, and the steamboats cease to run. Starting from Grand Rapids, where a tramway connects them with the Winnipeg steamers on the lake, they pass up by Cumberland House and Fort à la Corne to the Forks. Thence, one yearly trip is possible as far as Medicine Hat, on the south branch. By the other waterway the course is practicable as far as Edmonton until the beginning of September. Lake Winnipeg is never navigable until about the 6th of June ; and the lake boats do not go higher than Selkirk on the Red River. These Saskatchewan steamers possess broad stern paddle-wheels ; and their general build is similar to such craft on American rivers, and familiar to all, either by experience or illustrations.

On May 22nd General Middleton departed for Battle-ford. The craft were crowded, and gay with flags. Horses and guns occupied the lower decks, among which the Swampy Indians, who formed the crew, ran and climbed, and scrambled with the agility of monkeys. The balconies running around the many windowed saloons on board were filled with officers, in service forage caps and patrol jackets. The General was to be distinguished by a white helmet, with a grey tweed shooting suit on his portly form, and long boots and spurs. Mr. Henty, of the *Standard*, was visible among the staff. There was some delay in getting away from the moorings ; and the strains of the "Girl I left behind me" came from the band stationed on the poops. This was varied by the men singing "Sailing" in chorus. Then came a shriek from the whistles ; the paddles splashed, and the expedition steamed away gaily to the stirring tune beloved of soldiers, and were soon lost to view among the lovely islands.

The Winnipeg field-battery, under the command

of the genial Major Jarvis, remained as an additional garrison in the town. They removed their camp to the vicinity of the little wooden English church, and it was laid out in the form of an open square. A smart sentry, in white helmet and the familiar blue of that branch of the service, paced in front of the guns. These men were superior to the average lot of the Canadian militia. Among them I found one who at one time had resided a short distance from my home. Another was a member of the English bar, who had been at school with one of our fellows at Dulwich. But I think that the most extraordinary meeting that I have ever heard of was that of poor Lowry and Sleigh. Both of these had been together at the same school, under the eye of the same dominie. Both went forth into the world their different ways ; for we know what Kingsley tells us happens, when all is young, our lass a queen, and every goose a swan. It is " Hey ! for boot and horse, lad," and young blood must have its way, and every young dog must enjoy himself. From the commissioned rank of the Galway militia, which is a jovial school of good fellowship, Lowry drifted into the North-West Mounted Police. Sleigh reached the same goal by a widely different path. Neither knew of the other's proximity. They met again at Battleford after all these years, and both were shot in the head in the same action.

The authorities in the plenitude of their wisdom, from some dim idea that I had a remote knowledge of the mysteries of medicine, saw fit to place me in charge of seven wounded men ; and also considerately gave me the comic man of the corps as an orderly. The laughter which he brought to the faces of the recumbent sufferers will, I trust, be placed to the credit side of his account. A large kitchen was erected in the rear for his special use, and this, with a few choice spirits, he would nightly transform into a music hall.

" These men are to have whatever they want," said Authority, in the shape of field-officers and surgeons ; and I kow-toed accordingly. Of course I lived in clover until August, when my shattered warriors were removed, and I found my occupation gone.

The prisoners to the number of about thirty were taken heavily ironed to Regina, in waggons, surrounded by a strong escort of our men. We celebrated the Queen's birthday by a general holiday, and indulged in military sports of various kinds. On the General's arrival at Battleford, Poundmaker and his braves surrendered themselves at an imposing pow-wow.

Big Bear with his captives had wandered into the wild and trackless regions beyond the Saskatchewan. Major-General Strange was operating against him from his base at Edmonton, and Major Steel with his mounted police had followed up this wily savage's trail, which was impassable for wheeled transport. This column had engaged the enemy at Frenchman's Butte on May 28th. The redskins were fully six hundred strong, and attacked on every flank, even firing on the waggons which were coralled in rear. The white prisoners escaped. While the Alberta field-force were scouring the country to the west, an expedition advanced from Fort Pitt to Loon Lake. Colonel Otter was ordered to move to Turtle Lake, and Colonel Irvine marched out of Prince Albert to Green Lake, where the Hudson Bay post had been plundered. There were about 150 mounted police on this expedition. Green Lake is seventy miles north of Carlton. The intervening country consists of dense bush with lovely open glades and beautiful lakes.

We began to have some blazing weather in June.

On the 7th—Sunday—as I went up to dine at the Sergeants' mess of the Winnipeg Field Battery, the sun beat fiercely down from a cloudless sky, the broad bosom of the river shone like molten silver. My quarters near the water were haunted by mosquitoes. The mosquito is a species of humming-bird, for whom I do not entertain the least affection, and his nocturnal melody is anything but a sedative to exhausted nerves. No doubt he is fearfully and wonderfully made, and his architectural wonders are an interesting study— theoretically. Perhaps Sir John Lubbock will take him in hand, and answer the conundrum,—why was he built ? He possesses a lance, two meat-saws, a pump, a small Corliss steam engine, a poisonous syringe, and a musical box, in his diminutive interior economy. After he has experimented with his toxicological supply on the wound he has inflicted—having first practised phlebotomy—he sets his orchestra going, and dances round in glee.

The fish which inhabit the Saskatchewan are not up to much. Some lazy half-breeds used to take up a daily position in front of my window, with an ante-diluvian outfit, and sit on the bank for hours without catching anything. When cooked, these delicacies re-semble in taste what I should imagine boiled blotting paper would be like. Trout is plentiful in the Bow River at Calgary, and is most delicious. There is also a fish, in the lesser lakes, which they *call* sturgeon, and which is fairly good.

Big Bear after he had been abandoned by the Wood Crees, wandered off with a handful of his councillors and his youngest son. He crept, by Indian paths, between the forces of Colonels Otter and Irvine, and was finally captured, near Fort Carlton, by Sergeant-Smart and three men of the mounted police, who had been detailed to watch the crossing at this point. His son, a copper-hued boy with small, black, bead-like eyes, and one councillor, who rejoiced in the modest title of "All-and-a-half," accompanied him. They were brought to Prince Albert and entered the town in the early morning of July 3rd. A non-commissioned officer reported the fact to Captain Gagnon, who was in bed, and very much surprised at this unexpected intelligence. Big Bear was in a pitiable condition of filth and hunger. He was given a good scrubbing in a tub at the barracks, though this was anything but pleasing to him. A new blanket and a pair of trousers were procured him from the Hudson Bay store. His arms consisted of a Winchester, and he stated that his only food, for eleven days, had been what he was enabled to secure in the woods. A cell was placed at the disposal of himself and staff in the guard-room, and his skinny ankles were adorned with shackles. A little shrivelled-up looking piece of humanity he was, his cunning face seamed and wrinkled like crumpled parchment. Ever since the advent of the mounted police he had been in trouble, and when he finally agreed to take treaty he wished to have the extraordinary proviso inserted that none of his band were ever to be hanged. The Indians of his tribe were all disaffected. Little Poplar, one of his sons, escaped to Montana with some of the worst of the gang, leaving a trail marked with blood, and was finally shot by a half-breed at Fort Belknap in the summer of 1886. Captain Gagnon could now send a despatch to the General, announcing this welcome news, and the campaign of the rebellion was ended.

On Sunday, the 4th of July, in the evening, the Green Lake expedition returned. A heavy thunder-storm had just passed over the town, and black clouds were rolling their dense battalions sullenly away above

the pine-forest to the north-west. The rain was
falling in torrents as the column rode slowly down the
street, and the waggons rumbled in their midst. The
men certainly looked haggard and worn. Their long
blue cloaks were muddy and torn, their slouch hats out
of shape, their spurs red with rust, and their boots
indescribable. They had been away in the wilderness
for more than a month, without blankets, tents, or
change ! Food had been so scarce that for four
consecutive days each man had received nothing but
one biscuit a day. Thin, bronzed, and with beards of
scrubby growth, they were a grim, hard lot to gaze
on ; each man armed to the teeth, and carrying a
small magazine of ammunition. On horseback, they
surrounded the waggons on all sides, which contained
sixteen evil-looking savages of Little Poplar's cut-
throats. They were heartily glad to be back again from
ceaseless hardships. They had unearthed the " cache " of
plunder taken by the Indians from the Hudson Bay
store at Green Lake. The spare waggons were piled
with loot, and there was a brisk market for every kind
of goods, in town, for a day or two. Pipes, tobacco,
copper kettles, hats, stuff for dresses, furs, blankets, and
every imaginable article even to patent medicines,
were among the cargo. One man made 150 dollars out
of his package of lynx skins. The country through
which they had struggled was rough and infested with
flies. There was no trail to speak of, and they had been
obliged to make their way over stumps and fallen logs
as well as they could. The ambulance had been " bust,"
and the astonished doctor, who was riding therein, hoisted
into the bush, where he lay dispensing frequent blessings
to the universe.

Big Bear's "war bonnet" had been discovered in a
deserted camp. This head-dress of the mighty chief was

of skunk skin, adorned with feathers. To secure "plunder" seemed a great object in this campaign. Gabriel Dumont's house was sacked, and his billiard-table taken by one of the General's commissariat officers.

One lovely morning, the *North-West,* which made a special short trip from Fort Pitt, came steaming into the open water from the maze of islands to the west, and came to her moorings opposite the centre of the town. She brought the Maclean family, who had been prisoners with Big Bear. They were the observed of all observers. It was a blazing hot day, and Mr. Maclean carried his coat and waistcoat over his arm as he came ashore. In his white shirt and black clothes, with dark beard and portly form, he reminded me most forcibly of a merchant skipper in "shore-going togs." The girls were pretty and dressed in bright costumes, as though they were enjoying a yachting trip, or going to a fashionable watering-place. Mrs. Maclean, a thin woman with Indian blood in her veins, carried an infant in her arms. The young ladies could speak Cree like natives, and were taken to see their former captors, by Major Crozier, at Goshen. Here they gave the imprisoned aborigines a good telling off in their own tongue, and, in fact, performed a sort of secular general commination service. The braves were in irons, seated on the floor of the big room in our brick barracks under a strong guard.

CHAPTER XIV

Troops homeward bound—Big Bear goes to Regina—Mutual
Admiration Society—A good word for the police—*Esprit de
corps*—Sioux teepes—Squaws bathing—Riel sentenced—
Indian summer—The verge of the wilderness—Good-bye to
Prince Albert—Batoche bush-fires—A pleasant camp—A
chorus of coyotes.

DURING the week following the return of Colonel
Irvine's force from Green Lake—when the summer sun
was flooding with golden glory forest and prairie, when
the flowers were rich in blue, and crimson, and purple,
on the spreading carpet of green—the three returning
columns of the troops, under the General, reached Prince
Albert in steamers and barges, *en route* to Winnipeg and
the East *viâ* Grand Rapids. The mounted corps proceeded by land. The men enjoyed a run around the
town, and seemed in hilarious spirits, like schoolboys on
the occasion of a " breaking up." In the barges lashed
to the larger craft were many wounded, under awnings.
They must have suffered untold torments from the
mosquitoes. Big Bear was the focus of attraction, and
our barracks were surrounded by a mob of excited
soldiery. He was brought out for exercise, and seemed
rather afraid at the unexpected amount of interest he
was causing, as he shuffled along in his leg-irons, through
the long lane of eager, sun-burnt faces. When the
steamboats had taken a supply of wood, the flotilla
moved off down the Saskatchewan.

The Winnipeg Field Battery marched to Qu'Appelle,

and thence home by train.   They were relieved by "B" battery of the regular Canadian Artillery.   These men had fought beside the mounted police at Cut Knife, and consequently there was quite a spirit of *camaraderie* between us.   In a few days, Big Bear and his companions were escorted down to Regina by picked men of "B" troop, Colonel Irvine and his staff leaving at the same time, in a drenching rain.   Thus were we, once more, left to the dull routine of existence in that far-off settlement.   All the "D" troop men were under canvas in front, of the barracks, where a powder-magazine was being erected.

There were great rejoicings all over Eastern Canada when "the boys" came marching home again.   They were *fêted* and feasted everywhere, from Moosomin to Cape Sable.   Scrip and medals were at once voted to them by a grateful country.   By this scrip, each man who had been under arms, west of Port Arthur on Lake Superior, was entitled to receive 160 acres of land in any part of the Dominion, where Government free grants were open.   Of course, they were at liberty to sell this right, and many of them did so for a mere song. Speculators were on the *qui-vive* round every drinking-saloon, and the market was flooded with these military land-warrants.   The Montreal Garrison Artillery were encamped on the south side of the railway, at Regina, for a period, and the arduous service endured by these warriors was to be driven to picnics, and to see a sun-dance by Pieapot's braves.   They also received this reward, and their manly bosoms were afterwards decorated with the silver symbol bestowed by her Majesty.   But the mounted police, whose whole five years of service is one long campaign, who daily experience hardship in harrassing marches as a matter of course, and say no word of self-laudation, received—*nothing!*   We were told

that this was because we were regulars, and what we did
was only in accordance with our terms of engagement.
All over Canada a Mutual Admiration Society was
established, to the exclusion of the police.

A writer in an Ontario paper, a civilian, did say a few
good words for us exiles. He had ridden from Prince
Albert to Carlton to meet the Green Lake column on
its return. This is how he winds up his remarks :—

" Whether your readers may derive any information
or amusement from this rambling account of an ordinary
police fatigue we do not know, but we freely confess
that the force stood a hundred per cent. higher in our
estimation after this trip than before it. The matter of
fact, rough and ready, silent but systematic manner in
which these men grapple with the physical obstacles in
the path of their duty in this frontier country is worthy
of all admiration, and we feel certain that a closer
acquaintance with the N.W.M.P. would only confirm
this good opinion. We are glad to see their numbers
increased, as we believe that from the experience of
prairie life, which they of necessity acquire, they will
always, in case of trouble, demonstrate their superiority
over any ordinary troops which may be placed in the
field. Officers and men alike live a hard life, a lonely
life, a life in many cases almost as hard and lonely as
that of Alexander Selkirk, and this sort of existence is
dragged out by men, many of whom not long ago were
the pets of society in this and other lands. Many a
silent tongue in the ranks could tell a strange tale if it
chose."

I returned to barracks on the 12th of August.
After the middle of this month we enjoyed the most
lovely weather, calm days and frosty nights. The
days glided on in quietness, though occasional parties
were despatched to arrest Indians found to have been

implicated in the rebellion.   The late campaign was a
fruitful theme of discourse.   I recollect, one fine evening,
a certain non-com. was loudly bewailing the lack of *esprit
de corps.*

"That is what is wanted,—*esprit de corps,*" he emphatically announced, and several of his audience agreed
with him.   Then spoke a hitherto silent listener, in the
shape of a native of the Carse of Gowrie.

"Then, why dinna they requiseetion for some, frae
the quartermaster's store ? "

Between the Hudson Bay post and barracks were a
number of Sioux lodges, which were a nightly resort
for a good many of our men.   The interior of a teepe
is not, by any means, an æsthetic abode.   A fire of logs
smoulders on the ground, in the centre, and the smoke
makes its way through an aperture at the top.   A
blanket, swung in the form of a hammock, from one
pole to another, holds the papoose, if there be one.
There is no other furniture.   These teepes are formed
by a circle of poles, cut from spruce-trees, meeting at
the top.   Round these is fastened the outer covering of
skins.   Such is the lodge, or wigwam, of the mighty red-
man.

I think I have stated already, that the Saskatchewan
here widens into a broad lake, with lovely islands, tree-
fringed bays, and jutting promontories.   One of these
sequestered coves was the bathing-place of the squaws.
It was great fun to watch their antics.   They could
swim like musk rats, and seemed intensely fond of
splashing each other, and indulging in all sorts of rough
play.   It must not be imagined that they capered about
in the costume in which the Paphian Aphrodite is generally portrayed rising from the Ægean foam.   Oh, no !
The most fastidious British matron could not find fault
with the skirts and bodices which they wore ; as though

they were at a well-conducted, old-fashioned, sea-side village over here. There was no impropriety about these copper-hued naiads, when disporting themselves. These civilized remnants of clothing were only used for this purpose. At other times they were dressed in the ordinary blanket, and beaded, crimson leggings. It was a decided comfort to know that these dusky beauties did bathe sometimes.

Some few Indian prisoners, who were known to have committed depredations during the rising, were brought in at this time. I shall never forget the delight of my old friend of the "forty-twas" when one particular red-skin was carried to the guard-room. This brave had tried to throw a noose over him, when on patrol near Carlton. By-the-way, it is only in very cheap fiction that this operation is known as "lassoing," or "throwing a lasso." A genuine cowboy never uses the word, he always speaks of "roping" a steer, or horse. But "Deadwood Dick, the dismal desperado of Cut-throat Creek," uses the word "lasso" whenever he can.

The rebels had been tried and sentenced at Regina. Eleven Indians had been brought before Judge Rouleau, at Battleford, for murder, and were sentenced to death. Riel was to be hanged on the 18th of September, but as an appeal was made to the Privy Council, the execution did not take place until November 16th. As I was in Regina at the time, I shall speak of it in due course.

The Indian summer came in all its glory in September. It is much earlier here, in the north, and lasts for a month generally. A luminous mist floats over all ; and everything seems bathed in the tranced calm of one long summer's evening. The hideous mosquito has received his *quietus* from the nightly frost. The poplars and birch-trees begin to change their worn green gar-

ments for all the splendour of their autumnal robes of
russet, and bronze, and red. The roads are dry and
hard, and over lake and bush, open space and mighty
forest, over broad river and sere and yellow marsh, lies
the quiet slumber of the fall. One splendid afternoon,
a comrade and I sallied forth for a ramble over the
ridge to the south-east. When we reached the summit,
a scene lay spread beneath us beyond all words of
mine. Prince Albert, to the left, nestled in its amphitheatre of copsewood; its white toy-like houses peeping
out from amid their embroidery, and the great river
rolling gently by, with gem like islands on its gleaming
breast. To the north and east stretched the primeval
forest, all golden and olive; like a vast ocean of colour,
its billows spread sleeping and dreamlike. Such a
sight can never be forgotten. Here, on the south shore
of the North Saskatchewan, settlement has an end.
Beyond, as far as the desolation of the Coppermine and
Great Mackenzie Rivers, beyond the fertile meadows
of the Peace River Valley, beyond the wild Lac la
Ronge, as far as the moss-clad beach and lichened rocks
of the Arctic Ocean, stretches the unknown. Only a
few earnest missionaries, and the hardy servants of the
H.B. Co., the cunning Dog Rib, sullen Chipweyan, and
diminutive Esquimaux people these remote solitudes.
We stood, truly, on the verge of the everlasting wilderness—the extreme frontier of civilization! The Peace
River doubtless in due time will supplant the Saskatchewan, for it is said to have a better climate, and the
course of empire will roll further to northward and
westward yet.

Glad tidings came to me, suddenly, upon the 21st
of September. The officer whom I had accompanied to Prince Albert in the previous December
was returning to Regina. On this day I received orders

to pack my baggage and hold myself in readiness to go along with him, and in the afternoon we pulled out. As it was not considered expedient, somehow, for our small party to wear scarlet, we adopted mufti, of a somewhat varied and antique fashion. The inspector, his wife and child, his servant, a teamster, and myself comprised the whole. We took two waggons; one of them on springs and covered in. In the body of this reclined Mrs.—— and her baby, well wrapped in rugs, her husband handled the reins, while I sat alongside. The other vehicle carried our camp equipment, bedding and kit, cooking utensils, grub and forage, and a small "A" tent. We troopers were to sleep *sub tegmine fagi*, or rather *frigido Jove*.

We made a call at the Hudson Bay store, where many delicacies, and a plentiful supply of tobacco, were purchased to cheer us on our trip. We continued up through the town by the river, passing an exercise party, in half-sections, under the sergeant-major. I may state, that the majority of the Ontario horses died off, after the Green Lake expedition; thus demonstrating the superiority of the native-bred broncho, for these climates. A little further on we saw a squad of artillery-men, firing up the broad reaches of the river, with the Gatling. The store-keepers were standing at their doors, in their shirt-sleeves, looking half-asleep in the drowsy autumnal weather. It all looked pleasant now, the broad Saskatchewan and the russet woods. Often had I, on the long, weary, hot, summer days, cast wistful looks up this dusty trail, and wished I were going over it for the last time. And *O, terque, quaterque beate*, the day had come at length! Away we rattled, past the pretty convent, past the white palace of the bishop, past many-coloured villas with wide verandahs; —away through the yellow corn-fields, and by the snake fences around St. Catherine's. Here the country opens out into wide parks, and grassy slopes, and tiny lakes amid tangled copse. Past Scott's farm—still as dilapidated-looking as it was on that April night when we pitched our camp here, and received the astounding order to return. Scott had been tried at Regina for complicity in the rising ; but had been acquitted. Away through denser bush now, and so to the forks of the road, where our scouts had their headquarters, in the little log-house. Just beyond, in a bay of the surrounding bluffs, a little distance from the trail, from amid the long, dry grass, the smoke of a camp-fire rose straight into the still air. A police waggon was standing near, the horses were picketed alongside, and three recumbent figures were waiting for the kettle to boil. One of them rose, and came forward as we halted. He saluted, and made his report. They were two constables who had been left in charge of stores at Snake Plains,—between Green Lake and Carlton,—on Colonel Irvine's return. A certain malcontent had deserted from " D " troop, at Prince Albert, in August, and had proceeded into the wilderness, under the dingy banner of Mother Smoke, and some redskins. Unfortunately, when his money and supplies had given out, he had been " rounded on " by his dusky pals, and delivered into the hands of these two. They were now bringing him in. He subsequently adorned the guard-room at Regina for six months. Our drive now soon brought us to the comfortable homestead of Mr. Cameron, where we had stayed before. His snug house had suffered at the hands of the Sioux ; pictures and other cherished household gods had been wantonly hacked to pieces. We had a capital supper of eggs and beefsteak, and steaming souchong, and an enjoyable night's rest.

We were off again in the early dawn, the air keen but bracing ; and now one could enjoy one's matutinal pipe, without the juice freezing in the stem. The air was impregnated with smoke from the burning bush. It was on fire on all sides, in some places quite near the trail ; but fortunately there was not a breath of wind. The track soon meandered through the towering pines, sweet with the rare perfume of the woodlands. Half-breeds' farms here and there, stood in sheltered places. The shanties were plentifully plastered with adobe, and a general mosaic of dirt and disorder surrounded them. The trees were now shedding their leaves, and the slumber of the autumn lay upon the brown earth. About ten o'clock, we drew near to the South Branch of the Saskatchewan, opposite St. Laurent. This place consists of a church, and a few Metis' houses, and is about ten miles from Batoche. Here Mac—the officer's servant—shot a prairie chicken through the head with his Winchester. He had been in the corps for five years, and was one of our best shots. Game was plentiful all along our route, and as we had a breech-loading fowling-piece as well as our rifles we were never without duck or chicken. The smoke near St. Laurent was stifling, though the scenery here was very pretty. These fires have spread onward from the great prairie with devouring flames, and have eaten their way into and ploughed wide spaces through the forests of the north : hence the open glades, and curving bays of grass which line the outer edge of bluffs. Suddenly we came upon the crossing at Batoche. A cunningly devised rifle-pit stood upon the verge of the steep incline which led to the river, and a ruined store stood opposite. We camped for dinner upon a terrace above the gliding stream, overhung by many aspen-trees. Soon our camp-kettle was hung over the crackling faggots, and some savoury steaks were cooking in the pan.   On this journey, we were not reduced to the bacon and biscuit of our winter's march.   Now we had bread, and even condensed milk.   There had previously been a wire cable stretched across here for the use of the ferry ; but it had been destroyed.   After disposing of our meal, and washing our utensils, we commenced a vigorous chorus of shouts for our Charon, who made his appearance after some time on the opposite shore. This was no other than the former keeper of the mail station at Hoodoo.   Riel had kept his proud soul in dire bondage, for about two months.   He and his assistant brought the scow across with a pair of sweeps. It was a broad, flat-bottomed craft, with railings on either side and an inclined plane at both ends.   As the current was rather strong, we were obliged to start from a point at some distance above our proposed landing. The ungainly looking object, took our whole transport on board at once, each one of us standing at the horses' heads.   This is a dangerous proceeding, and frequent accidents occur.   Everything in this unfettered country is done in a happy-go-lucky manner, and rivers are crossed in the most primitive fashion.   We pushed out into the stream, and we swept gently over towards the opposite side, when a few strokes brought us to ground.   One of the horses was very restive in landing, and the inspector got a wetting.   The village of Batoche was deserted, and woe-begone, only two or three families remaining. The houses were battered and bruised with marks of war.   On the open ground to the west of the houses, were the remains of Middleton's zareba.   Scattered around were the rebel rifle-pits, which baffled a force of 800 men, supported by artillery, for four days.   The ingenuity and care displayed in the construction of these pits astonished the general.   They were completely masked and hidden by brushwood, stuck in the ground above them. At one of the houses, which contained inhabitants, we purchased some butter. The trail now led for some way along the edge of the rugged and shaggy heights that here line the course of the South Saskatchewan. It turns to the south about a mile beyond the cemetery. Away to the north, the great forest fires were rolling volumes of smoke into the air. We found also that the conflagration, was spreading from the west, on the southern side of the river.

We bowled along an even road through a pleasant, rolling country. What a terrible sense of haunted desolation fills this land ! It seems as though silence were a ghost, whose gruesome form is indefinably present everywhere.

A little before sunset we halted ; a pretty little lake reposed in a willow-fringed hollow, and bluffs of birch and poplar reared their lines of shelter to the west. Long grass shrouded the ground down beside the water, and here the bronchos were picketed. We pitched the tent in a picturesque recess, among the feathery birch-trees ; and soon the blue smoke-wreaths curled up from our fire. We stretched out our limbs upon the ground which was smooth and hard : the big moon showed her silver globe above the dim contour of the distant hills. Prairie chicken and fried ham, and excellent tea made us feel at peace with all mankind, and jokes were cracked without reserve. Then I unrolled my blankets underneath the waggon, lit my beloved pipe and fell into a meditative reverie. There are two things for which one never loses a craving on the prairie—tea and tobacco. And in this case I speak with authority, in spite of any counterblast from the Rev. Stiggins and his anti-tobacco humbugs. Then came forth the visions of the gloaming, the dreams of far away ; and the longing and the wild hope to see the old scenes once again. It must have been, I imagine, by the moon's position, about one o'clock in the morning, when I was suddenly awakened by the most unearthly row I ever heard. Evidently a Home Rule party of coyotes were holding an indignation meeting somewhere. First there was a peal of demon laughter, followed by a wild, despairing shriek, mingled with a howl from another portion of the orchestra. A series of sharp yelps—probably taking the place of our Hear! hear!—were now introduced, which were succeeded by another tumultuous burst of laughing. A grand *finale* of yells, shrieks, howls, barks, and screams of hilarity wound up the entertainment: it was evidently a great success. The cry of the coyote, breaking in upon the startled ear of night, as it invariably does, is about the most hideous I ever listened to. But this musical festival " banged Banagher," and came as a sort of " uncanny " surprise. The horses went on steadily munching their feed, the black shadows of the waggons lay upon the yellow grass ; and the air was calm and frosty. The lady in the tent was evidently alarmed, for I could hear a feeble voice saying something about " Indians," while the gruff voices of my comrades under the other waggon were giving vent to anything but prayers.

We turned out in the moonlight at 4 a.m., and to put some warmth in my veins, I grabbed a camp-kettle and ran to the sleugh for water. Mac had the fire ready, and we soon received the benefit of some hot coffee. Then the tent was struck and waggons packed, and away we went as the first pale streak of dawn gleamed over the Birch Hills.

Passing by some sedgy sleughs, I noticed, on the margin, the winter homes of the musk-rat, built of reeds and mud. He always puts up his little hut by the edge of the water, and projecting over it ; so that he has an unfrozen space through which to dive beneath the ice. We went through fifteen miles of rolling prairie to-day, over whose hilly surface, blackened with fire, the ground-squirrels were disporting in thousands. It was bleak and bare, and the sky was laden with leaden clouds. Numbers of the sheets of water here are so impregnated with alkali as to be unfit for use. In the afternoon we saw a huge lake to the right, with wooded islands and large lagoons along its silent shores. We could not see the other side. Its desolate waters slumbered mournfully in appalling solitude. In a tall bluff, to the north of Humboldt, we drew up our waggons at night. Here we immersed one of our wheels in a pond to tighten the tire. As I had a new pair of long boots on my feet, it was unanimously voted that I should wade in to extricate it. So much for having decent boots.

CHAPTER XV

Humboldt—A strange caravan—The salt plains again—The springs
—An unpleasant situation—Indian camp—Children—An Indian
masher—Fire bags—A game preserve—An early reveillé—
Skunk Bluffs—Qu'Appelle—Lord Lansdowne—Cigars—An
Indian legend—Harvest—Prairie fires—Pieapot's reserve—
The great prairie—Regina—A change—Leave of absence.

ON the following morning we passed the old mail
station at Humboldt, where I had endured such an
uncomfortable night in the preceding December. The
ground was worn bare with traffic all around, and bottles,
preserved meat tins, ancient forage-caps, and other
martial relics denoted the spot where the Quebec
(regular) cavalry had been encamped. All was deserted
now, and left to the nocturnal prowling of the wolves.

A large frame-house, painted green, stood on the
verge of the forest to the right of the trail, two miles
ahead. This was the new telegraph and mail station,
and here resided the operator and his family. Their
winter existence must have been inexpressibly lonely,
before the robbery of the stage in 1886, since when an
outpost of mounted police has been stationed here, and
at other places along the route. We halted a couple of
hours for dinner. The bush fires were creeping nearer
and our host was much concerned regarding his hay.
Soon after our departure, we met a remarkable caravan
in the shape of one of our men and his family returning
to Battleford, from furlough. He was one of our "old
hands," and much dwelling in the wilderness had caused

him to cast many of the prejudices of civilization to one side, as useless superfluities. Military smartness was evidently one of these. His wife was three parts Indian, and she reclined in a sort of *negligé* position on the waggon, with a dusky brood of youngsters sprawling around her.

In the trees, on the extremity of the Great Salt Plains, near the spot of nine months before, we pitched our camp to-night. No one can form any idea how the shroud of winter changes the aspect of everything out here. I hardly recognized the place again, when the inspector pointed it out to me. Indeed, I wished to argue the point, but when you are in the ranks it doesn't do to pitch argument against the wearer of a patrol jacket, with a star on the shoulder-strap. Here we had the usual yarns over our tea around the camp-fire, and the nightly pipe under the stars when blanket-time came and the owls began to cry in the woods.

We were up at dawn next day, and in a short time we were out upon the wide sea of stunted grass of the Great Salt Plains, an awful waste of grey and withered vegetation.

> " Nought to relieve the aching eye,
> But barren earth and burning sky ;
> And the blank horizon round and round."

The hut, standing on a slight mound in the centre, is only inhabited in winter, for the mail makes other stages in summer. A wooden cross, rising from a marshy quagmire, or muskeg, denotes " the springs." This is the only drinking-water for forty-five miles. It is strongly impregnated with iron. We camped to-night at the foot of the Touchwood Hills. Short, scrubby bush covered the wind-swept plateau which stretched away in darkening gloom to the west, where the sun was sinking in a mass of crimson fire. The watering-place was in a bad situation, the sleugh being surrounded by a thick hedge of willows. We indulged in a big feed of prairie chicken, though our camp was anything but comfortable ; for a cold breeze was scampering over from the north-west.

We were off again in the moonlight of the early morn. How reluctantly does one withdraw oneself from the warm covering in the chill, frosty air, sleepy and stiff ! On drawing away the blanket from my head I saw that everything was coated with frost. It is when sleeping on the prairie during this weather that one finds the benefit of a tuque pulled well down over the ears. Soon after entering the Touchwood Hills we met the mail stage, in which were seated some lady passengers. In winter we had found the Indians in huts, upon the reserve, but now they were encamped in teepes, which covered a wide hillside to the left of the trail. Some of the lodges were painted blue :—dark near the ground, but shading into turquoise at the top. There were only dogs and children about the camp. These youngsters were quite naked, and were capering about in wild gambols, in all directions. We pulled up at the Hudson Bay store, where we purchased some cigars ; but halted for dinner further on. One of the teams was on the point of remaining a fixture in the sticky bottom of the sleugh when taken to water ; but by frantic efforts was extricated in time. While we were engaged in disposing of our prairie chicken, ham, potatoes and tea, a young brave, on horseback, passed us with considerable pride in his port, and an extra amount of defiance in his eye. He was evidently a redskin masher, and a tip-top swell in Indian upper circles. This noble savage certainly made a nearer approach to the ideal Indian of romance than any I had yet beheld. His features were straight and regular ; his facial angle

being very good. His forehead was narrow ; one of the
leading characteristics of his race. His complexion was
clear, and he was really handsome. His hair of course was
parted in the middle, smoothed straight down on either
side, and was dressed in two long plaits which hung over
each shoulder, loaded at the ends with heavy ornaments
of brass. He had no cap, a buckskin shirt, fringed
and beaded with rare devices, fitted his agile form
like a glove. The crimson leggings and moccasins were
elaborately worked with beads, blue, white, green,
and scarlet, in flowers, and scrolls, and squares. His
saddle-cloth, or numnah, or shabraque, was also richly
embroidered with the same material. The rifle which
he carried was studded with brass about the stock.
The bridle on his little wiry black cayeuse was of
horse-hair, with beaded fringe upon the browband. I
reckoned him up, and I think—as he sat—he would
be worth about five hundred dollars as a curio. His
fire-bag, too, was a marvel of untutored æstheticism.
It is a pouch of deerskin which hangs from the belt, and
serves the same purpose as a Highland *spleuchan.*

We kept an eye to our horses to-night, as these gentry
have a very slight respect for the laws of *meum* and
tuum in that line. Every turn of the winding trail
showed us a chance at duck or prairie chicken ; but as
the ground is sacred to the Indians we could not fire a
shot. The whole reserve simply swarms with game.

We camped in a lovely spot—a gem of woodland
beauty, in the rich setting of the fall. Groves of
magnificent timber climbed the slopes, while a fairy
like peeped through the tangled screen. We lay awake
for some time under the starlight, smoking, and spinning
yarns of bygone times.

The moon was silvering the sleeping lake and the
shaggy clumps of copsewood when the inspector's voice

announced reveillé. It was a bracing morning. The
waggons threw long shadows on the grass, and the
horses lay resting in the hollow. Each of them, when
doing transport work receives a daily ration of fifteen
pounds of oats.

   To-day we lit our noon camp-fire on a gentle slope
above a winding, sluggish creek ; tall reeds fringing its
muddy banks. We reached a solitary farm-house in
the evening, near to which we halted for the night, and
next morning, about nine, we passed Skunk Bluffs,
bowling along a splendid trail towards Qu'Appelle.
The scenery bore such a resemblance to a well-kept
park, that I continually expected to see behind these
groves of white oak some fine old moated grange.
The bluffs were alive with game, and we of course
never missed a chance of replenishing our larder.
About half-past ten, we reached the height above the
V-shaped valley in which reposes the town of Fort
Qu'Appelle. What a different aspect it now wore !
The grey slopes were basking in the sunshine, the
Fishing Lakes glittered in the glorious light, and along
the beach were moored gaily-coloured pleasure-boats.
We stabled our horses down at the fort. We met some
old comrades, who informed us that the Governor-
General—Lord Lansdowne—had visited this thriving
settlement, with an escort of mounted police, on the
previous day. After a welcome shave, and a change of
underclothing, we lounged over to the hotel for dinner.
What a refreshing experience it was to be back among
the outposts of civilization ! The steel engravings in
oak frames upon the walls, the billiard-tables, the soft
carpets on the floors, were all a novelty to us poor
exiles from the wilderness. The cider, combined with
the magic weather, had quite an exhilarating effect ;
and the cigars proffered by the bar-tender, in the fulness

of his heart, were really good. I may remark that a decent cigar is a rarity in the North-West, though excellent tobacco is provided for the police at sixty cents per pound. It is a pleasant little place, Qu'Appelle. There is an Indian legend, which throws a poetic halo around the name. A young brave was obliged suddenly to leave the teepe, in which his beautiful squaw lay sick unto death. While the paddle of his canoe was flashing by the shores of these crystal lakes, he heard his name called softly from amid the rustling leaves that shaded the splashing waves. He asked, "Who calls?" And the voice of his beloved gave out his name twice again. He shot his skiff into an overhanging arch, and searched the bushes with nimble feet; but all was still, save for a startled deer that bounded from the thicket. On returning to his tribe, he found his bride had passed away in death—at this very hour when his name was whispered—in his far-off lodge by the rolling Kisaskatchewan. The French *voyageurs* translated the Indian name into Qu'Appelle.

A small weekly paper is published here, and a photographer had established a "gallery." This town was General Middleton's base of operations. After a capital dinner, at which were fish, flesh, fowl, and sweets in abundance, we ascended the narrow trail which leads to Regina. Our direction was westerly, and we should pass through Pieapot's reserve. There were a number of settlers around Qu'Appelle, who appeared to have comfortable farms, and who were in the midst of harvest operations. The frosts which had touched the Saskatchewan had not reached them here. It was a cold evening when we camped in a bluff near the log-house of a young Englishman. He had been scouring the country in search of some stray cattle, and rode up to us in a state of great excitement, requesting us to be careful of our camp-fire.

Considering that it formed part of our duty to search for the originators of all prairie fires, and to stamp them out when practicable, this *naive* request was rather amusing. But an enormous fire was at that time raging all over the Territory. The long-service man of our party said that in all his experience he had never passed over so much burnt ground. Sparks from the railway often cause immense destruction, and these conflagrations often spring from the American side of the boundary. The Indians, of all travellers on the plains, are the most systematically cautious in everything relating to their camp-fires ; never pitching their teepes till they make the site fireproof by treading down or burning the surrounding grass, and never leaving the embers to smoulder when they remove to fresh quarters.

Our compatriot became very friendly, on finding we were police, and offered us the hospitality of his shanty, but we preferred the open air. We were very merry— on this occasion—over the crackling blaze, for we hoped to be living in barracks on the morrow. However charming an occasional picnic may be ; with the popping of champagne corks, lobster salad, and the arch eyes of beauty to add a charm to the sylvan scene, it is apt to become monotonous when it is the normal state of existence, without any of the above pleasing accessories.

After breakfast, we passed through Pieapot's reserve, which is buried in the bush, on the edge of the plains. A few Cree braves and leering squaws were to be observed moving about, and one truculent-looking savage stalked across the trail with a rifle. These are the dirtiest and most immoral Indians in the Territories. We emerged from the woods about ten o'clock, and there stretched before us once more—in all its withered desolation—the Great Prairie.

We crossed Boggy Creek, and neared the clustering

houses of Regina, standing in the midst of the flat
expanse. Over the railway, to the east of the station,
some smart red-coats were passing up Broad Street. It
was like coming home, to see these troopers in all the
glory of scarlet and yellow. What trim swells these
fellows looked in contrast to us grimy objects.
Triumphal arches, laden with agricultural produce,
in honour of Lord Lansdowne, spanned South Railway
Street as we drove along. There was a mighty
change in this microscopic midget of a capital of
2,600,000 square miles. Stores, with plate-glass
windows, displayed the newest goods. There were
many hotels in all the splendour of gilded carving,
and dazzling mirrors. Broad side-walks had supplanted
the ravines and ponds of the year before. Telegraph
and telephone wires ran in all directions. Dainty, toy-
like dwelling-houses had sprung up as if by magic.
The Park, unfortunately, showed only a row of naked,
blighted trees. These will only grow from the seed, in
this climate; so that arboriculture is attended with great
difficulty. We recrossed the railway, where we met a
well-known Prince Albert face. The barracks were all
life and bustle. Two field-pieces were drawn up, under
the broad folds of the Union Jack. A feeling of pride
thrills through one as one gazes at that old rag ; whether
by the blue Mediterranean, in sweltering India, in the
Antipodes, or away in the Far West. The " morning
drum-beat that encircles the world " is no silly fable
now.

Between each block of buildings was a large square
tent for the accommodation of the increased number of
men ; for the strength of the force had now been raised
to 1000. A huge new barrack-room had been run up,
near the guard-room, and the recreation-room removed
to the prairie beyond. Horses were tied up in lines, in

the stable-square. Recruits were drilling under an Irish sergeant with stentorian lungs. The place swarmed with fine strapping young fellows, but all the faces were strange. We drew the concentrated gaze of every one upon us by our uncouth appearance, among all this purple and fine linen. I observed the eye of the adjutant fixed upon us with horror, and I almost guessed the result. I knew he nursed a rooted objection to men from the north being around headquarters. All the escorts who had brought down prisoners had been ordered to camp outside, and had thence been relegated to exile again. The free-and-easy manners of the wild camps did not suit the rigid discipline of this post, where a charge "in that he was improperly dressed" was sure to meet with severe punishment. I at once went to the quarters which the orderly sergeant informed me I was to take up ; and I took good care forthwith to don my most irreproachable war-paint. But the fiat had gone forth! In half an hour the orderly returned, with his fist full of the usual batch of papers without which no orderly apparently can move, and said,—

"You go to Battleford to-night."

I suppose my face would be what painters style "a study," but I immediately saw the inspector, who interviewed Major Crozier. The latter was in command here, as Colonel Irvine was with Lord Lansdowne at Calgary. The major was pleased to countermand the order, which he designated "preposterous." So I escaped being transported again to the dreary Saskatchewan. To show how unpopular this region was with men who had once been there, I may state that all sorts of dodges, sick-list, &c., were adopted to avoid being banished there.

No one troubled me to do any duty, as I belonged to

"D" troop ; so I made a pilgrimage to town. I found a new road had been laid out past the Lieutenant-Governor's residence, or Government House. This was a species of wooden bungalow, painted white, and surrounded with the universal verandah. There was a lawn in front, decorated with a flagstaff. The new road past this official dwelling was dignified by the title of Dewdney Street, after the Lieutenant-Governor.

But Victoria Square was only a patch of prairie ; Dewdney Street only contains this building, and that is two miles from town. At the other end were the chambers sacred to the deliberations of the North-West Council, the Parliament of the Territories. This has been now replaced by a Legislative Assembly. Here also were the offices of the Indian Department.

It seemed I was to await the return of our colonel, for promotion ; I missed it however by obtaining a pass and taking a trip to Brandon. When I returned I was too late, as some more fortunate individual, who was on the spot, obtained the billet. However, my absence enabled me to avoid being included in a reinforcement of 100 men who were being sent to that abomination of desolation, Battleford. I was now quartered in the large barrack-room among a crowd of recruits, and commenced to perform the usual routine of duties, such as guard, stable orderly, fatigue, and parade.

CHAPTER XVI

Louis Riel in prison—The guard-room—Guard increased—Riel doomed—Duty heavy—New organization—Mud and rain—A way to take up land—A *contretemps*—Riel's politeness—His devotions—*Apologia pro vita sua*—A prophet—Père André— Riel sane—St. Peter appears to Riel—An early breakfast— Exercise—The scaffold—Patrol—The execution.

THE irrepresssible *ego* has caused me to neglect for some time our friend Louis Riel, who was bewailing the failure of his ambitious schemes, in the seclusion of a guard-room cell at Regina. A few Indians and half-breeds, who had been sentenced to minor terms of imprisonment, were here also. Big Bear, Poundmaker, and One Arrow had been packed off to Stony Mountain Penitentiary, in Manitoba, for three years. They, along with a number of others, were amnestied in 1886.

The mounted police guard-rooms were the only prisons in the territory. The place of durance vile attached to the one in the Regina barracks had been extended a considerable distance to the rear, and a yard with a high stockade had also been added. It was a matter of common superstition that Riel would be eventually pardoned, and in all probability pensioned, so that he did not receive at first the many delicate attentions which were subsequently lavished upon him. There was only the ordinary barrack-guard on duty. *Le petit Napoléon* used daily to go out for an hour's exercise in the square, under the escort of two constables with loaded Winchesters. These weapons of the guard were always filled with three rounds of ball cartridge. Monsieur Riel was also adorned with a ball and chain, whenever he left his cell. Now to describe, as far as my feeble ability will allow me, this terror of Red River and Saskatchewan notoriety. He was a man about five feet seven inches in height, with a pale, flabby face, dark grey eyes closely set together, restless in their expression. His nose was slightly aquiline, his hair and beard were reddish in hue, his lips were thick, and his neck long. He spoke invariably in a low and gentle tone.

The Wood Mountain Division, the men from Southern Manitoba, and all those who had been engaged in watching the International Boundary were in barracks at the end of October. Forty recruits had also arrived recently. As soon as the parties had come in from summer duty on the plains the guard was considerably increased. Things had begun to look very serious for Riel. His appeal was considered shaky; and experts had pronounced him sane. It was at last expected that, in spite of all the hysterical yelling of the French Canadians, in spite of all political thimble-rigging, that he would have to "swing." The Government was on the horns of a dilemma. The people of Ontario and the North-West clamoured for his execution, the Catholics of Lower Canada enshrined him as a martyr. However, as will be seen, he was doomed.

Duty began to be heavy now. An officer took command of the guard, and, in addition, there was a sergeant and corporal. The officer of the guard, and four troopers under a corporal, always accompanied Riel in his walks abroad. Two sentries were on duty, night and day, in the corridors of the prison, the whole length of which could be commanded from the guard-room. The re-organization of the force went on apace; and there were

now three full troops, of one hundred men each, at
Regina. There were continual muster and mounted
parades.

On the 1st of November, 1885, the distribution of the
new divisions was published. The whole muster-roll of
1000 officers and men, with the different troops to which
they were posted, was affixed to the wall of the mess-
room. What a rush there was to see this ukase !

A troop (as before), Maple Creek and Medicine
Hat.

B troop, Regina. This was the troop to which I
found myself once more transferred.

C troop, Fort Macleod.

D   „   Battleford.

E   „   Calgary.

F   „   Prince Albert.

G   „   Fort Saskatchewan. This outpost is about
eighteen miles from Edmonton, on the North Saskatchewan River.

H troop, Lethbridge. This was a new settlement,
fifty miles from Fort Macleod. Coal-mines were being
worked there by the North-West Coal and Navigation
Company ; they had constructed a branch line to it
from Dunmore, on the C.P.R. H troop left Regina for
its new destination on December 1st.

K troop, Battleford.

Depôt troop. This was the permanent division at
Regina, and consisted of the headquarters staff and
recruits, with a sprinkling of duty men. In fact, it was
—as its name implies—the depôt.

The weather at this season was considerably milder
than that of the corresponding period in 1884. We had
much rain, and the barrack square and the approaches
to the stables were indescribable. A man had no need to
go through the formalities laid down in the Dominion

Land Act to acquire a free grant of 160 acres of " rich argillaceous mould." He had merely to walk from the barrack-gate to his room, and he had the legalized quantity attached to each foot. You mounted guard in all the pomp and circumstance of brilliant spurs and shining boots ; but when you entered the guard-room your spurs were invisible beneath the hideous geological formation on either heel. Mounted patrols were now established, and a couple of these were on duty in the daytime riding round the barracks, with orders to detain all suspicious-looking persons. This patrol was posted at reveillé and was taken off at retreat. At night a perfect cordon of sentries surrounded the place.

I was away on special service under a sergeant one evening, and I returned, leading his horse, at one o'clock in the morning. I was in a rough " costume," wearing a slouch hat. On my approach I was challenged by three sentries at once. The led horse and the head-gear, looming through the darkness, looked very fishy. Evidently I was a " breed," from Montana, who had turned up to aid Riel to escape. I could just see the gleam of the barrels as the carbines came to the " ready."

" Halt ! Who comes there ? "

" Friend."

" Stand, friend, and give the countersign."

" Hang the countersign ! Haven't got it. Policeman on duty. Call the non com."

" Halt ! "

How this *contretemps* might have ended I know not, for some zealous youth might have potted me. However, some one on the guard-room verandah recognized my voice, and I was allowed to advance.

I was now on continuous duty ; when not on mounted patrol, on guard. The barrack-guard mounted at 2 p.m., and I only enjoyed the luxury of going to bed every

second night.   The sentries were posted, as the guard
numbered off.   Thus the even numbers would find
themselves placed inside the prison one day ; and probably the odd numbers the next.   It was very frequently
my lot to find myself stationed inside.

My first experience of taking care of the rebel leader
was as follows.   I was marched into the corridor, and
given my orders by the corporal.   Then the provost
sergeant, who is responsible for the discipline of the
prison, came to me, and impressed upon me that I was
to keep a particular eye upon Riel, and see that, under
no circumstances did he communicate with, or speak to,
any of the other prisoners.

"He is sitting warming himself by the stove just
now, and you can turn him into his cell after a little
while."

The stove stood in the centre, between two blocks of
cells.   The passages ran down the front of the cells
from both sides of the guard-room.   Every door could
be fastened simultaneously by a lever worked from the
latter place.   Each of the little apartments possessed
an open grating in the centre of its wooden door, which
was the only space through which light could penetrate.
There were windows along the opposite walls, which at
night were hung with lamps with powerful reflectors.

I found Riel clad in a dark tweed suit, wearing a blue
knitted tuque upon his head.   There were a number of
other prisoners, including a few troopers, "in" for
breaches of discipline, standing around him.   He was
sitting on a wooden stool, with his feet up against the
stove.   It was necessary for him to move, that I might
pass.   "Excuse me, Mr. Riel, I wish to pass ; sorry to
trouble you."

"Oh ! no troo-bell at all.   If that was all the troo-
bell, it would be well."

This was said with a pleasant smile, French accent, and a soft tone of voice. He was always most studiously polite, and painfully deferential.

He occupied the cell next to the guard-room, on the left-hand side. Writing was his continual employment, when he was not praying or at exercise. A shelf formed his bed, and a small table stood alongside. In front of him was a metal statuette of St. Joseph; and when he was telling his beads he would carry this little image in his hands, and hug it. His countenance usually displayed a calm composure, and his grey eyes were nearly always bent on the ground, as though he were wrapt in contemplation and study. The literary work on which he was engaged was supposed to be a sort of *Apologia pro vita sua.* He commenced spouting French vigorously, one night, when all was still ; reading aloud from his manuscript. This brought the sergeant very briskly to the wicket ; he ordered me to " tell Riel to stop that racket ! "

I did so, and after he had subsided into silence, he came to his peep-hole and beckoned to me.

" I tell *you*—but, for the others—No ! " he exclaimed in a hurried *staccato.* " I *must* read. The Spirit tells me,--I *must.* I tell you—for fifteen years—it is since— that I have been a prophet on the Saskatchewan." This of course was a fable, and I knew it.

His confessor, Père André, was a constant visitor, with his unkempt beard and greasy cassock. This priest had left Brittany when quite young, to lead a hard life of exile amid far-off savages. His manners had become abrupt from much contact with the wily redskins. He was the very antithesis to the courtly abbé, of the glowing land of his youth.

A Medical Commission had been appointed to examine Riel as to the insanity alleged by his friends. When these gentlemen arrived, he was marched daily to the orderly-room, where the inquiry was conducted in private. Every one knows the result. I was standing by the open door of the cell, when Dr. Jukes, the principal medical officer of the mounted police, had a protracted interview with him. The doctor sat beside him for fully an hour, listening with exemplary patience to a random list of visions vouchsafed to this Metis apostle, which utterly eclipsed any of the mystic ecstasies of any ascetic of the Middle Ages. The doctor cross-examined him with considerable acumen; and it was amusing to note his skill in inveigling the astute Riel into contradictions. The arch-rebel, among a host of similar revelations, stated that St. Peter had appeared to him in the church of St. James at Washington, District of Columbia, and had ordered him to undertake his mission. This I heard him say.

I must say his conduct in prison was most exemplary, and he gave no trouble. Every request he made was most courteously worded. At 1.30 a.m., upon a certain Saturday, he requested me to endeavour to procure him some meat. Up till midnight he had fasted, as it was *un jour maigre*. Now, to look for meat in a prison during the small hours is about as forlorn a hope as to expect to find holy water in an Orange Lodge. However, I foraged among the cupboards in the corridor, and discovered a plate of hash, which I suppose had been put away by some unfortunate to serve as a *bonne bouche* at some needed moment.

On the Sunday previous to his execution I was on guard, and formed one of the escort when he was taken out for exercise. On this occasion we proceeded to the square patch of ground between the orderly room and the guard-room. The officer strolled about on the side-walk, while we stood at ease, one at each corner. Riel walked between us in a diagonal direction. A covered-in platform had been put up in the yard, at the rear of the prison, with all the grim accessories of the coming ceremony. Presently he asked me, pointing,—

" Is that the scaffold ? "

I said it was.

" Thank God ! " he exclaimed theatrically, " I do not fear the scaffold."

Then he grew excited, and appealed to the officer to send a telegram to his wife, who was at St. Boniface, the French suburb of Winnipeg. I remember the scene well : the figure holding the ball and chain on one arm, and gesticulating wildly with the disengaged hand.

Mass had been said every Sunday at a temporary altar in the prison ; Riel and the other Metis were always present. The guard at this time was very strict, and the walls of the place were hung with boards, each bearing a whole string of commands. The guard-room was terribly overcrowded every night, after the picquet mounted. It was very small, and resembled any other such building anywhere. There were guard-beds on either side, with racks for the carbines at their head. A stove was in the centre. A table stood opposite the entrance, with pen and ink, and a book to record the visits of the orderly officer and the surgeon. Above the table was a shelf, and over the latter ticked an ancient clock, which was a perpetual curse to all the watches in barracks. The bugler sounded the calls by this official timepiece, which either lost or gained one hour in the twenty-four.

The steeds which we were obliged to ride on patrol at this time were execrable. They were a lot about to be cast. We were not allowed to take our own troopers, and every man had a fresh mount on each

succeeding occasion.   At last the date of the execution
was definitely fixed, and extraordinary precautions to
prevent an expected rescue were taken.   Dismounted
bodies of men marched round the barracks at stated
intervals through the night.   Strong patrols, mounted,
were continually scouring the surrounding prairie.   The
date of this historical event was set down as the 16th
of November, 1885.

I was relieved from guard at 2 p.m. on the 15th.
Two hours afterwards I was warned for a special
mounted patrol at four o'clock on the following morning,
—the 16th—and I was also informed that I should be
for barrack-guard at 2 p.m. on the same day.   It was
not a bright prospect to a worn-out man.   My eyes
were sore and bloodshot.   I was haggard, and, in fact,
just properly done up, and of course I grumbled and
growled as every good soldier does.   Growling is his
especial privilege.   Did not "our army in Flanders"
swear terribly, and is not a trooper supposed to be a
past-master in this art?   This particular patrol, for
which I was detailed, was to consist of one corporal and
three men.

It was most bitterly cold and densely dark when we
turned out at half-past three on the eventful morning,
and stumbled over half-asleep to the stables, where a
dingy lantern was flashing about.   We saddled our
horses in silence.   Early as it was, Colonel Irvine was
here to inspect us, after we had mounted.   The only
road from the town, now, came past the rear of Government House, as the other bridge had been destroyed.
We were ordered to proceed to Mr. Dewdney's residence
and take up our station on the trail at that point, and
to allow no one to approach the barracks who did not
possess a pass properly signed.   We rode in half-
sections past the guard-room and out into the gloom of

the prairie. On our way to the bridge across the creek, we met the two priests, who were to attend upon Riel during his last moments, driving from town in a buckboard. The frost was very keen this morning, and our feet, in boots and spurs, suffered severely. When dawn stole gently over the plain, everything was white with hoar-frost. It was a magnificent sunrise! And on this heavenly morning, Louis David Riel was to look his last upon these prairies which he had loved so well. We rode quietly up and down, and whenever any object appeared we made it an excuse for a stirring gallop. When the sun had risen, we could see the polished arms of the sentries—a perfect ring,—around the barracks. Scouts were out in every direction, trotting off in the distance. Bugle-calls rang out in the clear air. An inner cordon of fifty men was posted around the guard-room at seven, and at the same hour a party of forty men, mounted, drew up at the end of the bridge opposite to us.

A crowd of people could now be seen advancing along the level plain from Regina, whose white houses were bright in the sunshine. Men on foot, on horseback, in buckboards, buggies, and "democrats," hurried along. There were visitors from Montreal, Toronto, Ottawa, and Winnipeg, and even from British Columbia. Those who were without passports were turned back, and we drew our horses across the trail, while the non-com. examined the papers. There was a good deal of pleasant chaff, and the voice of the great Nicholas Flood Davin, now Member for Assiniboia, in the Dominion House,—more power to his elbow!—was heard in the land; the brogue of the emerald isle sounding rich and racy. After the crowd had cleared away, a great silence seemed to have filled the air, save for the horses champing their bits and pawing the hard ground.

The *Regina Leader* gave the most minute description of the final scene in this drama, which has been of such importance in the history of the young Dominion.

Mr. Gibson, the deputy-sheriff, entered the condemned cell a few minutes before eight, and informed Riel that his hour had come. The latter turned ashy pale as soon as he realized his position, but braced himself together as well as he could. The procession was now formed. Riel was placed between Father McWilliams, who was first, and Père André, who was behind him. Mr. Gibson led the way. After this, Mr. White Fraser, who was our orderly officer, and ten men of the guard followed. Colonel Irvine and other officers of the mounted police, Dr. Jukes, and four members of the press brought up the rear. They ascended by steps to a room above the guard-room, which ran the entire length of the building. At the far end was a window, and through this was the scaffold. As they passed along, Riel exclaimed, " *Courage, mon père !* "

The hangman was Jack Henderson, who had been a former prisoner of Riel at Fort Garry in 1869. Verily the tables were turned with a vengeance! He was waiting on the platform. Before stepping out upon this, the priests and the prisoner knelt down in prayer ; all, except the guard, removing their hats. Riel made the responses in a firm voice. His whole demeanour betokened suppressed excitement ; his brow was covered with beads of perspiration, while he held a crucifix which had been lent to him by Madame Forget, the wife of the clerk to the N.W. Council. At twenty-five minutes past eight, the deputy-sheriff touched Father McWilliams on the shoulder, as an intimation that the time was up. Père André told Riel that they must cease. They all rose, and Père André asked the doomed

man if he were at peace with all men. Riel
answered in the affirmative.

" Do you forgive all your enemies ? "

" Yes."

Riel then asked if he might speak, but he was advised
not to do so. He then received the kiss of peace from
both priests, and Father André exclaimed,—

" *Alors, allez au ciel!* "

While the conversation was in progress, Henderson
had been engaged in pinioning the prisoner's arms. Dr.
Jukes, Colonel Irvine, with the two priests, and two of
the newspaper-men went out upon the platform. Riel
was placed upon the drop, where his legs were pinioned
and the rope adjusted. His last words were to say
good-bye to Dr. Jukes and to thank him for his kindness, and, just before the white cap was pulled over his
face, he said,—

" *Remerciez Madame Forget.*"

While he was praying the trap was pulled. Death
was instantaneous. His pulse ceased beating four
minutes after the trap-door fell. Thus ended the man
who had inaugurated and carried out two rebellions.
As for the wild outburst of political frenzy that swept
over the province of Quebec after the execution, is it
not written in the books of the chronicles of the time ?

Bugle-calls, the movements of men, and the returning
tide of visitors apprised us that the tragedy was over.
We fondly cherished a hope that now we should be
relieved, and that some welcome coffee and breakfast
would be waiting to cheer us over at the barracks. Nothing of the sort ! We were ordered to fall in with the
troop, and were kept marching and counter-marching,
merely to suit the whims of some one who was muddle-
headed enough to imagine it was of use. It was not
the colonel's wish, I am sure. He, and Lord Boyle, and

Colonel McLeod, C.M.G., were breakfasting together in his quarters.

At length came the order, "Leading-section, right!" And we went straight to the barrack-yard. "Form half-sections! Rear, halt! Half-sections, right! Halt! Prepare to dismount! Dismount! File to your stables" —and we trudged off with our reins upon our arms. As we were removing our saddles, the merry call to "stables" sounded, and consequently we had to wait until dinner-time to break our fast.

Now all these trivial details may not be of much interest to the ordinary reader. But it is the continual succession of such incidents that forms the reality of a soldier's life, and the wear and tear, and constant irritation therein. All is not beer and skittles. The whole duty of man in the ranks, is not simply to "slap your thigh with your cane and wink at the girls." And nowhere is the gilt so ruthlessly stripped off the gingerbread as in the North-West.

CHAPTER XVII

A miserable guard—Grand rounds—Riel's grave—Winter—1886—
A ball—Blizzards—Their power—Electric storms—Fatalities
—Newspaper amenities and fibs—Fort Macleod—Calgary—
Alberta—A garden—God's country—Chinook winds—Spring
—Usual rumours—Leave Regina—Moosejaw—A festive camp
—Easter Sunday—Out on the desert—Old Wives Lake—
Musings—Solitude—Wood Mountain.

I MOUNTED guard on the afternoon of Riel's execution
in no very enviable frame of mind. I possessed a disagreeable cold in the head, a sore throat, and the
conjunctivæ of my eyes were inflamed. The colonel
and the adjutant took possession of all the papers in
Riel's cell. I was on sentry at the back of the prison,
where the body was still lying, when "grand rounds"
came upon the scene, at 1 a.m. I was so hoarse, that
the captain asked me why I had neglected to challenge.
I replied I had done so.

Corporal : " Port arms ! Give over your orders."
An inaudible whisper crossed my lips, and floated into
space.

Orderly officer : " Send this man to hospital at sick-
call in the morning."

However, I waited until the guard was dismounted in
the afternoon, when the surgeon placed me on the
report as " off duty."

Riel's body was quietly removed to the Catholic
chapel in Regina, where it was watched by a squad of
our men in plain clothes. The remains were removed to
St. Boniface in a few days. Among the scanty trees, in

the little cemetery, beside the small cathedral on the right bank of the Red River, opposite Fort Garry, a plain wooden cross, bearing the simple words, " Louis David Riel—1885," marks the last resting-place of that uneasy spirit who was the cause of so much trouble, and who paid the fitting penalty of his unsuccessful treason.

The winter of 1885-6 glided over in the usual monotony of these far-off regions. The robe of spotless snow lay once more upon the prairie; and the icy winds howled around the wooden buildings, and piled the wreaths in fantastic shapes against the stables and barracks. In the early part of 1886 we gave a ball in the mess-room, which was tastefully adorned with lances, and trophies of arms, and mottoes. We sent the regimental sleighs down to Regina for our guests; all the rank and beauty of this sparse settlement attended, and officers' wives danced with men in the ranks.

In January also, a tearing, riotous blizzard swept across the desolate plains, and the night picquet was relieved every half-hour. The sentry-boxes were filled with snow, and, as no sane person would attempt to venture far, the shelter of the wash-house was used. The blizzard is a storm peculiar to the prairie regions, almost indescribable in its deathly power. It is the most terrible wind that rages upon earth ; a cloud burst of powdered ice, accompanied by a violent hurricane, with the thermometer away below zero. I am utterly impotent to describe the cold. During one blizzard in 1884 the thermometer in barracks showed thirty-seven degrees below zero, or sixty-nine degrees of frost, and the velocity of the wind—as measured by the anemometer on the top of the quartermaster's store—was fifty-five miles an hour! I refer the sceptical to the Canadian Meteorological Society. They give no warning.

Suddenly a small black cloud rises in a sky of brilliant blue, and the whole force of the storm is upon you in a few minutes.

These extraordinary storms are electric in origin, no doubt. During a blizzard in Regina in 1887, the stove and stovepipes in the guard-room and the iron bars in the prison emitted sparks when touched. One man received an electric shock when he lifted the poker. But the atmosphere in the North-West is often charged with electricity. I believe Lord Dunraven mentions this also in his book of travels, but I have not seen it for years.

In these terrible tempests, settlers have been known to have gone to feed their oxen in the stables, just a few yards from their own door ; and have been seen no more, alive. Some have been discovered when spring has lifted the shroud of winter ; their bones picked clean by the coyotes. Oxen have been frozen in their tracks. But any one can read the annual tale of devastation which is cabled across the Atlantic. It is utterly useless for the authors of emigration pamphlets to deny them. They do recur, and will continue to do so, in all the prairie lands, though in the dim future the increase of population may mitigate their severity.

When Dakota receives a visitation of this sort, Canadian editors flap their wings (non-angelic), and give forth a wild crow of exultation, and point to their own North-West, the great wheat-growing oasis, the magnificent, fertile belt, unvisited by blizzards at all. When this same North-West is enveloped in a whirlwind of this description, the Winnipeg or Toronto newspaper-man is silent, and is deeply absorbed in Fishery Treaties, or the affairs of Europe. Now is the time for him of Dakota to pile on the agony, and he whoops like a Sioux on the war-path. No storms like these visit the

American garden of Eden, which was the original cradle
of mankind. This absurd farce of trying to screech
each other down, like a couple of pugnacious washer-
women, does no good to either country. Blizzards are
just as severe in one place as the other. The reason
that so few lives are lost, comparatively, north of the
49th parallel of latitude, is that the population is
not there to suffer, and that is a very simple solution of
the problem.

While one of these hurricanes was raging we had to
wrap ourselves in buffalo coats to run a few yards to the
lavatory. On your return your towel was as stiff as an
iron target.

Fort Macleod is situated on the Old Man's River, and
near the Porcupine Hills, whose rounded forms,
scattered about, look like so many mole-heaps, against
the towering grandeur of the snow-capped Rockies.
The mounted police marched here, across the uninhabited
plains, in 1875, and founded the fort, living for the
first winter in " dug outs " in the ground. The present
site of the post is on an elevated plateau commanding a
superb view of the mountains. South of the town are
the extensive reserves of the Blood and Piegan Indians ;
members of the Blackfeet nation. Calgary is considered
the queen city of the far, far west, and is by far the most
prosperous and lively place in the Territories.

It stands, or reposes, in a basin ; which is walled in
by precipitous banks, and appears to be surrounded by
a couple of foaming, rushing, and tumbling torrents of
purest glacier water ; namely, the Bow and Elbow Rivers,
which here unite. A decade has not passed since the
buffalo grazed in the valley ; and now there are stone
buildings, theatre, rink, town-hall, churches, and banks,
and many costly and comfortable residences. Near
here is the Blackfeet reserve, with a population of 2200.

There is not the least doubt that the district of Alberta, in which these places are situated, is the garden of the North-West. It is peerless among the cattle countries of the world. I can unhesitatingly advise any one to go there. The class of settlers, too, is immensely superior to that in Assiniboia and Saskatchewan. This region was familiarly known as " God's country " amongst us.

Fort Macleod and Calgary were the two favourite stations of the mounted police ; as in these favoured localities the winters are shorter in duration, and considerably milder in temperature. The warm Chinook breezes, racing through the clefts in the mountain-wall from their home in the balmy Pacific Ocean, melt the snow as if by the touch of a magic wand. These winds receive their name from the Chinook, or Flathead, Indians of the western coast ; and blow periodically during the winter and spring. Fifty, forty, and sixty days have been the respective periods of the last three winters in Alberta ; and these days of cold were not consecutive. The nearer you journey to the Rockies, the milder becomes the climate. Men leaving Regina to reinforce the western posts, in the heavy furs of winter uniform, have discovered their comrades at Maple Creek wearing scarlet serges and forage caps ; and engaged in playing cricket, in March !

Spring came rapidly upon us at Regina, in 1886, after a comparatively mild winter. At the end of March, the brown of the prairie mud was everywhere in evidence; and the Wascana Creek was filled with its annual supply of turbid, yellow waters. The usual eruption of vivid scarlet and white, and yellow, with glittering brass and steel broke out upon the land ; as men swaggered off to town in the evening, or paraded on the square. The yearly rumours of intended movements were bartered

round, as soon as the first breath of the zephyrs began
to waft their spices over the plains.

"The Blackfeet have risen," whispers one mysterious
gentleman who is known to have a friend in the
cabinet, otherwise orderly-room. Another party draws
a fable from the myth-mine in his brain, and states it
as a fact that the sergeant-major has informed him that
"B" troop is going to Southern Manitoba. Some of
these legends are constructed with a skill that would do
credit to a Yankee editor, or a Russian *chargé-d'affaires.*
But they all end in smoke, for the unexpected invariably happens. As a matter of fact, the Blackfeet
nation generally do give trouble in the spring, owing to
the feverish restlessness of the younger braves, who are
anxious to distinguish themselves in some predatory
raid upon the Gros Ventres across the frontier. But
they are merely individual cases of crime, confined to a
few of the *mauvais sujets*, and not an organized opposi-
tion to lawful authority.

On the 1st of April, 1886, Colonel Irvine resigned
his post as Commissioner of the North-West Mounted
Police, to the regret of all. He was succeeded by Mr.
Lawrence Herchmer, who had been Indian agent at
Birtle, in ˌManitoba, and who, at one time, had served
as a subaltern in H.M. 46th foot. At this time the
mounted infantry system of drill, for all field movements,
and purposes of organization, was ordered to be adopted
throughout the force.

It began now to be generally known that our troop
was to proceed to the International Boundary, with
headquarters at Wood Mountain. This abandoned
post was 100 miles to the south of Moosejaw, and
twenty miles from the frontier-line, in the midst of a
wild region, devoid of settlement, and near the haunts
of the most notorious Western horse-thieves. It was

formerly one of the principal stations of the police, indeed one of the most important, for it was here that Sitting Bull and his braves, with all the squaws and children of the Sioux, had encamped after their massacre of General Custer and his command, and their flight for protection to British soil.

The log buildings of the old fort were ruinous now, but it was a great place for "high old times," when the teepes of the feathered and painted warriors were grouped around the walls. Major Walsh was commandant then. It was only after a good deal of correspondence with the Department at Ottawa that this summer rendezvous was fixed upon. A member of the N.W.M.P. can never lay any plans for his future. We had actually paraded on the barrack square, in full marching order,— baggage on waggons and bedding rolled up—for Battleford, when we were suddenly dismissed. And now, our destination was 500 miles in the other direction. Verily ' a policeman's life is not happy." A new scheme to defeat the contrabandists along the boundary was being inaugurated. Four troops were to be engaged in patrolling the whole extent of the United States frontier from Manitoba to the Rocky Mountains—a distance of 700 miles—during the ensuing summer. Permanent camps were to be established, at intervals, along this line. Parties, armed and mounted, were to leave these weekly, and meet at certain places on stated days. They were to arrest all horse-thieves, and "study the disposition of the half-breeds and Indians on both sides of the line."

The coulées and wooded ranges of the Missouri Valley were haunts of the most lawless desperadoes, who endeavoured to run their contraband cargoes of horse-flesh into the Territory. It is, in the first place, a crime to bring stolen property into Canada, and, moreover, there is a duty of twenty per cent. *ad valorem* on all horses, ponies, and cattle. Both these laws the freebooters try to evade. And the American Indians were also suspected of intended inroads. There were a good many disaffected redskins along the Missouri Valley, in Montana. Many had fled thither after the rising on the Saskatchewan. In addition, there were the half-breed settlements, which had been reinforced by Gabriel Dumont, Dumais, and other firebrands who had escaped from Batoche. Dumont was known to be stirring up the feelings of the excitable Metis in every direction.

Thursday, April 2nd, the day of our marching out, arrived in the warmth of brilliant sunshine. All around the prairie grass was springing green, and the trails were dry and firm. We paraded at 2 p.m., and went through the ordeal of inspection by the new commissioner. I wonder how many different horses I have ridden in the N.W.M.P. I could never keep a good trooper long, somehow, owing to my continued oscillation between duty and staff work. I was a sort of general utility man for the troop, and was pitchforked into the quarter-master sergeant's berth when he was on the sick-list, or given charge of the hospital, with the utmost impartiality. And still, the fourfold chevron never adorned my arm.

On our departure for Wood Mountain, I was mounted on a gigantic grey, a most ungainly brute from Ontario, whose back was more adapted for a howdah than a saddle. The barrack square was lined with officers, their wives, families and servants, and our comrades of the depôt, to see us march out into the desert, for an exile of seven months.

Our advance-guard had reached the canteen, when one of the men composing it was thrown violently from the

young broncho which he was riding, upon the back of
his head, and was carried insensible to the hospital,
suffering from concussion of the brain. He lost the
sight of his right eye by the fall, and was afterwards
invalided, with a pension of seventy-five cents per diem.

Our march westward was slow. The waggons were all
heavily laden, as they carried, in addition to our baggage
and rations for the journey, the complete equipment
for the summer-camp. And these ships of the American
desert toiled slowly on. The "prairie schooner" is
almost a thing of the past. It consisted of three
waggons lashed together, and drawn by a string of as
many as twenty oxen, the drivers of which were known
as bull-whackers. The prairie west of Regina, over
which our route lay, is flat and hideously monotonous.
The trail ran along the northern side of the railway.

We passed the station of Grand Coulée, a water-tank
and a house painted brown, above a ravine with smooth
and verdant slopes, where we made a short halt, and
reclined upon the turf with our bridles in our hands.
We encamped for the night at Pense, where there is a
station, and a ramshackle store of "miscellaneous notions,"
about seventeen miles from Regina. The waggons were
drawn round, and a corral constructed, inside which we
fastened up our horses; a guard-tent was pitched, the
others were soon standing in a double row. The glare
of the camp-fire lit up the darkness, and figures in cloaks
and boots and spurs stood in silhouette against the ruddy
blaze. The picquet was posted, and we lay down upon
the ground beneath the canvas, and slept the sleep of
the weary. *Reveillé* sounded amid the slumbering tents
at 5 a.m., and after a breakfast of tea and biscuit the
bugle called us into the saddle again. A fresh scampering breeze came gaily over the wide expanse of
waving grass. The horses tossed their heads with glee,

the jingling of the bridles and accoutrements made pleasant music, and every one felt the blood coursing rapturously through his veins, with the joyous exhilaration of the spring. I was given another steed to-day whose elephantine proportions had secured him the name of Jumbo. I must say Jumbo was the most delightful horse to sit, at the trot, I ever bestrode. His great fat form, of a dark bay tint, was soft and easy as an armchair. The same flat plain lay all around us, but we chatted and sung and joked as we went along. The freedom of the prairies was before us, where the saddle is one's home, and where a stirring gallop is worth a king's ransom. Only beware of gopher holes! The Ontario horse is never safe, but the wiry little broncho avoids them with the nimbleness of a sword-dancer. Give him his head, do not attempt to guide him, or you will pull him in, and over you go! We interviewed a camp of half-breeds, beside the railway, to-day. Massive piles of buffalo bone adorned the vicinity of their dingy, ragged tents, where unkempt women and children, in various degrees of nudity, were visible through the smoke. The men were engaged in gathering the collection of bone into Red River carts, bringing it to the line for shipment to the States, where it is supposed to be used in the adulteration of fine, white, powdered sugar. These children of the wilds receive about four cents a pound for it. Thousands of tons of this substance lie bleaching on the plains. At 3 p.m. we forded the dark Moosejaw Creek, a stream which brawled and foamed over a pebbly bed, between banks fringed with willows. The town of Moosejaw lies in a hollow of the prairie, and is the end of a section of the Canadian Pacific Railway. Here is a round house for engines. The population is 500, and there is the usual scattering of hotels and stores, standing at intervals upon the unromantic flat. Ugly square objects all of them, without the slightest pretence to architectural beauty. A prairie town is a more depressing object than a burnt forest.

We pitched our tents on the western outskirts, on a piece of level ground near the creek, and made the regulation corral with our waggons. To my great chagrin, I found myself on picquet to-night, first relief, and I was thereby prevented from enjoying the luxury of a "square meal" in town, as I had anticipated. At nine o'clock, there was a general disturbance all along the horse lines, owing to the high spirits of a few juvenile bronchos. It was a species of impromptu circus, and several steeds were tied up in their ropes in a manner which might have puzzled Messrs. Maskelyne and Cooke. The camp was deserted, and I did not care to disturb the other men of the guard, who were asleep. I set to work to free the struggling brutes, and my muttered prayers and benedictions brought out the captain. It was dark as pitch, and my lantern had been sent flying sky high by the heels of one unmanageable animal. The corporal of the guard was summoned from the tent, and as the orderly sergeant was unaccountably absent, our "centurion" suddenly gave the order to call the roll. This was a very simple proceeding, as no one was present but the picquet!

The captain retired, and by-and-by the men returned in half sections, or rather in skirmishing order, in a manner unprovided for by the articles of war. The ginger wine of the Moosejaw saloons and various other blandishments of the hospitable inhabitants had evidently been too much for the weak nerves of our troopers. A battery of the Canadian Artillery was, at this time, stationed here, and the two branches of the service had been fraternizing. In addition, there were a number of lodges of Sioux, to which many had repaired to study the manners and customs of the natives.

In the morning, I obtained a pass for the day, and enjoyed myself in town, after breakfast at an hotel. The whole command was up before the captain at eleven ; and when asked to account for their absence, on the preceding evening, they each and all declared that they were asleep beneath the waggons, as they could not think of sleeping in tents during such mild weather !

In an abominable drizzle in the raw, leaden dawn of Easter morning, we left Moosejaw and its' seductions, and bid farewell to human habitations for months. I was now mounted on horse No. 3, and Jumbo ornamented the off side of a waggon pole. South of the town, the lonely prairie is "rolling," or broken into low hillocks with shallow *coulées*. No house is visible on its surface. You may travel to the mighty Missouri and see no sign of man. We passed a long string of Red River carts and waggons, on the trail, bound for Wood Mountain with our stores, which were provided by a contractor in Regina. These were drawn by oxen, under the charge of Riel's executioner. We had our dinner by the shores of Rush Lake, which is nothing else than a sedgy pool, haunted by wild fowl, in the breeding season. A fierce sun shone out in the afternoon, though a keen wind was blowing. Not a sight nor sound to relieve the desolation of this lone land ! In the evening our white tents were ranged by the silent shores of Old Wives Lake—an immense sheet of water —behind the solitary waves of which the sun was setting in a blaze of crimson glory. The rosy light tinged ripple and island with a mystic hue ; adding a strange glamour . to the dream-like scene. A wild region, truly. To-night, as I lay smoking my pipe, and looked around the camp, in the stillness of this far-off *coulée*, my mind went back to the olden days, when first the rude adventurers pushed their way into the wilderness, the days of Da Soto and the rest.

What anticipations of the future filled the mind of the soldiers, of the bygone time, as they thus stood looking out upon the threshold of the Unknown? What visions of the El Dorado in the enchanted mountains beyond, must have thrilled their daring souls! What tales to tell on the marble quays of Genoa, and beneath the splendours of the throne of Spain! What riches would they carry to show to that old man, tottering about among his gardens and fountains at Versailles? And we, what a mere handful we seemed on these vast rolling plains! Yet it was only a day's march from the prosaic railway-cars. How must the giants of old have felt, when thousands of miles from their towering galleons? Or the intrepid French blackrobes, a thousand miles from the canoes that would carry them to Mont Royal or Hochelaga?

Old Wives Lake is of great area, and we could not see the opposite shore. A few grey gulls flew screaming over the unhealthy waters, which are undrinkable. It is useless describing the petty incidents of this lonely march. There was the same solitude, the same brown trail always visible, running like a ribbon for miles ahead, the same hillocks and the same silent lakes. The desert lay all around us, as we slowly marched southward. We saw the blue barrier of Wood Mountain rising through the haze, like a wall in front, along the horizon while yet far off. We passed the Thirty Mile Lake on our left, its green waters frothy with alkaline foam. It lay in a deep cup, with bare sides of seamed earth, rising sheer, like ramparts all around. It looked a haunted spot. We found ourselves among the hills on the third day. They were scarped and terraced and riven into ghastly chasms. Tier upon tier rose like giant stairs, in places, where the waters of this once mighty sea had left their mark as they subsided. Strange shells are still found upon the summits, and on the crumbling slopes. Green valleys here and there repose, deep and hidden, with bushes lining the crystal brooks that bubble through them.

It was a fine afternoon, as we descended into the broad valley where the old Mounted Police post lay. Far away below us, Mosquito Creek, like a silver thread, wound through between emerald slopes, while upon a level sweep of verdure, surrounded by a dense mass of bush, stood some long, low, grey log-buildings in the form of a square. This was the fort. Some cattle were grazing among the hills, and down in the lone meadows a few ponies were browsing. An ex-trooper of the force had married a Sioux squaw, built himself a hut, and squatted here. He made some money in the summer by bringing horses over from Montana, and disposing of them in Moosejaw, and, in addition, he was sometimes employed as a scout and guide, for Jim spoke Sioux to perfection. When we reached the ruinous barracks the view was very pretty. Behind, was a gently-sloping bank covered with a delightful grove of trees, through which many footpaths led to the creek. A wide vale ran up between the hills in front, and all around, except in front, were trees ; above which rose the rounded summits of the mountains, as they were termed, though but pigmies in comparison with any known range.

CHAPTER XVIII

Life at Wood Mountain—Unseasonable snow—Delights of rough-ing it—A capture—Gros Ventre Indians—Dirt—The old fort —Dust—Short rations—Fine weather—Patrols—Heat—A stampede—Antelope and sage hens—A sandhill crane—A primitive meal for a hungry man—Indian spies—Sign language —On sentry—Dawn—Gambling—Field-days—Indian graves —A ranche—Cowboys—A suggestion on dress—" Toughs "— Indian depredation and a skirmish.

A PLATEAU, running out like a promontory above the stream, was chosen as the situation for our camp, and, after unloading the waggons, we soon had the canvas streets laid out, showing white against the lofty back-ground of green. The unwelcome sound of *reveillé*, rang out at six on the following morning, and, as we turned out drowsily, the dismal scene sent us in again quickly to secure cloaks. Everything was covered with a soft damp snow, and the leaden atmosphere was filled with driving sleet. After the warm weather we had recently enjoyed, it was the reverse of pleasant to stand in the slush, ankle-deep, with icy feet, and by a spluttering, hissing camp-fire to eat granite biscuit and drink luke-warm coffee in the gloom of this execrable morning. We stood stamping our feet, and sipping the muddy concoction, while the sleet slowly melted in our metal cups. This sort of weather makes men morose. Let none of my younger readers, if there should be any such, ever be tempted by any romantic ideas to leave a comfortable home, merely for the sake of " seeing life." It is all very well in the path of duty, and by all means, when called upon, let them face it bravely and cheerily. But there is no romance about it at all. I know the prevailing idea among the 'rising generation is, " It must be awfully jolly, roughing it, and that sort of thing, don't you know ? " But in this case, it is distance which lends enchantment to the view.

We began now to make preparations for settling down here in earnest. The fort had to be cleaned out, and any buildings utilized that were not too ruinous. The square was deep with manure, even to the roofs. Indians, half-breeds, and horse-thieves had taken shelter here in the winter. Indeed, I have forgotten to state that a Norwegian was captured here in a snow-storm during the previous January, by a party despatched from Regina, under Inspector McGibbon. It was managed very cleverly, and he was taken completely, by surprise. This man had stolen forty-five ponies from the Gros Ventre Indians in Montana. He was escorted to Regina during the intense cold that reigned over this awful waste ; and was ultimately sentenced to a couple of years' imprisonment for bringing stolen property into Canada. The ponies were confined in a corral between two of the stables, and each fresh sentry had to count them over. One of the Gros Ventres and a half-breed came over from the American side to identify the stock. I have now a very high opinion of the Gros Ventres, and this is the reason. During his stay in our barracks, this native gentleman occupied a bed in No. 6 room, where I was quartered. Every morning he proceeded to our lavatory, and sedulously bathed his muscular, copper-hued arms and melancholy countenance. I often lent him my soap, and used to pat him on the back for his bravery. For an Indian voluntarily to wash himself, is about as revolutionary a proceeding as it would be for an archbishop to dance the *can-can*. The Sioux and Blackfeet bathe occasionally ; the Crees, never. Big Bear's horror of the cleansing process was comic. His breech-clout had done duty for a decade, and was as black as the ace of spades, which, by the way, it rather resembled.

After this digression, it will not require many words to explain that the nomads, who had used the old fort as a *Dâk bungalow* or caravanserai, had not left it a pattern of cleanliness and order. So the cleansing out process was our first general fatigue, and all hands were set to work with manure forks and spades. The four sides of this structure were about eight feet in height. The buildings were of logs, while poles, closely ranged together, formed the substratum of the roofs, which were flat. The top was coated with a thick layer of mud and clay. On the east, was a tall stockade of massive pieces of timber, with a couple of huge solid gates, which were now utterly useless. A long range of stables, with a flooring of poplar poles, ran along the south. The buildings on the west side were connected with the stables by a stockade in which was a wicket, or postern, opening on the wooded slope behind. The huts contiguous to this consisted of a carpenter's shop, quartermaster's store, and a small apartment with two windows, in which the troop baker was installed. The buildings on the north, at right angles to the foregoing, were in a much better condition. The windows actually possessed glass, and the floors were boarded. The corner shanty was appropriated by the sergeant major, and the one adjoining was handed over to the hospital sergeant and his pharmacopœia. Next to this came the saddle-room, and the cook-house followed. At the eastern end was the blacksmith's shop. A comfortable log-house stood on the edge of the wood, outside the barracks. This was fitted up as officers' quarters, and here also lived the telegraph operator.

There was a single wire between here and Moosejaw, solely for Government use. We luckily were not troubled with mud, as the camp stood upon gravelly soil. The dust, however, made up for this. It drifted into the tents, and covered up your plate at meal-times, with a thick, dingy powder. We hung our tunics and jackets on the centre poles, and they soon lost their bright scarlet tint, in the insufferable dust-storm. It filled our blankets, as we unrolled them on the ground at night. The looking-glass against the pole, which we used when shaving, was always more or less opaque. Our blue cloth pants were brown in no time. We lounged about in jerseys without jackets, and when we arose from a recumbent position (there were no seats) we were enveloped in a covering of this compound. On the day after our arrival our bacon gave out. As the stove had not arrived for the cook-house, and our mess-tent had not been pitched, we took our food *al fresco* by the side of the bubbling creek, which was convenient for the filling of the camp kettles. When we finished we wiped our knives on the grass and stuck them in the sheath which we each wore on a strap round the waist.

Owing to the failure of the pork supply, we were reduced to sugarless tea and hard-tack. There was no sign of old Jack Henderson and his train of supplies on the fourth day of our enforced fast, so the captain purchased a steer from the squatter, which we killed. As we had no salt, it was not much of a luxury. It was during this *régime* of tea and biscuit, and while we were working like navvies, excavating the mountain of manure, that the privilege of the British soldier, to growl, was used to its full extent. After driving a double row of posts well into the ground opposite the officers' quarters, and stretching a couple of long ropes their entire length, we fastened our horses to them and placed a picquet there every night. There was a big haystack alongside, which had been put up during the previous summer. The rumbling old Red River carts with our stores, did not come creaking and wheezing into the square of the fort till twenty-one days had elapsed from the time of their departure from Moosejaw! For slowness and "pure cussedness," generally, commend me to oxen.

Pleasant, sunny days set in, the breeze came laughing gaily from the west, the green leaves rustled on tree and bush, the birds carolled in the fragrant copsewood and flashed their brilliant plumage against the azure sky ; and the odour of the wolf-willow and the wild rose filled the air. The members of the staff were soon established within the stockade, the stores bundled into the dilapidated quartermaster's building, and a large mess-tent erected in the centre of the square. Our benches were simply square logs nailed upon stakes ; and our table was made of planks.

The patrols from this camp, along the frontier-line, were at once set going. One party left the camp weekly, proceeding westward to the crossing of the White Mud River, near to Pinto Horse Butte, where they connected with a similar patrol from " A " Troop, which was stationed in the ravines of the Cypress Hills. Willow Bunch is a half-breed settlement, forty-five miles to the east of Wood Mountain. Here a detachment was posted, which sent one man weekly to head-quarters, and a patrol eastward to meet another from the Souris River. These expeditions are fully armed of course, and remain out upon the prairie for a week. A transport waggon is attached to each, carrying tent, bedding, rations of tea, biscuit, bacon and oats, a spade, axe, camp-kettles and frying-pan, and wood. It is dreary work this everlasting monotonous ride, at a slow pace, over the same trail, dusty and hot, or muddy and cold, with nothing to brighten the weary view. On this eastern portion of the Boundary, there is not so much chance of meeting with any Indian adventures. Those left in charge of the post when the patrols were out, had a dull time of it; and of course each one had his share of this duty. In camp we loafed around, bathed in the creek, played cards under the sweltering canvas, sitting on the dusty ground, swept up around the horse-lines, did our turn at picquet and fatigues, smoked, yawned, slept on the grass in the shadow of the fort, or took the horses out and herded them. They were driven out every morning to graze in one of the many valleys, and brought in again for evening stables. Two men mounted and armed, were told off for this purpose each morning.

The heat, during the summer of 1886, was most intense, and never a cloud flecked the brazen sky. The ground was riven into gaping cracks, the prairie grass lay withered and dead, and a shimmering glare quivered on the surface of the yellow earth. A favourite walk of mine, in the cool of the evening, was away up among the hills, following the lean poles of the telegraph wire. About two miles from camp, was a deep *coulée*, clad in a dense undergrowth of bush, and surmounted by poplar and oak. The sides of this ravine were a perfect blaze of wild roses, for a time, and the air was heavy with their delicious fragrance. An awful solitude hung around as the wan light of the gloaming softly fell upon the scene. It was like living in a magic world.

A few of us were sitting upon a fallen log outside the

gate of the fort one still evening, puffing away at our
short pipes, and making casual remarks as we watched
the antics of a pet spaniel, when a waggon, full of
people, emerged from the hollow of the creek. It was a
police party ; and several dejected-looking men were
sitting upon a pile of baggage, with legs dangling down
over the sides. The sergeant sat, in front beside the
driver. These forlorn and sheepish individuals were the
members of the White Mud patrol, which had left camp
a few days previously. All their horses, with the
exception of the team, had stampeded, and gone off
into Montana. These stampedes arise from various
causes. One restless animal may start an entire herd.
A thunderstorm of unusual severity, mosquitoes, " bull-
dog " flies, or coyotes will each cause horses to break
away from their picket-pins.

It was exceedingly lucky that the men had been left
with means of transport, as this trail is deficient in water,
and at the time they were eighty miles from camp. The
sergeant in charge, was in a sad way. He used to
parade daily with a broken hopple, which he vehemently
declared was the *fons et origo* of the whole calamity.
Luckily some horse-traders, white men, *en route* from Fort
Belknap, found the missing bronchos and brought them
into Wood Mountain. They were discovered sixty miles
south of the frontier !

The land in the White Mud River district is very
poor, covered with cactus plants and wild sage. Out
here, we once managed to shoot a few sage hens. They
are larger than prairie chicken, to which I prefer them,
and are strongly flavoured with sage. We also bagged
a quantity of antelope during the season ; until we
became tired of venison. It is a pretty little animal,
weighing on an average 40 lbs. They are easily
secured, by displaying a white flag ; for, while they are

gazing at this strange object, you can generally manage to stalk them and pick them off.

One of our fellows shot a sandhill crane, on one occasion, while herding the horses. He brought this immense ornithological specimen to camp, when he came in to dinner, leaving his comrade in charge of the stud of troopers. This latter individual was the most ferocious *gourmand* in the troop; and was in a chronic state of famine. When the other returned, and he was at liberty to have his innings, he mounted, and galloped off at full speed, with joyous anticipations of dinner. After tying up his horse, he strode with his usual swagger (he had a pair of fierce black moustaches) to the kitchen.

"By the rock of Cashel, boys, I'm mighty hungry! Say, Dan, shure where's my dinner, at all?"

"Oh, we saw you coming, Dub. You'll find it over in the tent."

Dub vanished with fiery expectation glowing in his breast. What was his surprise, on entering the canvas dining-room, to find the gigantic bird, feathers and all, with wings outspread, on a clean table, with a knife and fork at either end! And what was worse,—*there was nothing else!* He never forgave that cruel joke.

Towards the end of the month of June many rumours were circulated regarding the movements of the Indians on the American side. Daily, scouting parties were sent out towards the frontier-line, proceeding by the Cart Coulée and Poplar River trails. A detachment of U.S. Infantry was stationed at Wolf Point, where the Poplar River joins the Missouri. Their commanding officer paid us a visit at Wood Mountain, and I heard him mention the distance as 120 miles.

A couple of tall, bony Assiniboine Indians rode slowly into camp one sunny afternoon. They were clad in dirty white blanket coats with tasseled hoods, and wore the usual leggings and moccasins; their heads were devoid of any covering, as is their custom. It is only on the war-path that the redskin adorns his head. Silently they moved across the Creek and pitched their teepe upon an eminence opposite to us. They had come from the reserve at Indian Head, and had had five "sleeps" upon the way; for by this method the noble red man calculates the length of his journeys. The language of each Indian tribe is totally distinct from the other. A Sioux cannot understand a Cree, or a Blackfoot, nor can any of them understand a Chipweyan or an Assiniboine. But they have a sign language, known to them all from the Athabasca to the Rio Grande. Thus by laying the head in the attitude of slumber upon the palm of the hand, they convey the idea of night. There are two tribes of the Assiniboines— or Stonies;—those of the plains and those of the mountains. The latter have been driven into these fastnesses by the Crees, and are expert hunters and splendid guides. Our two visitors drove a packhorse before them; it carried the teepe poles, skins, and provisions. They were fine specimens of the savage, and brought credentials to the officer commanding from the Big Chief at headquarters. The fact of the matter was, these two gentlemen were being sent over to the Missouri as spies, to discover, if possible, what truth there was in the persistent statements as to an intended raid. In ten days they returned, and reported all quiet in the camps which they had visited. Little Poplar, the bloodthirsty son of Big Bear, had been shot dead, in a fight with a half-breed near Fort Belknap. It is supposed that he was wilfully drawn into a quarrel so that there might be an excuse to get rid of such a nuisance.

On June 28th the Canadian Pacific Railway was

opened from Quebec to Vancouver, a total distance of
3065 miles !

Sentry duty at night is always, more or less, lonely,
except upon the well-lighted gate of a barrack at home,
where there are generally incidents enough to keep one's
interest alive.   But here the feeling of solitude weighed
upon you incessantly.   You turned out with cloak and
sidearms and carbine, for three hours and a half at a
stretch, and felt yourself the central figure in a sleeping
world.   Every one was wrapped in slumber but yourself.
The tents stood grey and ghostly in the darkness.   The
outline of the hills rose black, and solemn, and silent,
against the sky.   Not a sound save the movement of
some horse upon the lines or the far-off lazy murmur
of the Creek.   Sometimes the wild howl, and diabolic
laughter of some prowling coyote would startle you,
pealing suddenly from the darksome valley.   One would
wonder, often, in this far-away seclusion of the night
watches, if there actually existed a busy world.   Was it
really a fact that, far away beyond that dismal barrier
of lone and silent hills, the sun was shining on the gay
life of glittering cities, on park and boulevard ?   Could
it be possible that even then ; as you were wheeling
round to go over the beaten track once more ; in some
other quarter of the globe, dazzling ball-rooms were
gay with dancers, and theatres were all ablaze with
jewelry and bright eyes ?   One seemed to have died,
and to be walking in a spirit-land of dreams.

How often have I watched the day break here !   The
morning star would gleam alone, like some precious stone
suspended in the deep vault that sprang its arch from
behind the curved ridge in the range of hills, a little to
the North of East.   Then it would grow pale, and fade
away in the saffron light that came stealing up so softly,
and   a   strange   emerald   tint   would   mingle   with   it,

and rest upon the horizon. Then great bars of orange and crimson and amethyst would give place to a rosy blush all over the sky, and spears of light would flash around, and up would come, in splendour, the orb of day. The birds would twitter in the groves, and the waters flash into myriads of crystal gems.

After evening stables, when not on patrol, we amused ourselves in various ways. Quoits and gymnastics on the horizontal bar took up the time of many, while others went in for the subtle seductions of poker. Money is always plentiful in a camp like Wood Mountain, and many neophytes took to gambling, merely *pour passer le temps*. I have known a constable lose one hundred dollars at a sitting. Of course, it is prohibited, but—*quis custodiet ipsos custodes ?* Those of a contemplative turn of mind went for a stroll up the lonely valleys, all wrapped in the glamour of the glowing eventide. The dryness of the season and the heat were too much for the mosquitoes, and we were comparatively free from these pests.

Occasionally we were treated to a field-day, when we were put through the usual skirmishing drill of mounted infantry. And we would march away far into the heart of solitary glens and wooded *coulées*, never before visited by white men. Strange fantastic turns these miniature mountains take. They have the contour of a gigantic range of cloud-capped summits, and yet they are mere mole-hills of gravel, in comparison, even with the Cleveland or Cotswold Hills.

Numbers of Indian graves were to be seen around the camp. Each burial place consists of four lofty poles, supporting a platform of boughs. Upon it, the body is laid, tied up in buffalo robes with shagannappi. Gun and ammunition are placed alongside to help the brave in the happy hunting-grounds. Upon a lofty ridge, to the

right of the fort, rose the sepulchre of a squaw, who had
been killed because she had given birth to twins. The
medicine-men had pronounced this untoward circumstance as "bad medicine," and the unhappy woman was
executed accordingly, and the papooses buried with
her. The husband could not interfere.

The papoose of a Sioux squaw had died here in 1885.
The little body was hung up among the branches of some
trees beside the creek. When the Sioux camped near us,
this summer, the face of the tiny corpse was reverently
coloured with vermilion, every week ; just as we should
deposit a wreath to show our affection.

Colonel Scheetz, representing the Home Cattle
Company of St. Louis, Missouri, arrived at Wood
Mountain about the 8th of June, accompanied by an
American officer and some cowboys, to establish headquarters, and make the necessary arrangements for
their ranche, which was to be established in the
immediate vicinity of our post. Scheetz was a tall
fine-looking man, with long, dark moustache. He was
clad in a suit of brown courderoy. Each of the party
wore huge white sombreros of buckskin, and each was
armed with a revolver, carried in a leather holster,
attached to a cartridge belt. The Colonel's weapon
possessed an elegant ivory handle, inlaid with silver.
The cavalcade was mounted on splendid bronchos, and
was accompanied by a large covered spring waggon
drawn by a team of four magnificent bays.

En route from Helena, Montana, were 7000 head of
cattle, belonging to this company, which were to be
followed in a short time, by an additional 10,000.
They proposed to bring in a total of 26,000 head, and
had secured a lease of 700,000 acres for twenty-one
years.

These cowboys are quite at home in the saddle, and

ride with a perfectly straight leg. They are very expert with a *lariat* and running noose, sending it whirling through the air at full gallop, and catching the
wildest steer deftly by the foot. The *lariat* is attached
to the high pommel of their Californian saddles, which
are lined with steel to stand the strain, and their horses
are trained to a nicety to plant their four sturdy legs
firmly out, at a given moment.

Now these "cowpunchers," as they are sometimes
called, are written down by Eastern editors as desperadoes. The newspaper man, "down East," invests them
with a thick haze of fiction. He pictures them as generally engaged in revolver practice in drinking-bars, and
in the artistic occupation known as "painting the town
red." He imagines them to have been suckled by rat-
tlesnakes, and to live, in maturer age, on whisky and
ground glass. This educator of the public intelligence
thinks he has hit off an irresistible idea when he pens
such an item as the following. "The body of a man
was discovered on West Twenty-Fourth Street this
morning. As nothing was found upon him, but a six-
shooter, a deck of cards, and a plug of tobacco, we are
right in surmising he was a cowboy." I am really
almost ashamed to have to use such language, but I can
only characterize the above as arrant bosh. Does my
Oriental inkslinger know, I wonder, that on some
ranches there are schools, and reading-rooms. These
types of Western life, are, as a rule, quiet and unassum-
ing, though full of a reckless courage ; warm-hearted
and generous to a fault ; and given to the most unbounded hospitality. They must of necessity lead a
life of hardship, and often it is a life of danger.

A huge, soft-brimmed hat shades their sunburnt features, their legs are cased in *chaparajos* (or "shaps ")—
overalls of calf-skin—and they wear huge Mexican

spurs, with jingling pendants. They are invariably armed, owing to the exigences of a nomad life in a wild country. During this summer a band of them were encamped in the six-mile. coulée, and we fraternized the whole time. They were some of the best-hearted fellows I ever came across.

I regret to say that this ranche had to be abandoned because the Dominion Government was unable to remit the duty of twenty per cent. upon the proposed importation of cattle. In addition to the duty, there is also a charge of ten cents per head to be paid to the Government Veterinary Inspector, who examines all stock entering the Territory. Many large herds passed our camp during the summer, the cowboys riding in rear and hovering on the flanks of the dusty column, with long whips of raw hide. This was owing to the prevalence of immense prairie fires south of the Boundary, which rendered it necessary to bring cattle into Canada in order to drive them from Dakota to Montana. They were taken care of by the patrols, and handed over from one outpost to the other.

Our horses suffered severely from thirst during the intense heat, and actually, on the trail between Wood Mountain and Moosejaw, there was a distance of sixty miles between water, owing to the dryness of the season. As a rule, one of our waggons was despatched weekly to the latter place for supplies and mail, but our letters were uncertain. There was usually great excitement on the arrival of the mail, and when the team was expected we used to mount the roof of the fort, and eagerly scan the horizon with field-glasses. Bets would be made as to the exact time the waggon would reach the post.

On these patrols the bipeds suffered from want of decent drinking-water as well as the quadrupeds. This stuff had to be taken from brackish sleughs and carried in bottles or kegs, and became warm and sickening in the blazing heat of the sun. Our cavalry forage caps were utterly useless out on the burning plains. They afford no protection whatever to the eyes, and to wear them habitually injures the sight. The white helmets were far too heavy ; nothing at all like those in use in India. Therefore we purchased slouch hats, at our own expense. I think the Government should issue a dress for summer duty on the prairie, something after the fashion of that worn by the Cape Mounted Police. Major Jarvis has recommended a suit of dark brown cord, or velveteen breeches, long boots and spurs, a heavy blue flannel shirt, and a broad-brimmed hat of soft felt to complete the outfit. Certainly our scarlet and blue was utterly ruined after a little work round a camp fire.

We were not much troubled with horse-thieves in our section of the country, although a few " tough " looking customers were brought in by the patrols, and detained until the account which they gave of themselves was verified by telegraphic inquiries. A "tough " in Western parlance is akin to a " rough " at home ; only the former is a more finished ruffian, and conducts his operations on an extensive scale. Holding up a train and robbing the express car of its valuables, or riding into a frontier town and clearing out the bank, in broad daylight, are the exploits which this type delights in. Montana and Wyoming at one time swarmed with such outlaws.

A few half-breeds occasionally pitched their torn and blackened tents beside us and paid duty upon sundry bands of ponies. These cayeuses were generally purchased from the Gros Ventres, and the average declared value was thirteen dollars each. A patrol of " A " Troop, —our neighbours to the West—suddenly pounced upon a couple of horse-thieves in a deep valley of long waving grass, known as Davis' Coulée, in the remote recesses of the Cypress range. These two were sitting by their camp fire, smoking, in the gloaming of a summer evening, with their stolen herd grazing quietly around the verdant slopes of the lone glen, when our fellows rode down upon them, and told them to throw up their hands. They were moving arsenals, each of them having a couple of Smith and Wesson six-shooters, and a Winchester repeating rifle as well.

An outpost in the Cypress Mountains under Corporal Ritchie discovered a band of American Indians squatting by a camp fire a few miles from their quarters. On proceeding to the wooded hollow where the Indians were, the latter rose and cocked their weapons. The corporal asked them their business in the Territories, and for an answer received a shower of bullets, which fortunately flew wide of the mark. Ritchie at once ordered his men to dismount and fire, and one Indian dropped. The redskins surrounded their wounded companion, and, making for their ponies, succeeded in carrying him off. Shots were now frequently exchanged, and the chase kept up for some time, but the timber is dense in places among these hills, and the trail was lost.

CHAPTER XIX

Bird-life—Fireflies- Prairie fires—A surprised broncho—Sioux
Indians—Indian treaties—Reserves—Agents—A Sioux beauty
—Sweet grass—A lonely view—Thunderstorms—Hay-Spear
grass—Winchester carbines—A mail robbery—Arrest—Sentence—A cyclone.

ALL through the summer a number of pretty birds filled
the woods round the creek.   I am not much of an orni-
thologist, and therefore cannot describe all ; but the cat-
bird could be heard mewing among the branches, and
the meadow lark seen soaring aloft.   Myriads of fireflies
in the hot nights of July sparkled like a rain of diamonds
in the hollow in front of the tents.

The prairie fires came so dangerously near that we
were compelled to send and warn the ranchemen at the
six-mile coulée, in order that we might make a combined
effort to fight the flames.   There was such an amount
of dry undergrowth around our post, that the old fort
would most assuredly have been burnt.

The cowboys struck their camp and arrived with their
band of horses and waggons in the evening, just as our
herd was being driven through the creek, and the bugle
was sounding " Stables."

We possessed one notorious broncho, known as
" Sheep," who would never—well, hardly ever—permit
himself to be tied up at night.   He was as wily as a fox,
though his meditative eye and classic profile gave him
the guileless aspect of an ancient ewe.   Hence his
pastoral title.   He was particularly cute this evening

when it was most necessary that he should not be at large, and probably cause a stampede.

" I guess I'll fix him," said one of our allies.

In a few moments a lariat flew spinning through the air, and "Sheep" found himself fast in the noose, and lying on the ground. His astonishment was painful, and he spent a restless night in trying to work out the problem.

The prairie fire rolled away to the south, and left us undisturbed.

White Bull and his nomad band of Sioux camped on the slopes above the creek to the west of us, and remained for some time. The Sioux are refugees from the United States. In their own language, they are the mighty Dacotahs.

When this immense territory was purchased from the Hudson Bay Company, and taken over by the Government, treaties were made with the various Indian tribes, and certain areas of land set apart for their especial use, known as reserves. The negotiation and ratification of these important contracts extended over a number of years, as the noble red man is no mean diplomat. The basis of these treaties, in addition to the reserve of land, is an annual payment of five dollars a year to every man, woman, and child in the various tribes, with an additional sum for the chiefs and councillors. This money is paid annually in the autumn. The representatives of the Government are escorted by mounted police. The entire North-West is divided into Indian districts, each of which is under the supervision of an agent, who again is responsible to the Indian Department at Regina, controlled by the Commissioner of Indian Affairs.

Farm instructors are also stationed on the reserves, to teach the redskins husbandry. Many inducements are held out to industrious Indians, but the hereditary taint is too strong to permit of many taking advantage of this. The untutored noblemen look down upon work as degrading, and leave it to the squaws. Owing to the scarcity of game, rations are issued periodically upon all the reserves.

If any Indian wishes to resign his treaty, he can do so on the recommendation of the agent that he is able to maintain himself. He then receives a patent for 640 acres of land, which he may select upon any portion of the reserve.

These Sioux visitors of ours used to receive any food that might be left from our table, and nightly would they hold a "pow-wow," when tom-toms of bull hide would be beaten and flowery speeches delivered around the fire. I can't say much for the charms of Indian music. It is rather suggestive of the soft, sad cooing of the midnight cat. The Sioux women are, as a rule, virtuous, which is more than can be said of their sisters in other tribes. One young squaw (they are all squaws, married or single) in White Bull's camp was exceedingly pretty, with great wondering dark eyes. She was attired in garments worked wonderfully with beads of every colour. Her crimson trousers and moccasins were a marvel, and her dusky arms were adorned with silver bangles of barbaric size, and a necklace of strange shells, gathered on the prairie, hung around her neck. She had earrings in her tiny ears, and her firebag was richly fringed and embroidered. I wished to secure this as a curiosity, but my efforts were in vain.

These Indians made us several articles from a species of scented grass known as sweet grass. The Sweet Grass Hills take their name from it.

I am afraid I have harped too much for the patience of my readers on the utter loneliness of these regions.

But this sense of solitude is so overpowering, it towers above all other feelings. You experienced this in its fullest intensity if you climbed to the summit of any of the hills above the camp. There, far away below, nestled the white rows of tents, the grey haystack, and the brown buildings of the fort. The silvery waters of the creek could be seen winding through the valley of withered grass. All around rose terrace upon terrace of rounded hills, silent as though no foot had trod their slopes since the Creation. Not a sound to break the stillness of the noonday heat; not a moving figure to attract the eye. The burning furnace of the quivering atmosphere was stifling, and the horizon was dimmed by a Cuyp-like haze.

Apropos of the enterprise of trade, I may just mention that a Regina storekeeper planted an agent in a small tent at Wood Mountain, who dispensed sardines at seventy-five cents a tin, while a cake of soap, worth twopence in England, was sold for thirty cents. A half-breed supplied us with milk at ten cents per quart.

Thunderstorms burst upon us in August, in all the terrific grandeur of pent-up fury. A rain of fire literally poured down from heaven in continuous streams, with streaks of chain lightning. The rattle overhead was terrific, and simultaneous with every flash.

The hay used as forage at this post was simply the long grass which grew in rank luxuriance round the sleughs. It was coarse, and filled with the spear grass, which possesses a needle-like point upon a stem of wiry texture, curled in corkscrew shape. It is impossible to rear sheep where it grows, as it worms its way into their flesh.

During the latter part of August and in the beginning of September we were put through a course of mounted infantry drill, and we also fired the regulation amount of ammunition in the annual target practice. The Winchester repeating carbine has been pronounced a failure. The sighting of these weapons is lamentably deficient in accuracy, even at 100 yards, and the limit of their range is 500 yards. The trajectory also is very much higher than any other military arm. The initial velocity is 1234 feet per second. At 1000 yards the remaining velocity is 610 feet.

During the summer of 1886 a very impudent and extraordinary attack was made, single-handed, upon the Prince Albert mail. This involved some duty in searching the country for the daring "road agent," who was supposed to have made for that convenient refuge, Montana. As this was the first attempt at highway robbery in the Territories, it created a considerable amount of excitement, and all sorts of ridiculous stories were set afloat. One report stated that six masked men had committed the crime, and of course it was at once assumed they were American desperadoes from the Missouri. The facts, briefly, were these. It was the work of one man, who, in addition to robbing the mail, had " gone through " a party of five the same morning. When the mists were rolling away from the woodlands, they were awakened in their tent by the firing of a couple of shots outside. They were ordered out singly, and with the exception of two, tied up, one by one. This expert imitator of Dick Turpin then searched Mr. Swanston, a wealthy merchant of Prince Albert, evidently expecting to find a large sum of money upon him. Disappointed, he demanded the valuables and dollars of the other members of the party, and on receiving it he rode off, to treat the mail stage in the same way.

It was a lovely afternoon, as the light waggon, with its team of four black bronchos, came bowling along the dusty trail. Suddenly a figure appeared from a thick grove of poplars and stopped the stage, presenting a double-barrelled shot-gun. The passengers were peremptorily told to descend. They were all bound with cords, with the exception of one, who was detailed to attend to the horses. It seems astounding, that the passengers should have submitted to these arbitrary proceedings without making any show of resistance. Taking a knife for the purpose, the robber cut open the mail bags, abstracted all the registered letters, and, leaving all such articles as watches, he disappeared into the bush. The next day the driver of the mail going South found a package of opened registered letters on the trail, near the scene of the robbery. They contained cheques and vouchers, other than cash. He must have secured 260*l*. He took nothing belonging to the passengers, although he knew that one of them had 200 dollars in his possession. No attempt was made to disguise himself, and he evidently knew the country and the people.

On August the 18th Hart, the mail driver, called at the barracks and reported having seen the highwayman —a man named Garnett—in Prince Albert. He was at once arrested. In October he was tried at Regina, and received a sentence of fourteen years. When in the guard-room at the latter place, he confided to a fellow prisoner where he had hidden the booty. The money was buried in a can, on the south side of the South Saskatchewan, not far from the Hudson Bay Crossing. It was only by accident that one of our sergeants afterwards learnt this from a half-breed woman, but by this time Smith, the released prisoner who had secured the spoil, had escaped across the frontier.

A genuine cyclone came sweeping down upon us at

Wood Mountain in September, whirling the mess-tent from its moorings in the square and hanging it, like Macbeth's banners, " on the outward walls " of the fort. These storms are not so prevalent in the western parts of the Territories as they are in Dakota, where settlers are obliged to take refuge in their cellars.

On the following morning that restless spirit, " Sheep," performed the unusual circus feat of bolting clean through a bell-tent ;—rather a startling manœuvre to the two occupants who happened to be under their blankets. Luckily they were not hurt.

The summer gently passed into autumn, and nothing beyond the usual routine of patrol duty disturbed the monotony of our life. This fall was famous for a splendid Indian summer, the glory of this prairie land, when a holy calm seems to lie upon hill, and wood, and stream. Four successive Sundays were perfect days. Then, with one fell swoop, came the advance-guard of winter. Ice settled in the early part of November on the creek and marsh, and long strings of wild fowl were daily seen and nightly heard, flying south. We had no stoves in the tents, and our sufferings from cold became keen. A small detachment were to be left in exile here, during the coming winter, with a couple of men at Willow Bunch. We now spent our time in huddling—contrary to orders—round the cook-house fire, and in hazarding surmises as to the time when we should receive the glad marching orders for Regina. They came suddenly, as usual, on the 17th of November, and we were to move at dawn on the following morning. Universal peace and good will seemed to be established in the hearty bustle and confusion which ensued. Every one was thankful to get away from this dull and spiritless existence. We had not seen the face of a white woman for seven months.

CHAPTER XX

March from Wood Mountain—Springs frozen—Willow Bunch—
Dangerous descent—Alkali Lake—No water—Big bluffs—A
huge camp-fire— Intense cold—Sufferings—Frostbites—An
accident—The mirage—New riding-school—The cowboy
troop—1887—A blizzard—Drills—Blood Indians—Crees—An
Indian march—"Kinneekinick"—Indian religion—Handshaking—Pipe of peace—Squaws—A Sioux lady—"Medicine"—
Police fired on by Piegans—Kootenay Indians—Shuswaps.

OUR stumpy, broad-shouldered, little bugler threw an
extra amount of cheerfulness into his task when he sent
the notes of reveillé ringing through the grey tents in
the early morning starlight; and after stables, I saddled
my trooper, regimentally numbered 999, but familiarly
known as "Bosco." The waggons were loaded with
bedding and rations and camping outfit only, as our kits
were to follow in charge of some civilian freighters, who
had brought out the winter's supplies. Bosco was a
pretty chestnut broncho, and in excellent form. His
only fault, if it can be called such, was his exceedingly
tender mouth.

At seven o'clock the advance-guard trotted off up the
opposite slope, and away along the level of the valley in
front. We were to take a new route to Regina, by
Willow Bunch. The air was chilly, and leaden clouds
hung over the scene at first, but by and by the sun
broke through. It was my misfortune to be on rear-
guard, which; although it is supposed to be the post of
honour on the line of march, is a vexatious position with
such a small body of men. Waggons were continually

halting, one teamster in particular always having something to fix up. The trail at first led through the Hay
Field, a long, wide valley, with magnificent hills on
either side. The ranche men had put up two large
stacks of hay here. This vale was four miles in length
and one mile broad. The blood coursed wildly through
the veins this bracing morning; the bridles jingled
merrily, arms glittered in the sunshine, and the air was
laden with the healthy ozone of the prairies. Our
hospital sergeant accompanied us on rear-guard. He
was mounted on a broncho which was not accustomed
to his rider wearing a sword, and every time this weapon
of the luckless " poultice major" struck Baldy's side, he
was anxious to take an extensive tour of the surrounding district. Our disciple of Æsculapius was not
accustomed to equine exercise, and this added considerably to the hilarity of the proceedings.

At noon we reached a deep ravine, in which were
some springs. These were frozen, and the stream which
ran down the narrow gorge in the mountains was a
solid mass of ice. We halted on a species of natural
terrace, while above to the right a gigantic peak reared
its scarped sides of brown. It was a difficult and
dangerous task to lead our horses down the face of the
precipice to the watering-place by a zigzag path through
tangled brake, and over fallen boulders ; the poor beasts
went sliding and slipping in all directions, though
the broncho is very surefooted. The camp-kettles, too,
had to be filled, and carried up this wall-like steep.
After some warm tea and bacon, we resumed our march,
which for the remainder of the day continued along the
summit of a lofty plateau, commanding a wide view of
a lonely plain, with here and there a frozen lake
glistening in the distance. It was dark when we reached
the edge of the cliff overhanging the half-breed settle-

ment of Willow Bunch. We trusted to the instinct of our horses to keep this awful trail. One swerve to the right would have sent horse and rider crashing to the bottom of the abyss. However, we reached the valley in safety, and could see the yellow lights twinkling in the few log shanties. We had made a march of forty-five miles. We went rattling and clattering through the scattered village, and camped on a level space near a creek at the further end. Soon the camp fires shed their ruddy glare on the dark line of waggons and array of tents, while fur-clad figures grouped around the blaze, or led horses to their different stations. Sentries were posted, and after supper we were not long in seeking what comfort the hard ground provided, beneath the blankets.

Daybreak showed us a long, flat plain, stretching for miles from the foot of the mountains, which rose like a mighty wall. Bushes sprang from the seams in the slopes, and huts nestled at the foot or peeped out from amid the leafless branches, like châlets in an Alpine scene. After a hasty breakfast, we were off once more, steering north.

It was a brilliant day for the late autumn, and songs and yarns beguiled the tedium of the march. We halted in a rocky ravine at the head of a frozen sheet of water for our noonday meal. In the afternoon, the trail wound along over the everlasting prairie. For miles ahead you could see the light brown line. We camped at night near an ice-covered pond, the waters of which were alkali, fit neither for man nor beast. Some springs at a little distance were frozen, and the horses were unable to procure a drink. We melted ice in our camp kettles for tea. The stars shone brilliantly over the scene, but the sounds of the camp only made the surrounding solitude more apparent.

On the next day the sky was leaden, and a cold wind swept over the plains. We could obtain no water at noon. In the afternoon we met a cowboy returning to the ranche at Wood Mountain from Regina. The veil of dusk was falling when we reached the Big Bluffs on the Moosejaw Creek, and in a grove of tall poplars we pitched our camp. In one spot we managed to procure water for the horses, cutting a hole in the ice. The poor animals had not had a drink for thirty-six hours. We demolished the rations of tea, bacon, and biscuit, and the sentry was posted over the camp. Down in a sheltered hollow in the creek, where the grass grown slopes were clad with light timber, we made a blazing fire of dried trees. The night was most intensely cold, and there was no comfort in the tents. We all took seats around the small amphitheatre, and whiled away the hours before watch-setting with songs and jokes. When a cry for more wood was raised, axes would be plied, and a huge bush would be sent crashing into the centre beneath. It was a picturesque sight. The brilliant firelight shed its reflection on scarlet jackets and fur coats, and illumined the worn faces with a strange Rembrandt tint. Some were smoking, and all swelled the loud chorus of many a stirring camp song.

In the cold darkness of the following morning we rose with the prospect of reaching Regina before nightfall. It was Sunday, and we had thirty-two miles of dead level prairie before us. It was sheltered here in the bluff, but when we moved out in the grey dawn, the north wind met us in all its fierceness. There was nothing for it but to face the music as bravely as one could. Buffalo overcoats, mufflers, and moccasins were no shield against it. Every now and again it was necessary to dismount and lead our troopers, in order to keep from freezing to death in the saddle. We were soon frost-

bitten.   The thermometer to-day showed ten degrees
below zero (42° of frost), and this temperature with such
a wind was equal to double in a calm.   Long icicles
hung like heavy pendants from our moustaches, and
adorned our poor horses' nostrils.   I can recall the day's
march even   now, and the weary longing for it to end.
I never, during my whole term of service, felt the cold so
much.   Not even during our memorable march to Prince
Albert, for that was my first winter.   The oldest soldier
in the Mounted Police was riding alongside of me.   He
had penetrated this wilderness in 1874, with the first
batch of redcoats, when they crossed the desert to Fort
Macleod.   There were no settlers at all then, and the
buffalo, and Blackfeet, and Crees roamed at will over
these plains.   Jack was generally the cheeriest comrade
in camp or on the march, full of songs and old-time
stories.   The Force had become his home, and the
prairie seemed his native heath.   But to-day, he was
moody and silent.   He turned to me once, and said
bitterly, " No one knows what us poor beggars have to
suffer ! "

In this weird life of exile there is no blazoned
scroll of honour.   All is done as simple duty, far from
the plaudits of the world, and hardships become the
common incidents of your daily life.   They are taken
as a matter of course, and made light of when past.
To wear a scarlet coat out here is not to flaunt it
before the wondering gaze of lovely women, to the
entrancing strains of martial music !

When about fifteen miles from Regina, after we had
tramped on foot for   some distance, the order was
given to mount.   My horse was restive, and I was in a
hurry.   I suppose in my haste I must have pulled upon
his mouth, but my hands were numb and I neglected to
twist a lock of his mane around my thumb.   But, as I

had one foot in the stirrup, swinging, and the other off the ground in the act of springing into the saddle, he reared full upon his haunches, and fell back over upon me. He was given slightly to rearing, but never to this extent before. Luckily, a hollow in the trail where I lay helped to break his weight upon my thighs and the lower region of my body. I heard the bugler ask, "Is he dead?" and the others were soon around me. When they helped me up, I could barely stand. I may be very thankful that I am here to record the fact. It is a miracle that the horn of the saddle did not crash through my ribs and still the beating of my heart for ever. The sergeant-major wished to send a man forward to the main body to stop a waggon, but I requested the other fellows to hoist me into the saddle again, which they did, and I rode on in agony. We halted at a deserted farm, eight miles from Regina, and enjoyed some steaming hot coffee, made by our cooks. There was a wonderful display of mirage to-day. When we were yet twenty miles from the city, a huge windmill rose before us in the sky. This was for the purpose of pumping water, and was attached to a grain warehouse in the town. Yet there it was, magnified and lifted into the heavens, while the houses were invisible.

On resuming our march, I was so very stiff that I was at last compelled to mount a waggon and recline upon a pile of rolled bedding. The care and kindness of my brother troopers on this occasion I shall always remember with gratitude. It was a depressing scene all round. The sky to begin with was of ashen hue ; scattered over the prairie at intervals stood houses, bleak and abandoned. There had been no harvest at all this season. In the middle of the great plain stood Regina. To the left, the tower and roof of

the fine new riding-school rose above every other
building.

This structure was 224 feet in length and 123 feet in
width. It was erected at a cost of thirty thousand dollars,
and was entirely of wood. The aspect of the barracks was
entirely altered, as all through the preceding summer
the work of building had been going on. We could see
the brave old Union Jack floating gaily from the flagstaff. We skirted the town by the reservoir—a large
sheet of water formed by a dam upon the Wascana
Creek. A huge stone building stood in solitary
grandeur to the south of the city. This was the
future gaol. Number one sentry was pacing the side-
walk as usual when we entered barracks, and
turned out the guard ; we received and paid the proper
compliments. Regina is a pretty hackneyed subject now,
so I shall briefly jot down the salient features of our
sojourn in winter-quarters till we turned out again in
the following spring. The new barracks were a decided
improvement upon the old, each block being self-
contained, with lavatories and bath-rooms, and splendid
mess-rooms, attached by covered corridors. Every
room was large, and lighted by lofty windows, and heated
by hot air pipes. How pale our new chums of the
depôt looked, in contrast to our faces bronzed and
lined with exposure to wind and sun. On the morning
after our arrival we were treated to a howling snow-
storm, and in a brief time the whole prairie was wrapped
in its white sheet of virgin snow, which remained until
the next spring. In consequence of this our kits,
which had been left to the tender mercies of the
civilian teamsters, did not arrive until the following
week. Such dilapidated-looking scarecrows as we, after
a summer's work on the prairie, were hardly fit to be
seen amid the smartness and routine of Regina. We

found discipline in Regina to be extraordinarily strict, and the riding-school was utilized to its full extent. Our new adjutant had been in the 3rd Hussars, and our rough-riding sergeant in the 9th Lancers. This latter humorist hailed us as "the cowboy troop," owing to our seat in the saddle having been adapted to the exigences of long rides daily on the prairie. Moreover, the red book distinctly states that a Mounted Infantryman should be allowed to adopt that seat which suits him best ; it is impossible to sit in a stiff regulation manner out here. Ex-cavalrymen who have been out on the plains acknowledge it, but this genius of the *manège* had not left the barrack square since he landed. Drills and rides, rides and drills, was the everlasting programme for the winter. Long service men and recruits were kept hammering away with strict impartiality.

In the early part of December our troop was given a banquet by the buxom proprietress of the Windsor Hotel. Everything went off splendidly. Every night, by the commissioner's permission, a sleigh left barracks for town at 6.30 and returned at 9. We thus were saved a walk of five miles in our jaunts to the metropolis. What merry parties there were on the return journey ; songs would be sung all the way to barracks —the great plain lying white as burnished silver under the splendour of the moonlight.

On the 20th of December I was promoted to the rank of corporal, a slight step which carried no mean weight of responsibility in this corps. On New Year's Eve "B" troop gave a ball which was the event of the season ; and 1886 was sent away to the tune of "Auld Lang Syne."

1887.—January 29th, the worst blizzard ever known to have visited the Territory since the advent of settlement swept across the plains. It continued for forty-eight hours, and the Canadian Pacific train—called the Pacific " express " on the *lucus a non lucendo* principle, —was unable to pass Regina. There were many deaths and casualties. On this occasion the thermometer registered minus 37°, and the wind blew a hurricane, whirling the ice powder in a deathly density. This penetrates through every crevice, and covers beds and furniture with a robe of white.

Spring struggled into existence in 1887 after many a skirmish with the retreating winter. Muddy ponds, half ice and half water, stood with frothy surface all around the barracks, and caused much strong language on the score of polished boots prematurely spoiled ; for we were incessantly at work, practising vedette duty and scouting. We had field movements and sham fights on the prairie, and lectures on tactics in the drill-hall attached to the riding-school. Squads were formed also for instruction in signalling.

The Blood Indians have a magnificent reserve on the fertile banks of the Belly and St. Mary Rivers, far away in the extreme south-west corner of the Territories, in Alberta. They are a race splendid in physique, and the strongest in numbers of any of the Blackfeet nation. The number of the tribe, as laid down upon the police map, is 2240. A number of their young braves, anxious to distinguish themselves and tired of being kept upon their reserve, made a dash upon Medicine Hat. This is fully 120 miles from the St. Mary River, and numerous rugged coulées lie between. And it must be understood that no Indian is permitted to leave his reserve without a pass signed by the agent, and this is not given unless some valid reason is assigned. Another group of feathered and painted warriors made a *razzia* on the South Piegans in Montana, and lifted a considerable number of horses from the latter tribe. In consequence of these disturbances, reinforcements were sent to Fort Macleod.

At the end of April a sergeant and nine men of our troop were sent to Buffalo Lake, a pretty sheet of water north of Moosejaw, to intercept and turn back several lodges of Crees, who were reported to have left Pieapot's reserve. Our men discovered the deserters in a wooded ravine, and escorted them on their homeward journey. It is tedious and unpleasant work doing guard over travelling redskins, who are worse than Government mules for obstinacy. They will only move when they choose, and will only proceed a certain distance at their own pace. They throw all sorts of obstacles in the way of progress, and you are not allowed to use force, except on rare occasions. If you have not waggons to hold them, you cannot help yourself. It was once my misfortune to form one of an escort over thirteen Assiniboines, horse-thieves ; they were anything but agreable *compagnons de voyage.* You must never so far forget yourself as to go to leeward of them if you can help it. All their petty prejudices have to be considered. An Indian considers it the deepest disgrace to be deprived of his long hair. Consequently there is a very strict order against cutting the streaming locks of Indian prisoners, although they are thickets for the shelter of a certain species of live stock. I have accompanied various small groups of the aborigines, but it has never been my fortune to witness the march of an entire tribe. The following description of the movement of Poundmaker's people during the rebellion is taken from the *Montreal Star :*—

"As the (captured transport) train approached the Indian camp, squaws and toddling papooses poured out from every teepe, and advanced with cheers of joy to greet the returning braves. The females, at sight of

the prisoners, were especially boisterous, and shouted
to the braves to put them to death.   Through the
jeering, howling, yelling mass, the frightened drivers
were hustled, every moment expecting to be struck
down from behind.   Finally they were conducted to a
ravine close to the camp, and after receiving a parting
shout from the ugly squaws, they were left to their
own reflections.   A strong guard surrounded them, pre-
cluding all possibility of escape.   The Indians held a
formal council to discuss the propriety of shooting the
teamsters, but decided not to do so.   Shortly afterwards
Poundmaker put in an appearance in the ravine.   After
shaking hands with each man in turn, the redoubtable
chief assured them, through a half-breed interpreter,
that their lives would be spared.   He added that he was
aware there was a Manitou above, and that he could not
permit them to be slain without cause.   Poundmaker
then left, and shortly afterwards the Indians struck camp.
Teepe poles were thrown down in a twinkling by the
squaws, who, assisted by the young boys and girls,
rapidly packed everything away in carts and waggons
already in line for the start.   Bucks lolled around, whiff-
ing ' Kinneekinick ' from long-stemmed pipes, or attending to the trappings of their horses, while youngsters,
scarcely able to crawl about drove in the cattle.
Finally a start was made, and preceded by twenty five
or thirty scouts riding a mile ahead, the disorganized
mob moved eastwards on their way to reinforce Riel.
Instead of proceeding in column, the Indians moved along
in extended order, leaving a trail behind them over two
miles wide.   First came about three hundred and sixty
war-painted braves, mounted on wiry ponies, or on the
more powerful animals stolen in the early raids.   Next
came Red River carts, waggons, and every other variety
of vehicle ever manufactured.   Each was loaded with

plunder or teepe poles, while perched on top were seated old men, armed with bows and arrows. Behind followed a chaotic mass of waggons and carts, surrounded by lowing cattle and little boys on foot. Other Indian lads added to the grotesqueness of the scene, and, mounted on young colts, kept up to the moving outfit. Further in rear, at distance of half a mile, came other herds of cattle, while bringing up the whole came another herd of horses. Young girls and squaws were mounted, several of the females riding along on oxen. In this manner the followers of Poundmaker covered three miles an hour with ease."

While I am writing on the subject of Indians I may as well mention a few details, in parenthesis, which have been suggested by the foregoing. " Kinneekinick," is the dried bark of the red-willow, which is chopped up into small pieces and mixed with tobacco. Some white men affect to like it, but to my palate it is tasteless. The Indian worships two Manitous : the Good Spirit, and the Evil Spirit. He holds the Manichean doctrine that both are equally powerful. The evil god is to be propitiated. The Great Spirit is all good. He even ministers to your appetites, and he dwells in lonely lakes, in silent forests, and in weirdly-shaped rocks.

The Indian is very fond of shaking hands with white men. If one solitary redskin meets twenty police, he must shake hands with every individual. When the pipe of peace is smoked, it is strict etiquette to pass it with the right hand. It is not at all a pleasant ceremony, but it is not much more disgusting than the loving cup at Guildhall banquets. A squaw very soon loses the bloom and freshness of youth, and becomes wrinkled and aged. They are very coquettish damsels. One of our scouts married a Sioux, and brought her to Regina, She was not long in taking to oriental vanities, and shone forth in all the splendour of high-heeled boots silk costume, dress improver, and an immense hat of brilliant plumage. She also affected English, "as she is spoke," with horrifying effect upon her white sisters, as she indulged freely in several camp expressions which are not considered parliamentary in polite society.

Every Indian carries his "medicine" or charm about his person. For this he retires into the wilderness, where the Manitou reveals to him what it must be. It may be a piece of deerskin, or a pebble, or a twig. Whatever it is, is known to him alone, and henceforth it becomes a part of his life. If he is unlucky in his undertakings, it is "bad medicine."

On April 27th, a party of police, under Sergeant Spicer, were fired on by either Bloods or Piegans, in the Cypress Hills, and some freighters received a shower of bullets on the 29th near Kipp's Coulée, a considerable distance from the former place. The Blackfeet were also restless. Crowfoot, the chief of the Blackfeet, is a very loyal and truthful man, but he confessed himself unable to restrain the roving propensities of his young braves.

The Kootenay Indian , in British Columbia, had been attracting some attention, and Major Steele was ordered to move into their country with " D " troop. There are the Upper and Lower Kootenays and Shuswaps among the Rockies, near the frontier of the United States. The Upper Kootenays have their reserve on the north side of St. Mary's River, and at Tobacco Plains. The Lower Kootenays dwell on the Lower Kootenay River, near the Kootenay Lake. The Shuswaps occupy a Reserve at the Columbia Lakes. The Upper Kootenays and Shuswaps are horse Indians, the Lower Kootenays use canoes. The British Columbian whites in this district had been thrown into a state of alarm during the preceding winter by the action of Isadore, head chief of the Upper Kootenays. He had forcibly released from gaol an Indian, named Kapla, who had been arrested by Provincial Commissioner Anderson.

On the arrival of " D " Troop, there was no further trouble, and special commissioners were sent to inquire into the Indian grievances. Major Steele in his report says :—" The Indians here are more industrious and moral than any in the north-west, except perhaps, the Mountain Stonies."

On the 1st of May we were still in Regina, and the weather was gloriously bright and warm. The authorities seemed to be holding " B " Troop in readiness, in case anything of consequence occurred in the west. Mounted parades, drills, and carbine practice, filled up the day-time, and at night we played cricket or walked to town.

CHAPTER XXI

Wet weather—A sudden order—Off to the Souris—Mud—A
caboose—Broadview—A big spill of whisky—Moosomin—The
Big Pipestone valley—Indians on the trail—Travoies—A
lovely camp — Cannington — Moose Mountain — Game —
Carlyle—Indian deserters—The sun dance—Initiation of
braves—The Souris—Alameda—The frontier.

I HAVE, I think, mentioned before the suddenness with
which movements are decided upon in the N.W.M.P.
It was known in May that Major Jarvis and the troop
headquarters were to occupy their former station at
Wood Mountain. I was detailed to accompany a
subaltern officer, who was to command the Moose
Mountain district, and the extreme eastern section of
the frontier-line.

The morning of Friday, May 13th, broke under a
leaden sky, and torrents of rain were falling, as reveillé
rang across the gloomy square. At breakfast in the
mess-room, every one was glum, for we were tired of the
perpetual grind of riding-school, drill, parades, stables,
and guards, and longed once more for the comparative
freedom of duty away out on the plains. We sipped
our coffee, and ate our eggs and hash almost in silence,
while the rain splashed in the stable-yard without. One
corporal wished to wager ten, twenty, or fifty dollars
that we should not move out of barracks for another
month. As he was vociferating his infallibility of pre-
diction, an officer entered, and we immediately sprang
to attention. Beckoning to me, he said,—

" Have your party ready in half an hour to march down to the station, the waggons loaded, and everything complete, parade mounted in the square. The train will be at Regina in half an hour."

This sort of thing must be expected, but no one seems ever to be ready for such an emergency. Brown has his washing out, Jones is up at the hospital, while Robinson is off on pass. I hastened to look up my men, and a nice flutter and hurry there was in the barrack-rooms. The horses had to be saddled, the two transport waggons were to be loaded with supplies of all kinds, including camp equipment; the men to dress in marching order, pack up their kits, roll up their bedding, be in the saddle, on the square, and down at the railway station, all in the brief space of one half-hour! Any one who knows the amount of a mounted policeman's kit, will appreciate the difficulty. Luckily, the Wood Mountain party were not to leave until the following day, so our comrades came to the front with cheerful alacrity, and willing hands, to help us. Each of us had five different attendants busied in various ways. One was engaged in fixing up a man's accoutrements, another had hurried off to saddle up his horse, a third was employed in rolling up bedding, while a fourth was ramming his kit into its proper receptacle. I was supposed to possess the miraculous properties of Sir Boyle Roche's famous bird, for, in addition to performing all the above duties for myself, I was to watch the loading of the waggons, and check every article off on form No. 12,070, or some such figure. The circumlocution fiend is triumphant in this branch of the Canadian service, and there is a form to be filled in at every turn, in triplicate. At length, with soddened cloak and pulpy helmet, I was at liberty to splash through the lake in front of the stables, and mount my

trooper, Chocolate George. This was a fine-looking
animal, and one of the few remaining Ontario horses.
He was always on the dance. A series of musical rides
had taken place in the school since the establishment of
the band at headquarters, and this species of dissipa-
tion seemed to have imbued him with a frantic desire to
excel as a circus horse. Consequently, his chief happi-
ness was in attempting some new ornamental move.
If I took him out for exercise alone to town, he must
needs "passage" up the street. Fortunately, every one
was on parade in time. The major gave us a very
short inspection, saying curtly, "March them off,
Mr. McGibbon."

We went out of the square at the trot, and away over
the soaked and sloppy prairie at the gallop. We were
bespattered with mud from head to foot, and the pipeclay from our white helmets came down in a Niagara
of dirty water. Our gauntlets were saturated. It was
a foretaste of the coming summer's wet. On entering
the town, we observed the two box-cars, which were to
receive our horses and waggons, standing on the line.
These were to be attached to the freight, or luggage-
train by which we were to travel to Moosomin. The
loading of these cars was not by any means a labour of
love in all the rain and mud. We had to take off our
juicy gauntlets, and "wire in." The cincha—as the
woven horse-hair girth is termed on a Californian
saddle—upon one of the saddle horses, slipped back,
and he, in consequence, commenced a vigorous course
of buck-jumping, and did not cease throwing his heels
to heaven until he had sent the saddle flying into a
convenient pond, whence it was dragged in anything
but a regulation condition. The waggons had all to
be taken to pieces, and the component parts and
contents lifted into the car. The slimy mud was upon

everything. Then the harness and saddlery was piled
in. After this the horses had to be marched up the
railed-in "shoot," into their compartment. The bronchos
went up readily enough, but the Canadian horses
seemed to regard it as a species of cunning trap to be
obstinately avoided.

But after much tugging in front, and persistent
walloping behind, we got them safely housed, and as soon
as the doors were fastened, the train made its appearance
in the distance, steaming slowly over the level prairie.
We were a rough-looking lot, streaked with dirt, and
plastered with mud. The inspector handed me the
men's tickets, which I distributed, and when the train
came alongside the platform, we all entered the conductor's caboose. This is a house upon wheels, and is very
comfortable. At one end is a cooking-stove and cupboards, and a table. There is an elevated platform
where the conductor and brakesman sit when on duty,
they can see ahead through small windows above the
roof. The body of the car is furnished with cushioned
seats along the sides. There was a small lavatory also,
where we gladly performed our much-needed ablutions.
We carried towels and soap in our haversacks. The
private car of the superintendent of the line was also
hooked to this freight train, and the officer was invited
therein. As we neared Qu'Appelle, he came out and
informed me that the above official had kindly consented
to allow of a delay of half an hour at this station
(formerly Troy), so that the men might have dinner. I
was to see to this, for which he gave me the requisite
funds, and I had also to take care that the allotted time
was not exceeded. On our arrival, a good repast was
ready for us at the Queen's Hotel, the conductor having
telegraphed ahead. We created some excitement in the
quiet village, and many "citizens" asked me if the

Indians had broken out anywhere. On our return we made ourselves cosy, and smoked and sang, while the rain pattered against the blurred and streaming windows. Broadview was reached at six o'clock in the evening. The surrounding landscape was almost under water, while the rain continued to pour down with a steady persistency. We here discovered that we should be unable to proceed until the following morning. Our cars were shunted, and we watered and fed our chargers. One man entered the car, and the buckets of water and forage were handed up to him. This is a risky proceeding with strange horses, as they are simply packed loose in the caravan, head to tail. Rooms were engaged for our party, and we took our meals in the refreshment-room. The Pacific express came clanging into the station, and fresh arrivals from England stared wonderingly at us, as we stalked about in rusty spurs, muddy boots, bedraggled cloaks, and dingy helmets. All liquor permits, for the entire Territory are cancelled here, and a good deal of illicit stuff is captured and spilled. An excursion party of Ontario farmers were somewhat astonished at this station in '88, when 700 dollars' worth of whisky was emptied out before their eyes. Broadview is 264 miles west of Winnipeg, and is in the centre of a fairly good farming country. According to the pamphlets, it is a well laid-out town, and I have no doubt it is—on paper. There are three or four stores, and a handful of houses, which are prettily situated at the head of Wood Lake, and the C.P.R. have workshops here. We set off for Moosomin, on the morning of the 14th at seven o'clock, and passed through a level country sprinkled with birch and poplar bluffs, and drew up at Moosomin at half-past ten. After unloading the cars, putting together the waggons, and taking our horses to water, we went to the hotel for dinner. Lovely clumps of trees, with lakelets gleaming through the foliage, all round this town. There are churches and stores in abundance, and the growth of timber gives Moosomin an advantage over other prairie towns, and saves it from the generally unfinished appearance which distinguishes these rising cities. It is 219 miles west of Winnipeg. We marched out at two in the afternoon, amidst an enthusiastic group of the inhabitants. The corporal in charge of the detachment here had kindly volunteered to saddle Chocolate George for me, while I was engaged in looking after the purchase of some supplies, and this I acquiesced in to my subsequent discomfiture. The trail led through a finely wooded and well settled country. Good frame-houses, neat and brightly painted, characterized all the farms we passed. Lady Cathcart's crofter colony is situated out here. All this air of snug prosperity seemed strange to me, accustomed as I had been to life in the wilderness. This is the most thriving grain-farming country in the Territory, and is conterminous with the western boundary of the province of Manitoba.

My trooper had been in the most exuberant spirits since starting, and in order to allow some of his superfluous joyousness to evaporate, as I was with the advance guard, I gave him his head and myself a little practice in the sword exercise. As I was bending over to a low guard, my saddle turned completely round, and off I went like a bolt from a catapult! My face was almost bare of skin, and I am afraid I was not very grateful for my brother non-commissioned officer's laxity in fixing up my saddle-girth.

Reaching the edge of the lofty cliffs that stand above the Big Pipestone Creek, we made a careful descent into the broad valley, by the rugged trail of stones and yellow mud that turned and twisted among the hanging bushes.

We pitched camp for the night by the side of the swollen stream as the sun was setting.

We were to proceed to the prairie settlement at Carlyle, about eighty miles south of Moosomin, and to pick up a sergeant and five constables, who had been stationed at that outpost during the winter. Thence our march would lie in a south-easterly direction, and a camp was to be established on the Souris, where it crosses the frontier into Dakota. Leaving a detach-ment at this spot, the officer was to move westward with the rest of his command, following the boundary-line, and set up his head-quarters upon Long Creek, a sluggish stream that winds through the plains to the north of the Missouri Coteau. Our camp upon the Pipestone nestled in a most romantic scene. The towering heights were robed in shaggy woods ; and white farm-houses with roofs of red, or brown, peeped out from among the foliage. The vale was cultivated and laid out in fields with snake fences. Our horses were picketed by long ropes attached to iron pins by a ring. These pins were shaped like corkscrews, so that you could wind them into any ground. A broncho, when startled, is apt to draw the straight style of picket-pin. If a horse per-sistently drags his fastening from the ground, your best plan is to attach the rope to a hopple around one of his fore-feet ; as a rule it is fixed around the neck by a loop. A couple of men were told off to look after the horses, dividing the night into two watches. Then the blankets were spread in the tents ; and only loud snores, or the puffs of a pipe were heard from beneath the canvas.

A cold and cloudy morning, with occasional showers of snow, ushered in the 15th. We often grumble and growl, in this tight little island of ours, at the fickleness of that arch coquette, spring ; but her smiles are never

to be depended upon in any climate. Even in the
Riviera, a day of genial warmth may be followed by
one on which the hideous mistral sends you shivering
home. Evidences of prosperity and good farming lay
on every side during the first period of the day. But
any degree of success, out here in the north-west, is only
to be attained by stern determination, and rugged
perseverance. The life of a pioneer is lonely and dis-
heartening at first. And let him not hope to win a
fortune from the soil. If he make a living, he should
rest content. This is, emphatically, a *hard* land to
dwell in ; and existence is a struggle. Want of rain
may paralyze his efforts one season ; and a blighting
frost in August may shatter his hopes the next. And
for any one to stake his hopes on grain alone, is utter
folly ; but if he goes in for mixed farming, he may suc-
ceed. The scenery through which we were passing was
park-like and dotted with lovely groves of white oak.
We entered a bleaker stretch about noon, and lit a fire,
on the edge of the little Pipestone, to cook our bacon
and boil our water. The surroundings were very bare,
and a searching breeze swept down the slopes. The
horses were picketed in different places where the feed
was good ; and we rigged up a shelter by hanging horse-
blankets from the waggons, to windward, behind which
we lay upon the grass and smoked or slept. As we were
riding down into the hollow, before we halted, I noticed
the tops of some teepes peeping above a few bushes upon
the opposite hills. I mentioned this casually to the
inspector, but he made no reply, as it was not a startling
incident. We rested about two hours, and when we
resumed our march, these nomad dwellings had disappeared. When we had proceeded a few miles upon the
trail, which was now dry and dusty, we came upon a
band of Indians moving in extended order across the

prairie. They seemed to increase their pace on our approach ; but we merely exchanged the usual saluta- tion of " How ! How Koola ! " and went ahead. Away in front a young brave and a pretty squaw were walking together, evidently bound by that one touch of nature which makes the whole world akin. A few Red River carts contained blankets and sprawling youngsters in rags of gaudy hues. Some pack-horses carried bundles of teepe-poles. The men were mounted, while the women trudged on foot. This is the noble red-man's way. He rides on horseback while the patient squaw shuffles alongside with her papoose strapped to a board behind, like a knapsack. Comic-looking objects are these same papooses, peeping from their dirty swaddling clothes with little black bead-like eyes. A few sick were borne on travoies ; which consist of two long poles crossed and attached to the neck of a horse ; while the other two ends drag on the ground. Between these two sticks behind the animal's tail a blanket is slung, and in this uncomfortable couch the invalid reclines. It is truly a case of the survival of the fittest.

Towards evening we again entered a lovely country magnificent in rolling woodlands, with the blue range of the Moose Mountains rising behind. We camped in a beautiful glade, with a velvety carpet of bright green ; in the centre sparkled a tiny lake, its limpid waters were tinged with the hues of a blushing rose by the long lines of crimson light flashed from the setting sun. It was a glorious evening, though cold, but we were well sheltered here. The white tents made a picture against the vivid emerald of the boughs, clad in their freshest tints. The birds sang among the leafy branches ; and the gophers scampered off, sitting on their haunches with drooping paws and arch look for one brief moment before making a sudden dive into their burrows. The horses rolled upon the sward, and munched the grass, and the grey smoke of our fire curled up into the magic sunset. I told off the picquet, and after some welcome tea, entered my tent, unrolled my blankets on the clean springy turf and lit the soothing pipe. No one knows the comfort of that good-night pipe, who has not experienced the worry of a trying march, harassed by the weight of responsibility. For be it understood, if anything goes wrong, the full torrent of official wrath falls on the shoulders of the non-com. At this place we were one mile and a half from Cannington, a flourishing English settlement. It is essentially a moneyed, aristocratic colony; in fact the village is a model one. There is a mill, a pretty church, and an excellent hotel, well-furnished, and possessing a most courteous host. It has also a club, a school, and town-hall. Captain Pierce, formerly of the Royal Artillery, is the moving spirit, and holds 2000 acres of land. Things are carried out to such perfection that there is a surpliced choir, and everything has a flavour of home. Flocks of Cotswold and Leicester sheep roam over the green slopes of this undulating country.

When winding our way over an excellent trail through thickets, vocal with the music of birds, it did not need a very strong imagination to make one fancy we were moving through some fine old park in merry England. A flourishing homestead stood on a gentle rise, with barns, and byres, and folds. Sheep and cattle clustered round the out-buildings, some plethoric ducks waddled down to a pond, poultry cackled round the doors, and a group of chubby children gazed in awe as the red-coated soldiers went jingling by. After passing this glimpse of comfort, so painfully suggestive of the dear land across the sea, we faced once more the desolate plains, with lonely, ugly log shanties standing in hideous solitude here and there. A line of bush fringed the base of the Moose Mountains which rose to the right. This range is beautifully varied with wood and water ; and there are three Indian reserves in its recesses. The inhabitants are Assiniboines under the three chiefs, Pheasant Rump, Ocean Man, and White Bear. The total population amounts to 311. Elk, deer, partridge, and rabbits are fairly plentiful as yet, the lakes swarm with wild fowl and fish, while prairie chicken and snipe abound on the plains. The view here across the prairie shows a line of thick bush to the left, and in front the everlasting level stretches as far as the eye can reach, till it blends with the horizon.

We arrived at Carlyle about mid-day, and could see the familiar scarlet on some figures moving among the few houses while we were some distance off. These were the men of the winter detachment, and they were extremely glad to see us. They occupied a barrack-room attached to the hotel, and took their meals at the table d'hôte at Government expense. We pitched our row of tents some short way from the village. Carlyle is situated in the centre of a vast flat plain, as I have stated, and is the centre of a fairly settled region. I have seen more buildings around a farm-house at home and yet this bantam hamlet is styled a city. It consists of three or four dwelling-houses, a general store, a blacksmith's shop, and the hotel. One of the houses was built of stone and fancifully decorated. The population were clamouring for railway accommodation ; this might be given by the extension of the southern branch of the Canadian Pacific from Deloraine. The only markets for the settlers were at Virden or Moosomin ; and the cost of transport to these places was more than the value of the produce. It was mail day at Carlyle, and the place was thronged with people who had come in for

their weekly supply of letters and newspapers, which
arrive by stage from Moosomin.

There was also a civil trial proceeding, which seemed
to excite some interest. The court of justice was an
empty log-house, and tobacco-juice was freely squirted
on the floor by the mob of settlers who crowded around
in patched and seedy garments of homespun. These
pioneers often flutter about in rags, and every one wears
a battered slouch hat. After a wash and a shave in the
barrack-room, the sergeant and I proceeded downstairs
to dinner. On regarding my features in a mirror, I
found that I resembled a Tonga Islander in full fig, or
an urchin after an interview with an irate cat. My face
was a mass of scrapes and scratches from my tumble.
The morning of the 17th was spent in an inspection of
the Carlyle detachment by our commanding officer, in
fixing up stores and equipment, and in making arrangements for the ensuing summer. The merchant at
Carlyle had obtained the contract for furnishing us with
provisions. We were to receive half a ration extra,
daily, per man, all through the season's campaign.
This would give each individual, per diem $2\frac{1}{4}$ lbs. beef,
$2\frac{1}{4}$ lbs. bread, $1\frac{1}{2}$ lbs. potatoes, and other things in pro-
portion,—an exceedingly liberal allowance,—and I will
venture to say no other troops in the world receive so
much. Any surplus, at the end of each month, we were
at liberty to exchange for luxuries we fancied.

One of the Moosomin detachment came galloping
into camp this afternoon, bearing a telegram for our
officer, to the effect that nine families of Indians had
left the Crooked Lakes Reserves, and that, if we came
across them, we were to escort them back. These
reserves are four in number, and lie along the right bank
of the Qu'Appelle River, which widens into two lakes,
bearing the above name, at this point. The chief,

Mosquito, holds sway over 136 Indians on the west side.
Next comes O'Soup,—a name suggestive of an Irish
King—with 345 redskins ; and the nine families had
deserted from his patriarchal jurisdiction.   Alongside
the former rules Kakewistahaw, over 170 souls.   The
reserve of Kakeesheway is to the east, with a population
of 427.

It was at once surmised that the parties wanted were
those Indians whom we had passed near the Little
Pipestone ; and men were at once despatched to watch
the various trails.   On the 18th, one of the constables
returned with the intelligence that he and his comrade
had run the Indians to earth on the trail in the mountain.   He had left his companion to hold them there,
and had himself ridden in, " with hoof of speed," to
report the matter.   A party of us were at once ordered
off with waggons ; but when we conducted the captives
to the interpreter's house, on Pheasant Rump's reserve,
we found them to be Sioux from Oak Lake, in Manitoba, on their way to the Assiniboine camp at Indian
Head, for the annual Sun Dance.   We allowed them to
proceed on their journey, which they did with much
hilarity.   The Sioux are not a long-faced race by any
means, but are rather jovial and pleasant fellows.   One
of White Bull's braves used to invariably greet me with
the most comic grin, and hearty hand shake ;—a contrast
to the frigid *hauteur* of the dignified savage of
romance.

The Sun Dance is a mighty festival, attended with
many barbarous ceremonies.   A large council lodge is
erected, fully 100 feet in diameter.   The sides are
formed of poles, with boughs of trees interlaced.
The roof is constructed in the same manner with strong
cross beams.   In this all the tribe and their
visitors assemble ; the medicine-men are in full uniform,

wearing many charms; and the chiefs, councillors, and braves are in all the glory of paint and feathers. The squaws are seated on the ground. Those of the young bucks, who are to be initiated as braves, are stripped of all clothing except a breech-clout. Two parallel incisions are made with a knife in the neighbourhood of each breast, and through the muscles of the chest, thus laid bare, thongs of raw hide are passed. The other ends of these are attached to the beams above. The tom-toms are beaten, there is a wild shouting, the medicine-men vociferate invocations to the Manitou, and a species of fierce frenzy—epidemic in such scenes as these—seizes upon all. The candidate dances in ferocious ecstasy at the extremity of his bonds, and if the sinews of the chest give way and he has borne the torture well, he is forthwith saluted as a brave. If, however, the lariat should break, then it is very "bad medicine" indeed for the unlucky youth. Sometimes the incisions are made in the back. I have seen Indians point to the cicatrices with a glow of pride. They are the badges of their manhood.

On Sunday, May 22nd, our arrangements being completed and our men all gathered together, we resumed our march to the south. A detachment of one corporal and one man who had been stationed at a settler's on the Souris during the winter, were to join us *en route*. After leaving Carlyle, we had nothing but the prairie before us, with here and there a few scattered homesteads, looking gaunt and depressing amid their bare surroundings. We made a halt at noon by the side of a reed-fringed sleugh. At sunset we reached Alameda, dusty and tired. We had ridden the entire thirty miles at a walk. We were leg-weary and thirsty at the finish. It was this officer's fad to travel at a snail's pace. He had a pleasant theory that a horse was of more value than a man, and he once had the politeness to express this idea aloud before all his command. Unfortunately for the truth of his remark, all men were not of the same value as himself. I found to-night that a thoughtful teamster had brought a keg of cider in his vehicle, and I enjoyed a hearty draught.

Alameda, in spite of its flowery title, consists of a few log shanties stuck here and there about the prairie above the valley of the Souris. There is a frame store, and post-office. The Souris River rises near the Yellow Grass Marsh, south of Regina. It flows in a south-easterly direction at first, to within six miles of the American frontier, thence its course winds away northward to Alameda, where it takes a semicircular curve and enters Dakota. Once in American territory it becomes the Mouse River. After forming the letter U, it sweeps into Manitoba and joins the Assiniboine, not very far from Brandon.

We forded this stream, which brawls and babbles over a pebbly bottom at Alameda. Oak, ash, poplar, elm, and a species of bastard maple ramble over the slopes that run up to the prairie. A fringe of oaks lay between the river and our camp, which soon nestled in a secluded hollow. Caio Moreau, a half-breed and ex-interpreter to the police, was hunting and trapping in the valley. He reported that Gabriel Dumont was among the Metis in the Turtle Mountain district of Dakota, endeavouring to incite them to make a raid into Canada.

The morning of the 23rd was lovely, the river prattled gaily, the dew sparkled on the grass, the birds trilled out their orisons, and a thousand pleasant perfumes floated in the air. We struck camp, and climbed the southern boundary of the valley, on our way to cross the Ox Bow. This is the name given to the stretch of prairie between the two arms of the river, from the peculiar form taken by the windings of the Souris. It is a sparsely settled region. Those who have pitched upon this spot hail for the most part from that abode of pine-trees, rocks, and bears, Manitoulin Island, on Lake Huron. They have chosen the lesser of two evils.

In the distance, to the south-west, we could see the hazy contour of the low hills—the Grand Coteau du Missouri—blending with the sky. Nearer still rose the lofty ridge of the solitary Hill of the Murdered Scout. A march of five hours brought us to the Souris again at the point where it enters American territory. The trail led through a gully into a lovely vale, still and hushed. Oak and elm trees of vigorous growth spread their shade in dense clusters by the river's side, or stood in pleasant groves in the rich, tall meadow-grass that grew in fragrant richness up to the foot of the hills. It was a charming scene, tinged with the gilding of a summer's afternoon. The trail which was formerly made by the Frontier Delimitation Commission crosses the Souris at this point by a dangerous ford just upon the boundary. This line follows the 49th parallel of north latitude, and is marked by mounds at intervals of half a mile. There was some difficulty in finding a comfortable spot upon which to make our permanent camp for the summer. The commanding officer left it to my judgment, as I was to be in charge, and I pitched upon a small level terrace with the slopes of the valley behind, and about 200 yards from the river in front.

On the morning of the 24th of May, the officer, sergeant, and party set off for Long Creek, and I was left in undisturbed possession of my outpost.

CHAPTER XXII

Life on the Souris—Flies—Mud turtles—A lovely scene—Thunderstorms and cyclones—A tent scattered—Man lost—A cloud of mosquitoes—A narrow escape from drowning—Saved by a comrade.

THE Queen's birthday in 1887 was blazing hot on the banks of the Souris River. Down in the valley the trees drooped, the river murmured lazily, and up above, the prairie quivered in the blinding glare. The mosquitoes rose in noisy swarms and settled venomously on neck and hands, and their bloated bodies gleamed crimson with blood. This was a holiday over all the land, and the rumbling old waggon of a settler went creaking up the vale, the wife and family under sunshades sitting beside the sunburnt farmer, bent on a visit to some distant friend. Caio Moreau, who had followed us, paid a visit to our tents, where we lay sweltering in the shade outside engaged in an incessant fight against our insect pests. I gave him a pair of boots and received in return a fine robe of white rabbit-skins, woven like a net, with the fur covering the interstices.

I had a junior corporal and five constables to bear me company, and one transport waggon. The two tents were pitched close together, facing the river, and properly trenched. In a few days, a cooking-stove and some utensils were sent from Carlyle. At first these were set up in the open air; and when the rain fell, as it always does here, in torrents, it was often hours before we could coax our fire to burn. Some deserted shanties were

purchased by our contractor and subsequently removed
to this spot, and erected by us.   One we very soon put
together as a kitchen, and the other was eventually got
in order as a barrack-room, to be used when the cold
weather commenced in the Fall.   It was never destined
to be inhabited, however.   There was a deep sleugh in
a depression of the valley, a little to the left of the camp,
and, amid the long grass surrounding it, we picketed
our horses as long as the feed continued good.   Our
supply of rations was to be sent monthly from Carlyle,
and as we were unable to consume the full government allowance, we exchanged the surplus for delicacies, such as butter, and eggs, and preserves.   Eggs
were sold at this time at the rate of ten cents (5*d.*)
per dozen.   Our flour we sent to a settler on the plains
two miles to the north, whose daughters, two strapping
highland lasses, baked our bread.   There was a small
log-house on the opposite side of the river in a clearing
amid the bush.   There were no outbuildings attached to
this small ranche, merely a corral for cattle and a sadly
neglected garden.   A stockman with his mother and
sister occupied this one-roomed shanty, through the
roof of which the rain would pour in streams upon the
beds ; his cattle used to roam at large upon the plains,
or in the deep meadows which fringed the windings of
the Souris.   One of us crossed the river daily to his hut
for milk, which he sold at ten cents per quart.   Our
transit was by means of a dangerous natural bridge of
driftwood, the deep river gleaming sulkily between the
openings at your feet as you scrambled over.   The men
undertook the cooking in turn, and some brilliant attempts were made in that line.

All along the valley, ravines, or coulées, long and
winding, clad in matchless verdure, led up for miles
right into the heart of the prairie.   Daily I used to

explore these romantic gorges, on horseback. One of our men recklessly shot a deer, two days after our arrival ; but the flesh was bad, being out of season. We often saw the pretty animals flitting nimbly across the open glades. The jutting rocks, the wide meadows of rich, waving grass, the masses of foliage and the clinging tendrils of the creepers, the sparkling atmosphere, the wild delight as you galloped at will over the velvety sward, the songs of the birds and flashing of the plumage, the cool waters of the babbling rills, the magic sunsets, the hush of evening, the silvery moonlight on brake and river, the golden glory of the orange lilies, and the purple blossom of the buffalo apple, and the peaceful lowing of the cattle,—all made up a living picture that memory loves to conjure up.

Unfortunately, we were not well off for drinking-water, being reduced to use that of the river, and that was often warm. Many bottles of Eno's Fruit Salt were added during the excessive heat. A shady pool at the bend of the stream was our daily bathing-place. There were numbers of mud turtles in the Souris and its affluents, their shells being a species of checkered red and green upon a groundwork of olive. As I have said, the mosquitoes were a perfect torment, as their natural haunts, wood and water, were near ; and their numbers were increased by the wet summer. We had various kinds of insects which visited us in succession. The mosquito, like the poor, was always with us. The small black flies came on the scene shortly after our arrival. They were very severe upon our poor horses, which soon had their withers bereft of hair. They hung in clusters around the eyes of the frantic animals, and we had to guard against a stampede. After swarming in dense masses for three weeks, they suddenly disappeared. Then came the bull-dog species, a huge creature that would take a comfortable bite out of you, causing the blood to spurt like an ornamental fountain, and giving a momentary sting of intense pain. This voracious brute was followed by the flying ant, who generally made for your neck, at the·head of the spinal column. To wind up the procession, the house-fly came in squadrons, and continued till November.

The system of patrols, leaving this outpost, was as follows :— One of us two corporals, with two men, left camp for Winlaw, near the Manitoba Boundary, every Thursday. It was twenty-eight miles to the east, and consisted of a solitary post-office. The Souris was crossed at the ford on the Boundary Commission trail ; and this patrol returned upon the following day. Another party set out, every Monday, for the west, meeting the patrol from Wood End at some springs, thirty miles distant. The mid-day halt was at the Hill of the Murdered Scout. Our post-office was named Boscurvis, a lonely farm on the prairie, ten miles westward, and the limit of settlement in that direction. Beyond this, as far as the Rocky Mountains, lay the desert. No habitations, save the camps of the Mounted Police.

In the early part of June my camp was aroused at midnight by a mounted constable from Moosomin. He brought me a telegram from headquarters, which informed me that a settler had been murdered by four half-breed desperadoes near Wolsely. The whole country was scoured by our men ; and there was a great deal of excitement, as two other farmers were also murdered at the same time and in the same locality. I sent a mounted man with a despatch to the officer commanding at Wood End, and stationed a vedette daily on the high ground above the camp, where he commanded a view of the ford and the surrounding prairie. I also scouted the country myself, and made inquiries among the few scattered settlers. It was reported that the murderers had made their escape by way of Moose Mountain, and the whole of our detachment were turned out to search that neighbourhood, while special patrols from Wood Mountain scoured the country along the boundary-line as far as Deloraine; and one of the parties went south to the Turtle Mountain district, but without success. These patrols were recalled at the end of June. Two of the criminals were eventually arrested by the United States Marshal at Fort Shaw in Montana. They were handed over to us, and executed at Regina on the 13th of June, 1888.

During the whole of this summer we experienced a succession of terrific thunderstorms, accompanied by cyclones and torrents of rain. These visitations came every other night at first, and arose without the slightest warning. Not a breath would stir the groves, while the birds were hushed in the rich green of the foliage, and the drowsy hum of the insects alone murmured in the deep ravine, and on the grassy plain. The sun would set in a blaze, flooding the broad valley, the slumbering woods, and peaceful river with a stream of ruby light. Then the wan and mystic gloaming would steal down among the hills, and the world would seem at rest. At first we never thought of pegging down the curtains of our tents, until we became wary by experience. You are never safe from the vagaries of the climate in the north-west. It is a land of surprises and the French proverb, about the unexpected happening, holds good here. This general uncertainty has a good deal to do with the wily character of the aborigines. We turned in to roost in unsuspicious innocence, and were rudely awakened about midnight by all the tumult of a first-rate storm. Now, a thunderstorm in Ontario is a fearful thing; but a thunderstorm on the prairies bears the same relation to one in Ontario, as the phenomenon in Ontario does to one of ours in England. It is indescribable in its grandeur. The black darkness is illuminated by a ceaseless, quivering fire of crimson and purple, which seems to rain from heaven. Every few minutes, sometimes seconds, a bolt of steely blue comes down and shivers this burning cataract in two. Thunder rattles and rolls, and shakes the earth in awful bursts of sound. The wind roars with an eldritch shriek, and the rain splashes down in one sheet, as though a sea were falling.

On the night of the 14th of June I went under my blankets in all confidence, beguiled by the glamour of a summer's night. My bed in this permanent camp consisted of four thick stakes driven into the ground, to which were nailed poles, making a parallelogram. This was covered with the staves of a biscuit barrel, the concave sides being uppermost. These were beautifully adapted to the shape of the body, and were nailed upon the poles at the side. Upon these my palliasse was laid, filled with dried grass. The other corporal and I shared one of the tents, but upon this occasion he was absent on duty. Between our beds was a rough deal table, which we had made ourselves. On this were a couple of small reading-lamps, a few books, and writing materials. Underneath was a tin box filled with official stationery, and certain forms,— offered monthly as a sacrifice to the god, Red Tape. Our clothes were hung around the centre pole, and our arms fastened against it. On the ground was stacked a supply of flour, tea, bacon, butter, bread, sugar, and other rations. All our other property was lying about the tent, and our valises and bags were open. Tobacco, pipes, and matches lay exposed upon the table. A bull terrier of ferocious aspect, the property of one of the detachment, used to reside principally in this tent also. The camp, as I have said, was trenched according to the "custom of war in like cases," but I am afraid on this night. I had forgotten to slacken the guy-ropes before retiring. About half past twelve I awoke. The interior of my canvas dwelling was filled with a lurid light that danced and tremulously vibrated. A river was rushing with arrowy speed across the floor, and a heavy shower was pouring from the roof. The roaring patter of the streaming rain was hideous. I could hear also the trees crashing by the river. The earth was trembling under the deafening noise of continual shocks of thunder. Peal upon peal followed each other almost instantly. I looked around, under the lifted curtain the gleams of the chain lightning were almost blinding in their intensity and nearness. Poor Sweep was sitting on his haunches in the moving lake of water, shivering and wretched. The tent was swaying to and fro. I was simply wearing shirt and drawers, my cloak was over the foot of my bed. Presently the pole went down, as the whole canvas covering was lifted and whirled away by the cyclone. I wrapped my cloak hurriedly around me and hurried through the pitiless, drifting cataract to the other tent. I was nearly blown through the soaking canvas. The other fellows were sitting in boots and cloaks upon their respective rolls of bedding in the water. The floor of this tent was a pond, and the canvas above was dripping like the well at Knaresborough. How we dragged through that beastly night, I do not know. We could only sit with our elbows on our knees, and our chins in our hands, looking savage, though we laughed and jested as though it were a lively spree. In the morning the sun came bounding over the wooded spurs with fiery heat, and sent his fierce rays beating down on the steaming valley, and upon an almost comic scene of desolation. Fragments of my chum's correspondence lay scattered in skirmishing order all around, every sheet of paper blurred and illegible. The fugitive tent was in the bushes by the river. The provisions were in a state of juice. Lamps and table were smashed and hurled to the ground.

Upon a similar evening of deceptive loveliness one of the men set off for a pleasant ramble over the prairie, where the mosquitoes were not quite so thick. He was wrapt in reverie and time stole upon him, unconscious of its course. Night came down and he was on the measureless plain bewildered. He had lost his bearings. Then came a thunderstorm, with all its accessories, in full force. But it is the simplest thing in the world to get lost on the prairie in broad daylight. You may even get turned upon a trail, and be utterly unaware that you are retracing your steps. At four o'clock in the morning, this unlucky wight found himself fortunately at a settler's house in Dakota, twelve miles south of the line! We were scouring the country in search of him when he came tramping up the valley, having been driven some distance in the kindly farmer's buckboard. We neglected to take a tent upon one of our patrols to the springs. Our camping place at night was upon a hill. We lit our camp fire and consumed our regulation supper, as the sun was sinking low down in the west. Then we laid our blankets beneath the waggon. But in the twilight the plague arose. Clouds of mosquitoes that darkened the sky came from every direction and assailed us. We made fires of damp grass, but to no purpose. These are called smudges and we were obliged to have one in our tent every night before retiring to rest. Every aperture was closed, and

as soon as our enemies had been suffocated by the
smoke, we withdrew the smudge, and dived rapidly in,
fastening up the door quickly lest our tormentors
should follow us. On this night torrents of rain fell
before morning, and we rode back thirty miles to camp
in no very enviable frame of mind. This is merely one
of the small delights incidental to " roughing it."

Upon Thursday, June 23rd, I left our camp at 8 a.m.
in charge of the patrol to the Manitoba boundary. It
was a glorious morning, and the air was balmy and
laden with the odour of blossoming shrub and prairie
flower. The sun gilded the quivering leaves of the trees
and waving grass, as we moved down to the ford.
There were only three of us ; I was mounted on
Chocolate George, and a teamster and dismounted man
occupied the waggon with the bedding and grub. On
reaching the crossing the waters were yellow and muddy,
but they did not seem to have risen much above the
average level. We got through all right with a few
slight inconveniences. My long boots were full of
water, and the waggon box was swept by the rushing
stream. One roll of bedding floated out, but was recovered. Our rations, of course, were rendered worth-
less. But we laughed it off as usual, and chatted gaily,
and lit our pipes as we jogged along the level prairie,
the surface of which was shimmering in the heat. Here
and there a solitary homestead was lifted up in air by
the mirage. We halted at a settler's for dinner, which
consisted of greasy bacon, eggs fried to an abnormal
hardness, and green tea. All Canadians of the rural
class go in for green tea. How miserably dirty are the
log-houses of these settlers from Ontario ! The one
room in the interior possesses a rickety table, a few un-
reliable chairs, and a broken stove. The bed is usually
in a state of frowsy disorganization, and a few hideous

prints begrimed with smoke adorn the dingy walls : of course there are exceptions, but this is the general state of affairs. I have a high admiration for the Canadians, but I cannot say I care for the Ontario backwoodsman, who of course is not a representative specimen of this nation.

In the evening we pitched our camp on the South Antler, in a lovely spot. A pretty house stood in a grove above the creek. It was built of cement, and nestled among the trees. The limpid waters babbled and prattled through fields of the richest green, and bushes were mirrored in the pools. The house was of two storeys with large windows, and each apartment was a picture of old-world comfort. This settler hailed from Dumfries in Scotland, and his wife was a bonnie, fresh-looking, kindly Scotswoman. Pleasant it was to hear the Lowland accents bidding the red-coats welcome. They would not hear of us camping outside, and we all sat down to a table furnished with toothsome luxuries and a snowy cloth. Part of the surrounding land was enclosed in a wire fence, there was a flourishing garden, and everything around showed solid industry, backed up by capital. Had it not been for the mosquitoes, one might have fancied oneself on some picturesque farm in Scotland. There were cows in well-ventilated byres, calves in the folds, sheep on the slopes, and poultry around the barns. The garden was hidden in the dense bush, through which led well-ordered paths. On our return to the Souris, at the edge of the ford the teamster drew up his horses, blocking the narrow trail.

"The river has risen a little, shall I go in ?" he asked.

"Go on," I replied.

I observed that both men lifted their feet upon the dashboard in front. I followed immediately after them.

I saw the body of the waggon sink, and the box leave the bolsters, floating for a moment on the swollen tide. Then both the occupants were striking out with lusty sinews. They were heavily handicapped with ammunition, revolvers, tight pants and long boots, and I was in the same predicament. I saw the broncho team—game little beggars—swimming down the stream, and over towards the tangled brake opposite. My horse, being an arrant fool, would not swim, but plunged and reared and made frantic struggles in the water. This came out in evidence afterwards, when an inquiry was held into the loss of the Government property. All this time we had been drifting down the current, which was very strong, and on either hand were steep banks with over-hanging branches. I received a blow, somehow, and was knocked completely under my trooper in thirteen feet of water, and when in that position my face and head were cut open in many places by his shoes. The others, who had gained land, were watching the antics of Chocolate George, and Constable Drummond swam over to my assistance. When I came to the surface, almost help-less, he clutched me, but we sank again at once. However, on once more rising, he held me bravely, and brought me to the edge, holding by a bough till I was helped ashore. To him I owe my life. Never shall I forget that scene, and the solemn silence that, but for the sound of our breath, reigned in that leafy arcade, as we struggled for life, in the surge and eddy of the sweeping torrent. The sun was sending shafts of golden glory athwart the river. All nature seemed hushed at the contest between man and the treacherous Souris. In the meantime the camp had been alarmed. All the horses had reached the side. Men swam in, cut the traces, and released the team. Chocolate George was entangled in a screen of undergrowth, his bridle was caught by a branch, holding his mouth open, and he was nearly *in extremis*, swallowing water rapidly. Three carbines were lost—mine was washed off the saddle— and a great deal more Government property. The majority of this was afterwards recovered by a settler in Dakota, but our bedding was never brought to light. A board of officers held an inquiry into the matter, and I was acquitted of blame. But I should not like to state what the decision would have been had any of the horses perished. There was no apparent cause for this sudden flood, which continued for days, and we had to swim the river for our supply of milk. When I was assisted out of the water my face was streaming with blood; Chocolate George has left his sign-manual on my cheek. These North-West rivers are a constant source of danger, as there are no bridges. A settler was drowned, six miles higher up the Souris, a few days after the above occurrence.

In July, I received orders to proceed to Wood End, as the camp on Long Creek was named, and report for duty, as another non-commissioned officer was needed at that post. Two men, also, were to accompany me.

CHAPTER XXIII

Off to Wood End—Hill of the Murdered Scout—Crees and Blackfeet—A storm—Long Creek—A happy valley—Wild fruit—A
Helena girl and culture—Patrols—Wild horses—Wild hops—
Prairie fire—Winter-quarters—The Souris coal-fields—Good-
bye.

IT was a pleasant morning when I bid good-bye to
the Souris camp, and set off for Wood End. In addition to the waggon there were two mounted constables,
the officer and his servant in a buckboard, and myself.
In this country it is necessary to travel with wheeled
transport, as you must carry all the requisites for camp-
life. At noon we halted by a sluggish creek at the base
of the Hill of the Murdered Scout. The grass was
luxuriant in the hollow, and the heat was intense. In
the days when warfare raged between the redskin tribes
upon the plains, an Indian scout was killed here by the
Sioux. Their country—the land of the Dacotahs—lay
to the south and east. To the north was the nation of
the Crees; and away to the west roved the restless
hordes of the Blackfeet, magnificent horsemen and
daring warriors. The buffalo in countless herds roamed
the wild prairie from the Missouri to the Saskatchewan.
He furnished the red-man with robes to protect him
from the winter cold, and with skins for his teepe. The
flesh was.bruised, and dried in the sun, and placed in
bags, as pemmican.

When the pale faces came from the land of the rising
sun, these children of freedom found a ready market for

the hide of the shaggy bison of the plains. So he was hunted by whole armies of painted braves, who hovered around the thundering phalanx, riding on flanks and rear and sending the unerring arrow quivering in the giant's flesh. And this whole region was one vast slaughter-house. The squaws had many beads and gaudy blankets, and the men obtained rifles and fire-water.

On the summit of this lonely mountain which stands sentinel over the engirdling plain, is seen the outline of a recumbent figure. It is the natural contour of the hill, and probably from it has arisen the tale of the murdered spy, for it is a peculiarity of the redskin mind to hitch on a fable to any strange phenomenon of nature. In the evening we reached the springs. These wells were called the "'74 springs;" they were made by the mounted police in their celebrated march from Fort Garry to the Rocky Mountains. The officer's tent was pitched at some distance from ours, and our horses were picketed in different places on the plateau.

About one o'clock in the morning a tornado, with thunder and lightning, visited our exposed camp. The rain came down in bucketfuls, and there was no more rest for us. We were compelled to rise and roll up our blankets, and hold on to the pole and skirts of the tent to prevent it being blown away. The level space outside was soon changed into a lake, and at every flash we could see our poor horses standing in this sheet of water with their backs humped up, and turned towards the pitiless storm. Morning brought no improvement. Every inch of the horizon was walled in with black masses of loaded clouds.

Our breakfast and dinner consisted of soaked biscuit, nothing else. Everything was saturated with wet. There was no appearance of any break at one o'clock; so it was decided we should resume our march. We

struck camp, loaded the waggon, and saddled our shivering horses, in the downpour and terrible wind. We
pushed on with bent head, over the black plain, and
down into the abyss through which rush the arrowy
waters of Short Creek. We luckily managed to
ford the foaming torrent without any accident. Great
cliffs, gaunt and rugged, frowned down on the canyon,
as our little band climbed up the zigzag trail to the
prairie on the other side. The wilderness stretched
before us ;—that desert of the sunset land spreading to
the west, where the snow-clad sierras lift their summits
through the clouds. A driving hailstorm, of stones like
pebbles, with awfully near lightning, nearly drove us
from the saddle.

At last, during a lull in the wild storm, we could see
far beneath our feet, on a lovely lawn, the tiny tents of
the camp on Long Creek. There is here a riven chasm
as if the Great Prairie had been burst asunder, and the
deep waters of the creek flow through a belt of bush at
the base of this rugged fissure, here wide enough to leave
swards of level grass. In this happy valley is the station
of Wood End. We went down a breakneck declivity,
and I was put up in the sergeant's tent. There was a
beaver dam at the bend, which made a magnificent pool
for bathing, and a wooden pier ran out towards the centre.
There was a large square tent for stores, and a mess-
room with kitchen, built of poles, with a roof of thatch.

We obtained fish from the creek, the patrols often
brought in a supply of venison, and for a time we
enjoyed saskatoon berries in abundance, a delicious
fruit eaten with cream and sugar. Wild strawberries,
too, are plentiful on the prairie. Every day we were
served with some sort of pudding, and we always had
beef three times a day. Of course, when out on patrol
we did not fare so well. When I arrived, the detach-

ment was engaged in putting up a sod house, thirty feet by eighteen feet, to be occupied as a barrack-room. It was completed in August, and was a welcome addition to our comfort in the autumn. It was constructed entirely by our own labour, the Government only paying for doors and windows and flooring. Fatigue duty is very heavy in the North-West Mounted Police, as everything has to be undertaken by the men themselves. A carpenter, blacksmith, baker, saddler, and tailor are attached to each troop, and receive extra pay.

Life at this camp was very pleasant, though the wearing isolation was sometimes trying. Here we were entirely out of the world, beyond the outposts of Canadian settlement. Fort Buford was eighty miles away across the frontier. The Northern Pacific were extending their line this summer to Helena, in Montana. Numbers of settlers from the Territory took their teams over, to secure the high wages paid in the work of construction. On returning, they invariably attempted to smuggle some stock across the boundary.

Society, among our neighbours over the way, was in a very crude state. Tradition says that a Helena girl was once asked by a Boston young lady, if they had any culture out West.

"Culture!" she replied, "you bet your variegated socks! We can sling more culture to the square inch than they can in any camp in America. Culture! Just loosen my corset, till I smile!"

There was no house to the west of Wood End nearer than Willow Bunch, a distance of two hundred miles. A patrol was despatched weekly in this direction, leaving camp every Monday, and returning on the following Saturday. Buffalo Head, where we met the Willow Bunch party, was ninety miles to the west, and we traversed a great desert of withered grass, cactus plants, wild sage, and alkaline lakes. Our route followed the boundary-line for fifteen miles, and then trended in a northerly direction. The place of rendezvous was simply a buffalo skull placed upon a pile of stones. We reached this spot on the Wednesday afternoon, leaving it again on the Thursday morning. Those dreary marches, in all weathers, were hideous in their monotony. We generally made our camping place about five in the evening, and pitched our tents by the edge of some creek or sleugh. Then there was nothing to do but lie down, and smoke, and dream of home, or read. There was no game to stalk on these journeys. Sometimes we shot a deer, and in the fall we secured plenty of duck and chicken. We used to picket the horses in front of the tent, so that we could keep an eye upon them. I never bothered to post a sentry over the camp. A band of wild horses used to haunt some low hills, where we generally halted on our first night out. Thus the place received the name of the " Wild Horse Buttes." Sometimes we tried to disable one of these nomads by a bullet ; but it was hopeless. They were too many for us. When we heard that we should have to hand any captives over to the Government, we gave up the chase. In these long rides my party only once came across any human beings. These were a party of trappers encamped at the second crossing of Long Creek, and they had killed a quantity of beaver. A beaver skin is valued at three dollars, but here they are not of such good quality as up in the north. The nearer the south, the lighter in colour do they become.

In August I sent in an application for my discharge by purchase. Only three men per month were permitted to go by this method, and sometimes it was necessary to wait for eighteen months, unless you possessed political influence, and could work the ropes at Ottawa.

Many grew tired of waiting and took, what is vulgarly termed, French leave. To procure your discharge by purchase, you must pay three dollars for every unexpired month of your term of service.

This is a life as hard and lonely as that of a castaway, at times. It seems to take the spirit out of you, and ages you before your time. My readers will naturally imagine that men went in, vigorously, for all sorts of sport. This is not so. There is no sport of a sufficiently exciting character to be obtained. We occasionally indulged in a rifle match, among ourselves. But gambling and card-playing, in the tents, went on amain.

Colonel Herchmer inspected the detachment in September. He was brother to the commiss'oner, and held the post of assistant commissioner. An excellent officer in every way, he was keenly alive to the interests of the men under his command. He first came to the North-West with the Red River Expedition. In connection with his duties as assistant commissioner, in 1887 he travelled the following number of miles.

By rail	10,461
By water.	900
With horses	3,620
On foot, snowshoes. . . .	200
Total . . .	15,181

From the middle of the month of September till the end of October we had superb weather for six weeks in succession, with very slight cold. A magic glamour seemed to lie on all the land ; the glistening pride of the sparkling creek, the hushed twitter of the birds, and the beauteous tints of the leaves all bronzed and scarlet and olive filled in the details of the landscape. Wild plums and cherries were plentiful in the woods, and wild hops thick in every brake. These latter could have been sold for eighty cents (three shillings and fourpence) per pound in Moosomin.

But pleasant weather has an end, like everything else, and I was in charge of the Buffalo Head patrol at the ending. On the Thursday night of our return journey we went under our blankets with the cosy assurance of an agreeable finish to our trip. On the morning as I gazed out, our dreams had vanished. A blinding snowstorm was drifting over everything. There was no help for it but to push on to our next camping-plaçe. Breakfast and dinner were out of the question, so we munched our soddened biscuit in morose silence. I lay down under my blankets in the wet tent, on the sloppy ground, supperless at five o'clock in the evening.

A devastating prairie fire was raging when we started out on this patrol, far away to the west. When we were camped at the third crossing on our outward voyage, we were obliged to strike our tent at midnight, and ride through it. We had been warned of its approach, by hearing its distant roar, as we lay on the ground. It was a magnificent spectacle in the dark. No pyrotechnic display could equal this effort of nature. The reader must understand that the grass is short, and, in a calm, the fire burns in a thin line of a few inches in width which you can step over. It is like a row of advancing footlights, winding and twisting in a dance of flickering tongues of flame. The hills of the Grand Coteau du Missouri were on fire, and seemed like some fabled city of the gods, illuminated with myriads of lamps, towering into heaven. When we had passed through the luminous ring, the darkness in front was intense. At our feet the ground was blackened, and charred, and the trail was lost. The dust was sent flying by our horses' feet, and our faces in the daylight would have fitted us to perform in the most select troupe of nigger minstrels. To-night we had to trust

implicitly to the instinct of our horses, and we trotted
along with a loose rein.   After travelling for twelve miles,
they turned to the right suddenly where a sheet of water
lay shining under the stars.   This was known as the
Duck Pond, and was a camping-place where we kept a
cache of wood.   We were always obliged to carry fire-
wood with us on patrol.   We soon had our canvas up
once more, and after some hot coffee, took to our hard
couch again and the unfailing pipe.

So the Indian summer wrapped in its regal robes had
given way to the first snap of the coming winter.   We
were anxiously awaiting the summons to snug quarters.
The creek rapidly became coated with ice, and some of
us enjoyed skating.   Buffalo overcoats became a necessity.   A rude shelter or corral had been made of brushwood, and in this the horses were placed at night.   In
the daytime they were allowed to roam at large upon
the scanty pasturage, for the prairie fire had not touched
us here.   The wild geese had passed, flying overhead on
their southern pilgrimage, and the lonesome lament of
the loon had wailed from the marshes.   Mallard and
teal, frozen out, had sped to milder lands and water.
What little foliage there was had slowly fluttered earth-
ward.   The long sleep of winter was falling slowly on
this western land.

In the latter part of November, marching orders came
to our shivering outpost.   I was to be stationed at the
house of a settler on the Souris (in the region known as
the Coal Fields) with one constable under me, for the
ensuing winter.   A sergeant and four men were to be
left at Carlyle, two at Alameda, and a couple at Bois-
curvis, the post-office on the frontier south of Alameda.
Many a camp-ditty and negro melody sounded through
the valley on the receipt of this joyful intelligence.   On
the following morning, breakfast of strong coffee, meat,

and bread was hastily devoured by the light of candles stuck in forked sticks. Many lanterns went flashing about in the struggling dawn.

"Tom, you've got my head-collar."

"Your head-collar be blowed! Don't I know my own number?"

"Has any one seen my head-rope?"

"Bill, lend me your hoof-pick."

"Stop that chewing the rag there!" sang out the voice of authority, "and look sharp in saddling up."

Amid these amenities, the very horses on the lines were infected with the spirit of unrest, as if they also knew that they were going to enjoy the warmth of winter-quarters with clean bedding to lie upon. Men carrying saddles on their shoulders were hastening to the horse-lines, while others were pitching baggage and camp equipment into the waggons. Then the detachments for Carlyle and Alameda moved away. After this the main body destined for Regina, was formed up, and away went the fur-clad cavalcade, in the amber morning light. My destination was only thirteen miles distant on the Alameda trail, and my comrade and myself had been ordered to wait for the settler's waggon which was to carry our *impedimenta* to our new quarters. He arrived about eleven o'clock, and I rode on ahead, telling S—— to follow on in rear in case of anything falling off. We had borrowed sundry articles of furniture from the officer's hut.

The sun was shining brightly as I cantered off. I had been given a new mount, and Chocolate George now cut his capers in front of the Inspector's buckboard. "Bummer," as my latest trooper was called, was a little bay broncho with white points. He was a game little fellow, and many a lonely winter's ride we had together over the plains. You could rein him by the neck, or you could turn him in a circle with either leg. If he were at full gallop he would stop if you dropped the reins. His head was pretty as a deer's, and he was intelligent and docile to perfection. He used to lift his foreleg the moment you asked him to shake hands, and no distance, and no continued hard riding, would play him out; after a rest he would start again as fresh as ever. Poor little Bummer, where are you now? Have you been "cast" I wonder, and sold to some sordid mossback? Or has your brave little heart given way at last, and do your bones bleach on those great dreary plains you knew so well, and has your flesh formed food for the cowardly coyotes? Wherever you may be, *Waes hael!*

As I rode along, the Souris—into which Long Creek empties two miles from Wood End,—too large and rapid for the frost as yet, babbled and rushed over its rocky bed. The air—so dry, and sparkling like champagne, on the prairies—was mild to-day, yet bracing, as it often is in the fall. The peaceful slumber of the dying year lay upon rock and valley. A haze of filmy gold softly veiled the tranced scene. A covey of prairie chicken, with startled whirr, flew into a clump of birch-trees. A solitary prairie wolf (larger than the coyote) stole across the trail, and a black-tailed deer bounded into the bushes. It was an exhilarating ride, and I somehow felt as if I had never thoroughly appreciated the beauty of these surroundings before. But the fall of the year is the only time when life is enjoyable out here.

I arrived at Hassard's at 1 p.m. and soon had Bummer stabled. The house stood about two miles from the frontier line on the north side of the Souris valley, and was posted like a vedette in advance of the army of settlement. Here savagery and the wilderness began,

You might now travel for many days and see no human life. The stable lay at a little distance from the white-washed house, and was also built of logs, against a cut bank, so that the back of the place was of earth. The roof consisted of hay which could be forked off for use in the spring. There was also a haystack above the stable on the ground behind. A deep coulée ran down from the edge of the plain to the Souris, which took a bend at this point and wended its way through a broad, beautiful valley mantled with brushwood and timber. Seams of coal which here crop to the surface were burning in places along the cliffs, the wreaths of smoke curling up as from a line of miniature volcanoes. Here the prairie is so flat, and the descent into the ravine so abrupt, that at the distance of a mile or two a horseman would never suspect that there was any depression in front of him. Straight ahead stretched the unbroken plain, till in the distance the dim outline of the hills of the Missouri Coteau ran along the sky-line. A few log buildings thatched with straw or manure, stood a short distance from the dwelling-house, and did duty as folds for the cattle and sheep. A few head of cattle and some ponies and sheep grazed peacefully and roamed at large over the extensive pasture, hundreds of thousands of square miles without a fence.

We lived in a small barrack-room attached to the house, taking our meals with the family, the Government paying one dollar a day for the maintenance of each man and horse.

Our host and his family treated us with extreme kindness. We decorated our room with photographs and books, and hung up our arms. We were snug all winter. Headquarters was 300 miles off, Carlyle sixty miles. The sergeant used to make monthly visits with our pay. It was our duty to keep a general look-out for horse-thieves and contrabandists from Dakota and Montana, and to collect duty—twenty per cent. *ad valorem*—on all stock brought across the line. The principal trails leading from the above territories converged upon Short Creek. Alameda was thirty miles distant to the northeast, and thither one of us had to ride weekly for the mail, over an uninhabited plain. When the snow lay thick over all the prairie, obliterating every familiar landmark, this was no light task. You were always liable to be caught in a blizzard, which means almost certain death. If you are lost on the plains, when snow is on the ground you can always retrace your trail, *if it remains calm*. But in a blizzard, or even a breeze, you are done for, when you are "out of sight of land." It is so very, very easy to get lost. Many a time, when I felt the wind rising, has Bummer instinctively hurried on, struggling through crusted drifts, to gain the low rise whence we could see the house. Sometimes he would sink to his belly, and I had to dismount to let him extricate himself. It was often a close race between my plucky little horse and the gathering storm.

Time glided away quietly without anything worthy of record, for the days of the white desperado and the red-man are numbered. In the month of April, 1888, after I had left the service, a notorious horse-thief, named McIntyre, was captured in the Cypress Hills with a band of fifty stolen horses, which he had taken from Fort Shaw. He was sentenced to fourteen years by Colonel Macleod, C.M.G. (formerly commanding N.W.M.P.), for bringing stolen property into Canada.

Hassard's coal-mine was in the ravine in front of his house, and he worked it himself with the assistance of a hired man. Their only machinery were picks and ordinary felling axes. This coal was really as good in quality as any I have seen, and it was sold to the

settlers at one dollar a ton. The Dominion Government receives a royalty of ten cents on every ton
excavated. The whole prairie, as far as Wood Mountain, is traversed by beds of coal. The following article
appeared in the *Regina Leader* in February, 1888. It
shows that very few are aware of the mineral wealth
which lies hidden in these regions. The fact of the
matter is, the Government, being interested in the Galt
Mines at Lethbridge, do not care to develop the
resources of the Souris.

"THE SOURIS COAL-FIELDS.

*Valuable Facts about these rich and Comparatively Un-
known Mines. Perpetual Fires Burning.*

(From an occasional correspondent.)

"Alameda, January 10th.

" Having paid a recent visit to the Souris River coal-
fields, I wish to dissipate a little of the ignorance
prevailing regarding these comparatively little known
regions. I never regretted more than at the present
moment that I have not the pen of a ready-writer, in
order to describe in full what I saw, but I shall
endeavour to do as well as I can. On coming across
the prairie you suddenly reach the bank of a deep
ravine, all seamed and scarred, rugged and gaunt, red
and brown with the action of fire long ago. Down in
this hollow, burrowed under the lofty bank, Mr. H.
Hassard is working his mine. The seam is eight feet
in thickness, and he has made his way inward about
100 feet. The coal is of excellent quality for domestic
purposes, and though soft at first, is now becoming firm
and hard. It burns with a good heat, and is infinitely

superior to the Banff coal. (Banff is in the Rocky Mountains.) Mr. Hassard has had a mining expert at his pit, and he pronounced the coal to be A1 lignite.

"Recently, I believe, the place has been all life and bustle with settlers hauling away supplies of the black diamond. Some of them came from as great a distance as eighty miles. There is no wood to speak of from Turtle Mountain to the Cypress Hills, except a little, fast disappearing, on the Souris River. The trail from Alameda to this place has been cleared of stones, and farmers anticipate being able to haul coal all winter.

"There is limestone in unlimited quantities all down the valley. Mr. H. has a kiln, and sells lime at 20 c. per bushel.

"It seems to me that a thriving settlement will one day spring up around this nucleus, for there is timber enough on the river to roof houses and erect outbuildings with, and there is plenty of stone if it be worked. Sand abounds in plenty.

"One thing, however, catches the eye, and that is an alarming circumstance when considered in all its bearings. Fires are burning all over this promising district, eating their insidious way into the bowels of the earth, and consuming an immensity of coal, besides being injurious and positively dangerous to the surface. Prairie fires have frequently originated from this source. Considering how much fuss has been made about these destructive agents, it seems astonishing the Government does not take steps to have something done to remove at least this one cause. I understand the matter was brought before the North-West Council, with what result I am not aware.

"Another great consideration is that there is abundance of water along the edge of the prairie, and the fires could easily be subdued with little expenditure.

" Commissioner Herchmer, considering this such an important district, has a detachment of police stationed here.   Corporal Donkin and Constable Stewart represent the red-coats.

" At one time I hear that settlers in this region were obliged to sleep under arms in their stables at night. Owing to the system of patrols originated by Commissioner Herchmer, and the establishment of winter detachments, this undesirable state of things has happily passed away.

" VISITOR."

The writer of the above, with true Western gush, has exaggerated matters when he hints at coals being transported over the prairie in winter.   The idea is ridiculous. No one came, after the snow fell at Christmas. Major Jarvis ordered me to send in a complete report on this district in February, and I did so.

In March, I was surprised by the advent of an officer, with a constable to relieve me, bringing the welcome intelligence that the discharge which I had applied for, during the preceding August, was lying ready for me at headquarters.   I returned with the officer in his sleigh, having handed over everything in the shape of Government property to my successor.   I was suffering intense agonies from snow blindness, having for the three previous days in succession been in the saddle on the prairie exposed to the terrific glare of the reflected sun.   We remained one day at Alameda and I had applications of tea-leaves to my eyes.   The pain was almost beyond endurance at times.   When we left for Moosomin, I had to be led to the sleigh.   We reached the latter place in three days from Alameda, and proceeded to Regina by the morning of the 10th.   A board of officers sat on the 12th, " to verify and record the services, &c.," and in two hours I had said good-bye to the North-West Mounted Police.

In conclusion, I should like to express my thanks to the Comptroller of the North-West Mounted Police for the blue-books containing the Commissioner's reports for the years 1886 and 1887, and for the maps, one of which accompanies this volume.

And I must also mention the courtesy of the officials under the High Commissioner for Canada, in London, who kindly obliged me with the loan of certain works of reference from the library of the department.

THE END.